Survival Communications in Ohio: South East Region

John E. Parnell, KK4HWX

10 ISBN 1479244341
13 ISBN 978-1479244348

Cover design by:
Lynda Colón
FREELANCE GRAPHIC DESIGN &
MARKETING COMMUNICATIONS
www.hirelynda.webs.com

I do wish to acknowledge the hard work of **Angie Shirley** in putting together the database required for this book. Without her efforts, this book could not have been done.

Titles available in this series:

Survival Communications in Alabama
Survival Communications in Alaska
Survival Communications in Arizona
Survival Communications in Arkansas
Survival Communications in California
Survival Communications in Colorado
Survival Communications in Connecticut
Survival Communications in Delaware
Survival Communications in Florida
Survival Communications in Georgia
Survival Communications in Hawaii
Survival Communications in Idaho
Survival Communications in Illinois
Survival Communications in Indiana
Survival Communications in Iowa
Survival Communications in Kansas
Survival Communications in Kentucky
Survival Communications in Louisiana
Survival Communications in Maine
Survival Communications in Maryland
Survival Communications in Massachusetts
Survival Communications in Michigan
Survival Communications in Minnesota
Survival Communications in Mississippi
Survival Communications in Missouri

Survival Communications in Montana
Survival Communications in Nebraska
Survival Communications in Nevada
Survival Communications in New Hampshire
Survival Communications in New Jersey
Survival Communications in New Mexico
Survival Communications in New York
Survival Communications in North Carolina
Survival Communications in North Dakota
Survival Communications in Ohio
Survival Communications in Oklahoma
Survival Communications in Oregon
Survival Communications in Pennsylvania
Survival Communications in Rhode Island
Survival Communications in South Carolina
Survival Communications in South Dakota
Survival Communications in Tennessee
Survival Communications in Texas
Survival Communications in Utah
Survival Communications in Vermont
Survival Communications in Virginia
Survival Communications in Washington
Survival Communications in West Virginia
Survival Communications in Wisconsin
Survival Communications in Wyoming

The above titles are available from your favorite online or brick-and-mortar bookstore or directly from the publisher at Tutor Turtle Press LLC, 1027 S. Pendleton St. – Suite B-10, Easley, SC 29642.

TABLE OF CONTENTS

Survival Communications in Ohio 1
General Mobile Radio Service / Family Radio Service 1
Citizens Band Radio 1
Ham / Amateur Radio 2
Standardized Amateur Radio Prepper Communications Plan 2
Nets and Network Etiquette 3
Topics for Technician Amateur License Exam 4
Call Sign Numbers 6
Topics for General Amateur License Exam 7
Topics for Extra Amateur License Exam 9
Canadian Call Sign Prefixes 13
Common Radio Bands in the United States 14
Common Amateur Radio Bands in Canada 14
Call Sign Phonics 21
Morse Code and Ham Radio 23
International Call Sign Prefixes 24
Third Party Communications 31

Appendix A – Ohio Ham Radio Clubs

ARRL Affiliated Amateur and Ham Radio Clubs – By City

Akron .... App A – 3
Alliance .... App A – 3
Ashland .... App A – 3
Athens .... App A – 3
Avon Lake .... App A – 3
Bay Village .... App A – 3
Beachwood .... App A – 4
Bellbrook .... App A – 4
Bellefontaine .... App A – 4
Bowling Green .... App A – 4
Brook Park .... App A – 4
Cambridge .... App A – 4
Canton .... App A – 4
Chesterland .... App A – 5
Cincinnati .... App A – 5
Cleveland .... App A – 5
Columbus .... App A – 5
Conneaut .... App A – 6
Coshocton .... App A – 7
Cuyahoga Falls .... App A – 7
Dayton .... App A – 7

Delaware .... App A – 7
Eaton .... App A – 7
Elyria .... App A – 7
Fairfield .... App A – 7
Findlay .... App A – 7
Galion .... App A – 8
Georgetown .... App A – 8
Hamersville .... App A – 8
Hamilton .... App A – 8
Hebron .... App A – 8
Hillsboro .... App A – 8
Huron .... App A – 9
Independence .... App A – 9
Jackson .... App A – 9
Lancaster .... App A – 9
Lebanon .... App A – 9
Lewisburg .... App A – 9
Lima .... App A – 9
London .... App A – 10
Louisville .... App A – 10
Mansfield .... App A – 10
Mantua .... App A – 10
Marengo .... App A – 10
Marietta .... App A – 10
Marion .... App A – 10
Massillon .... App A – 10
Medina .... App A – 11
Miamisburg .... App A – 11
Middletown .... App A – 11
Milford .... App A – 11
Monclova .... App A – 11
Mount Vernon .... App A – 11
New Philadelphia .... App A – 11
New Springfield .... App A – 11
Newark .... App A – 12
Painesville .... App A – 12
Pickerington .... App A – 12
Port Clinton .... App A – 12
Portsmouth .... App A – 12
Ravenna .... App A – 12
Salem .... App A – 12
Sandusky .... App A – 12
Springfield .... App A – 13
Steubenville .... App A – 13
Strongsville .... App A – 13
Sunbury .... App A – 13

Tiffin .... App A – 13
Toledo .... App A – 13
Van West .... App A – 13
Warren .... App A – 14
Wauseon .... App A – 14
Waverly .... App A – 14
West Chester .... App A – 14
Westerville .... App A – 14
Wilmington .... App A – 14
Wooster .... App A – 14
Youngstown .... App A – 14
Zanesville .... App A – 14

Appendix B – Ohio: South East Region Ham Licensees by City

Adams Mills .... App B – 3
Adamsville .... App B – 3
Adelphi .... App B – 3
Albany .... App B – 3
Amesville .... App B – 4
Athens .... App B – 4
Ava .... App B – 9
Bannock .... App B – 9
Barnesville .... App B – 10
Barton .... App B – 11
Beallsville .... App B – 11
Beaver .... App B – 11
Bellaire .... App B – 11
Belle Valley .... App B – 13
Belmont .... App B – 13
Belpre .... App B – 13
Bethesda .... App B – 15
Beverly .... App B – 16
Blaine .... App B – 16
Blue Rock .... App B – 16
Bridgeport .... App B – 17
Buchtel .... App B – 18
Byesville .... App B – 18
Caldwell .... App B – 19
Cambridge .... App B – 20
Carbon Hill .... App B – 24
Chandlersville .... App B – 24
Chauncey .... App B – 24
Chesapeake .... App B – 25
Cheshire .... App B – 25
Chesterhill .... App B – 26

Chillicothe .... App B – 26
Clarington .... App B – 33
Clarksburg .... App B – 33
Coal Grove .... App B – 33
Coal Run .... App B – 34
Coalton .... App B – 34
Coolville .... App B – 34
Corning .... App B – 35
Creola .... App B – 36
Crooksville .... App B – 36
Crown City .... App B – 36
Cumberland .... App B – 37
Cutler .... App B – 37
Deadman .... App B – 38
Deshler .... App B – 38
Dexter City .... App B – 38
Dresden .... App B – 38
Duncan Falls .... App B – 39
Ewing .... App B – 39
Fairpoint .... App B – 39
Fleming .... App B – 39
Flushing .... App B – 39
Frankfort .... App B – 39
Franklin Furnace .... App B – 40
Frazeysburg .... App B – 40
Friendship .... App B – 41
Gallipolis .... App B – 41
Garfield .... App B – 44
Glenford .... App B – 44
Glouster .... App B – 44
Gratis .... App B – 46
Graysville .... App B – 46
Guysville .... App B – 46
Hamden .... App B – 46
Hannibal .... App B – 47
Haverhill .... App B – 47
Haydenville .... App B – 47
Hide-A-Way Hills .... App B – 47
Ironton .... App B – 47
Jacksonville .... App B – 50
Jacobsburg .... App B – 50
Jerusalem .... App B – 51
Junction City .... App B – 51
Kerr .... App B – 51
Kimbolton .... App B – 51
Kingston .... App B – 52

Kitts Hill .... App B – 53
Lafferty .... App B – 53
Langsville .... App B – 53
Lansing .... App B – 54
Latham .... App B – 54
Laurelville .... App B – 54
Lewisville .... App B – 54
Little Hocking .... App B – 55
Logan .... App B – 56
London .... App B – 60
Londonderry .... App B – 63
Long Bottom .... App B – 63
Lore City .... App B – 63
Lowell .... App B – 63
Lower Salem .... App B – 63
Lucasville .... App B – 64
Macksburg .... App B – 66
Malta .... App B – 66
Marietta .... App B – 66
Martins Ferry .... App B – 72
McArthur .... App B – 74
McConnelsville .... App B – 75
McDermott .... App B – 76
Middleport .... App B – 76
Millfield .... App B – 77
Minford .... App B – 77
Morristown .... App B – 78
Mount Perry .... App B – 78
Mowrystown .... App B – 78
Murray City .... App B – 78
Nashport .... App B – 78
Neffs .... App B – 80
Nelsonville .... App B – 80
New Boston .... App B – 82
New Concord .... App B – 82
New Lexington .... App B – 84
New Marshfield .... App B – 85
New Matamoras .... App B – 85
New Plymouth .... App B – 86
New Straitsville .... App B – 86
North Waterford .... App B – 86
Norwich .... App B – 86
Oak Hill .... App B – 87
Otway .... App B – 87
Patriot .... App B – 88
Pedro .... App B – 88

Philo .... App B – 88
Piketon .... App B – 89
Pleasant City .... App B – 89
Pomeroy .... App B – 90
Portland .... App B – 91
Portsmouth .... App B – 91
Powhatan Point .... App B – 94
Proctorville .... App B – 95
Quaker City .... App B – 97
Racine .... App B – 98
Radcliff .... App B – 98
Rarden .... App B – 98
Ray .... App B – 98
Reedsville .... App B – 98
Reno .... App B – 99
Rio Grande .... App B – 99
Rock Camp .... App B – 99
Rockbridge .... App B – 99
Roseville .... App B – 100
Rutland .... App B – 101
Saint Clairsville .... App B – 101
Salesville .... App B – 105
Sarahsville .... App B – 105
Sardis .... App B – 106
Sciotoville .... App B – 106
Scottown .... App B – 107
Senecaville .... App B – 107
Shade .... App B – 107
Shadyside .... App B – 108
Shawnee .... App B – 109
Somerset .... App B – 109
South Bloomingville .... App B – 109
South Point .... App B – 110
South Salem .... App B – 111
South Webster .... App B – 112
South Zanesville .... App B – 112
Stewart .... App B – 113
Stockport .... App B – 113
Summerfield .... App B – 114
Syracuse .... App B – 114
The Plains .... App B – 114
Thornville .... App B – 115
Thurman .... App B – 117
Trimble .... App B – 117
Trinway .... App B – 117
Tuppers Plains .... App B – 117

Union Furnace .... App B – 117
Vincent .... App B – 117
Vinton .... App B – 118
Wakefield .... App B – 118
Waterford .... App B – 118
Watertown .... App B – 119
Waverly .... App B – 119
Wellston .... App B – 121
West Portsmouth .... App B – 122
Wheelersburg .... App B – 123
Whipple .... App B – 125
White Cottage .... App B – 126
Willow Wood .... App B – 126
Woodsfield .... App B – 126
Zaleski .... App B – 127
Zanesville .... App B – 127

Survival Communications in Ohio

Perhaps you have prepared for WTSHTF or TEOTWAWKI with respect to food, water, self-defense and shelter. But what about communication?

Whenever there is a disaster (hurricane, earthquake, economic collapse, nuclear war, EMF, solar eruption, etc.), the normal means of communication that we're all reliant upon (cell phone, land line phone, the Internet, etc.) will probably be, at best, sporadic and at worst, non-existent.

As this author sees it, short of smoke signals and mirrors, there are three options for communication in "trying times": (1) GMRS or FRS radios; (2) CB radios; and (3) ham or amateur radio. Let's consider each of these options to come up with the most acceptable one.

GMRS (General Mobile Radio Service) / FRS (Family Radio Service)

GMRS (General Mobile Radio Service) / FRS (Family Radio Service) radios work optimally over short distances where there is minimal interference. Originally designed to be used as pagers, particularly inside a building or other such confined area, these radios are low-cost and convenient to carry. Unfortunately their small size and light weight comes with a trade-off – short range and short battery life. These radios are supposed to be able to communicate for up to 25-30 miles. Right. That's on level terrain, without buildings or trees getting in the way. While battery life technology is constantly improving, you will need spare batteries to keep communicating or someway of recharging the ones in the radio. In this author's opinion, GMRS/FRS radios are not first choice when concerned with medium or long range communication.

CB (Citizens Band)

CB (Citizens Band) radios operate in a frequency range originally reserved for ham or amateur radio operation. Because of the overwhelming number of people wishing quick, low-cost, regulation-free communication, the FCC (Federal Communication Commission) split off a portion of the frequency spectrum and allowed anyone to purchase a CB radio and start communicating. No test. No license. Just personal/business communication. Today, CB radios are readily available in such outlets as eBay and Craigslist. This author has seen them at yard/garage/tag sales and at flea markets.

CB radios come in a variety of "flavors." Fixed units, sometimes referred to as base units are intended for home use. For the most part, they derive their power from the utility company. In the event of loss of electricity, most base units can also be connected to a 12-volt battery, like that in your car/truck. If you choose to obtain a fixed unit, make sure you know how to connect the unit to the battery – ahead of time. Trying to figure this out when you're under extra stress is not a good situation.

A second type of CB radio is designed to be mobile, that is, installed in your car/truck. It gets its power from the vehicle's battery. You can either attach an antenna permanently to the vehicle or have a removable, magnetic type antenna.

The third type of CB radio is designed for handheld use. They are small and light. Most weigh less than a pound and operate on batteries. Yes, using batteries in a CB poses the same limitations as those by the GMRS/FRS radios, but have the added advantage that most handheld units come with a cigarette lighter adapter. Comes in handy when you are on the move and wish to be able to communicate both from a vehicle and also when you have to abandon it.

While they have a greater range than GMRS/FRS radios, CB radios are, legally, limited to operate on 40 channels, with a power rating of four (4) watts or less. Yes, it is possible to alter CB radios to get around these limitations, but not legally,

Ham/Amateur Radio

Ham/Amateur radio is very appealing. With a ham radio, you are not limited to less than 50 miles, but can communicate with anyone in the world (who also has access to a ham radio, of course).

Standardized Amateur Radio Prepper Communications Plan

In the event of a nationwide catastrophic disaster, the nationwide network of Amateur Radio licensed preppers will need a set of standardized meeting frequencies to share information and coordinate activities between various prepper groups. This Standardized Amateur Radio Communications Plan establishes a set of frequencies on the 80 meter, 40 meter, 20 meter, and 2 meter Amateur Radio bands for use during these types of catastrophic disasters.

Routine nets will not be held on all of these frequencies, but preppers are encouraged to use them when coordinating with other preppers on a routine basis. Routine nets may be conducted by The American Preparedness Radio Net (TAPRN) on these or other frequencies as they see fit. However, TAPRN will promote the use of these standardized frequencies by all Amateur Radio licensed preppers during times of catastrophic disaster. The promotion of this Standardized Amateur Radio Communications Plan is encouraged by all means within the prepper community, including via Amateur Radio, Twitter, Facebook, and various blogs.

Standardized Frequencies and Modes
80 Meters – 3.818 MHz LSB (TAPRN Net: Sundays at 9 PM ET)
40 Meters – 7.242 MHz LSB
40 Meters Morse Code / Digital – 7.073 MHz USB (TAPRN: Sundays at 7:30 PM ET on CONTESTIA 4/250)
20 Meters – 14.242 MHz USB
2 Meters – 146.420 MHz FM

Nets and Network Etiquette

In times of nationwide catastrophic disaster, the ability of any one prepper to initiate and sustain themselves as a net control may be limited by the availability of power and other resource shortages. However, all licensed preppers are encouraged to maintain a listening watch on these frequencies as often as possible during a catastrophic disaster. Preppers may routinely announce themselves in the following manner:

• This is [Your Callsign Phonetically] in [Your State], maintaining a listening watch on [Standard Frequency] for any preppers on frequency seeking information or looking to provide information. Please call [Your Callsign Phonetically]. Preppers exchanging information that may require follow up should agree upon a designated time to return to the frequency and provide further information. If other stations are utilizing the frequency at the designated time you return, maintain watch and proceed with your communications when those stations are finished. If your communications are urgent and the stations on frequency are not passing information of a critical nature, interrupt with the word "Break" and request use of the frequency.

For More Information

Catastrophe Network: http://www.catastrophenetwork.org or @CatastropheNet on Twitter The American Preparedness Radio Network: http://www.taprn.com or @TAPRN on Twitter

In order to use a ham radio, legally, one must be licensed to do so by the FCC (other countries have analogous governmental bodies to regulate ham radio). To obtain a license is quite easy – take a test and pay your license fee. There are currently three classes of license – Technician, General, and Amateur Extra. With each of these licenses come specific abilities.

Technician class is the beginning level. The exam consists of 35 multiple choice questions randomly drawn from a pool of 395 questions. The question pool is readily available online for free downloading (http://www.ncvec.org/downloads/Revised%20Element%202.Pdf) or in such publications at *Ham Radio License Manual Revised 2nd Edition* (ISBN 978-0-87259-097-7). The current Technician pool of questions is to be used from July 1, 2010 to June 30, 2014. Be sure the question pool you are studying from is current. You will need to score at least 26 correct to pass. (Do not worry, Morse Code is no longer on the test, although many ham operators use it anyway.) You do not need to take a formal class in order to qualify to take the exam. You can learn the material on your own. Most people spend 10-15 hours studying and then successfully take the exam. The cost of taking the exam is under $20. The exam is given in MANY locations throughout the US. Usually the exam is given by area ham clubs. You do not have to belong to the club to take the exam. Check Appendix A for a listing of clubs in Ohio.

Topics for the Technician License in Amateur Radio

The Technician license exam covers such topics as basic regulations, operating practices, and electronic theory, with a focus on VHF and UHF applications. Below is the syllabus for the Technician Class.

Subelement T1 – FCC Rules, descriptions and definitions for the amateur radio service, operator and station license responsibilities

[6 Exam Questions – 6 Groups]

T1A – Amateur Radio services; purpose of the amateur service, amateur-satellite service, operator/primary station license grant, where FCC rules are codified, basis and purpose of FCC rules, meanings of basic terms used in FCC rules

T1B – Authorized frequencies; frequency allocations, ITU regions, emission type, restricted sub-bands, spectrum sharing, transmissions near band edges

T1C – Operator classes and station call signs; operator classes, sequential, special event, and vanity call sign systems, international communications, reciprocal operation, station license licensee, places where the amateur service is regulated by the FCC, name and address on ULS, license term, renewal, grace period

T1D – Authorized and prohibited transmissions

T1E – Control operator and control types; control operator required, eligibility, designation of control operator, privileges and duties, control point, local, automatic and remote control, location of control operator

T1F – Station identification and operation standards; special operations for repeaters and auxiliary stations, third party communications, club stations, station security, FCC inspection

---

Subelement T2 – Operating Procedures

[3 Exam Questions – 3 Groups]

T2A – Station operation; choosing an operating frequency, calling another station, test transmissions, use of minimum power, frequency use, band plans

T2B – VHF/UHF operating practices; SSB phone, FM repeater, simplex, frequency offsets, splits and shifts, CTCSS, DTMF, tone squelch, carrier squelch, phonetics

T2C – Public service; emergency and non-emergency operations, message traffic handling

---

Subelement T3 – Radio wave characteristics, radio and electromagnetic properties, propagation modes

[3 Exam Questions – 3 Groups]

T3A – Radio wave characteristics; how a radio signal travels; distinctions of HF, VHF and UHF; fading, multipath; wavelength vs. penetration; antenna orientation

T3B – Radio and electromagnetic wave properties; the electromagnetic spectrum, wavelength vs. frequency, velocity of electromagnetic waves

T3C – Propagation modes; line of sight, sporadic E, meteor, aurora scatter, tropospheric ducting, F layer skip, radio horizon

Subelement T4 - Amateur radio practices and station setup

[2 Exam Questions – 2 Groups]

T4A – Station setup; microphone, speaker, headphones, filters, power source, connecting a computer, RF grounding

T4B – Operating controls; tuning, use of filters, squelch, AGC, repeater offset, memory channels

Subelement T5 – Electrical principles, math for electronics, electronic principles, Ohm's Law

[4 Exam Questions – 4 Groups]

T5A – Electrical principles; current and voltage, conductors and insulators, alternating and direct current

T5B – Math for electronics; decibels, electronic units and the metric system

T5C – Electronic principles; capacitance, inductance, current flow in circuits, alternating current, definition of RF, power calculations

T5D – Ohm's Law

Subelement T6 – Electrical components, semiconductors, circuit diagrams, component functions

[4 Exam Groups – 4 Questions]

T6A – Electrical components; fixed and variable resistors, capacitors, and inductors; fuses, switches, batteries

T6B – Semiconductors; basic principles of diodes and transistors

T6C – Circuit diagrams; schematic symbols

T6D – Component functions

Subelement T7 – Station equipment, common transmitter and receiver problems, antenna measurements and troubleshooting, basic repair and testing

[4 Exam Questions – 4 Groups]

T7A – Station radios; receivers, transmitters, transceivers

T7B – Common transmitter and receiver problems; symptoms of overload and overdrive, distortion, interference, over and under modulation, RF feedback, off frequency signals; fading and noise; problems with digital communications interfaces

T7C – Antenna measurements and troubleshooting; measuring SWR, dummy loads, feedline failure modes

T7D – Basic repair and testing; soldering, use of a voltmeter, ammeter, and ohmmeter

Subelement T8 – Modulation modes, amateur satellite operation, operating activities, non-voice communications

[4 Exam Questions – 4 Groups]

T8A – Modulation modes; bandwidth of various signals

T8B – Amateur satellite operation; Doppler shift, basic orbits, operating protocols

T8C – Operating activities; radio direction finding, radio control, contests, special event stations, basic linking over Internet

T8D – Non-voice communications; image data, digital modes, CW, packet, PSK31

Subelement T9 – Antennas, feedlines

[2 Exam Groups – 2 Questions]

T9A – Antennas; vertical and horizontal, concept of gain, common portable and mobile antennas, relationships between antenna length and frequency

T9B – Feedlines; types, losses vs. frequency, SWR concepts, matching, weather protection, connectors

Subelement T0 – AC power circuits, antenna installation, RF hazards

[3 Exam Questions – 3 Groups]

T0A – AC power circuits; hazardous voltages, fuses and circuit breakers, grounding, lightning protection, battery safety, electrical code compliance

T0B – Antenna installation; tower safety, overhead power lines

T0C – RF hazards; radiation exposure, proximity to antennas, recognized safe power levels, exposure to others

Once your name and call sign are available in the FCC database, you have the privilege of operating on all VHF (2 m) and UHF (70 cm) frequencies above 30 megahertz (MHz) and HF frequencies 80, 40, and 15 meter, and on the 10 meter band using Morse code (CW), voice, and digital mode. For a Technician license in Ohio, your call sign will consist of a two-letter prefix beginning with K or W, the number eight (8), and a three-letter suffix. The single digit number in the call sign is determined according to which area of the US you obtain your first license. Even though you may move to another state, you keep this number in your call sign. This is also true should you upgrade to a higher license and get a new call sign. The numeral portion of your call sign stays the same.

Call Sign Numbers

Below is a chart showing the various numbers and the state(s) in which you would obtain the number.

Call Sign Number	State(s)
0	CO, IA, KS, MN, MO, NE, ND, SD
1	CT, ME, MA, NH, RI, VT
2	NJ, NY
3	DE, DC, MD, PA
4	AL, FL, GA, KY, NC, SC, TN, VA
5	AR, LA, MS, NM, OK, TX
6	CA
7	AZ, ID, MT, NV, OR, WA, UT, WY
8	MI, OH, WV
9	IL, IN, WI

Residents of Alaska may have any of the following call sign prefixes assigned to them: AL0-7, KL0-7, NL0-7, or WL0-7. Likewise, residents of Hawaii may have the prefix AH6-7, KH6-7, NH6-7, or WH6-7 assigned.

Once you obtain your Technician license, do not stop there. Go and get your General license.

General is the second of three ham license classes. Like the Technician license, to get a General license, you merely have to take a 35-question multiple choice exam and pay your license fee. Passing is still at least 26 correct answers and the fee is the same (less than $20). Again the question pool is available for free online (http://www.ncvec.org/page.php?id=358). It is also available in such print publications as *The ARRL General Class License Manual 7th Edition* (ISBN 978-0-87259-811-9). The current General pool of questions is to be used from July 1, 2011 to June 30, 2015. Be sure the question pool you are using is current. Being a bit more comprehensive than the Technician license, the General license usually requires 15-20 hours of study to learn the material. Check Appendix A for a listing of clubs in Ohio where you might take your exam. Once your name and NEW call sign is listed in the FCC database, you're good to go. For a General license in Ohio, your call sign will consist of a one-letter prefix beginning with K, N or W, the number eight (8), and a three-letter suffix.

Topics for the General License in Amateur Radio

The General license exam covers regulations, operating practices and electronic theory. Below is the syllabus for the General Class.

Subelement G1 – Commission's Rules

(5 Exam Questions – 5 Groups)

G1A – General Class control operator frequency privileges; primary and secondary allocations

G1B – Antenna structure limitations; good engineering and good amateur practice, beacon operation; restricted operation; retransmitting radio signals

G1C – Transmitter power regulations; data emission standards

G1D – Volunteer Examiners and Volunteer Examiner Coordinators; temporary identification

G1E – Control categories; repeater regulations; harmful interference; third party rules; ITU regions

---

Subelement G2 – Operating procedures

(5 Exam Questions – 5 Groups)

G2A – Phone operating procedures; USB/LSB utilization conventions; procedural signals; breaking into a OSO in progress; VOX operation

G2B – Operating courtesy; band plans, emergencies, including drills and emergency communications

G2C – CW operating procedures and procedural signals; Q signals and common abbreviations; full break in

G2D – Amateur Auxiliary; minimizing interference; HF operations

G2E – Digital operating; procedures, procedural signals and common abbreviations

Subelement G3 – Radio wave propagation

(3 Exam Questions – 3 Groups)

G3A – Sunspots and solar radiation; ionospheric disturbances; propagation forecasting and indices

G3B – Maximum Usable Frequency; Lowest Usable Frequency; propagation

G3C – Ionospheric layers; critical angle and frequency; HF scatter; Near Vertical Incidence Sky waves

Subelement G4 – Amateur radio practices

(5 Exam Questions – 5 Groups)

G4A – Station Operation and setup

G4B – Test and monitoring equipment; two-tone test

G4C – Interference with consumer electronics; grounding; DSP

G4D – Speech processors; S meters; sideband operation near band edges

G4E – HF mobile radio installations; emergency and battery powered operation

Subelement G5 – Electrical principles

(3 Exam Questions – 3 Groups)

G5A – Reactance; inductance; capacitance; impedance; impedance matching

G5B – The Decibel; current and voltage dividers; electrical power calculations; sine wave root-mean-square (RMS) values; PEP calculations

G5C – Resistors; capacitors and inductors in series and parallel; transformers

Subelement G6 – Circuit components

(3 Exam Questions – 3 Groups)

G6A – Resistors; capacitors; inductors

G6B – Rectifiers; solid state diodes and transistors; vacuum tubes; batteries

G6C – Analog and digital integrated circuits (ICs); microprocessors; memory; I/O devices; microwave ICs (MMICs); display devices

Subelement G7 – Practical circuits

(3 Exam Questions – 3 Groups)

G7A – Power supplies; schematic symbols

G7B – Digital circuits; amplifiers and oscillators

G7C – Receivers and transmitters; filters, oscillators

Subelement G8 – Signals and emissions

(2 Exam Questions – 2 Groups)

G8A – Carriers and modulation; AM; FM; single and double sideband; modulation envelope; overmodulation

G8B – Frequency mixing; multiplication; HF data communications; bandwidths of various modes; deviation

Subelement G9 – Antennas and feed lines

(4 Exam Questions – 4 Groups)

G9A – Antenna feed lines; characteristic impedance and attenuation; SWR calculation, measurement and effects; matching networks

G9B – Basic antennas

G9C – Directional antennas

G9D – Specialized antennas

Subelement G0 – Electrical and RF safety

(2 Exam Questions – 2 Groups)

G0A – RF safety principles, rules and guidelines; routine station elevation

G0B – Safety in the ham shack; electrical shock and treatment, safety grounding, fusing, interlocks, wiring, antenna and tower safety

With a General license, you can use all VHF and UHF frequencies and most of the HF frequencies. You would have access to the 160, 30, 17, 12, and 10 meter bands and access to major parts of the 80, 40, 20, and 15 meter bands. Of course, this is in addition to all bands available to Technician license holders.

Amateur Extra is the third of three ham license classes. Like the Technician and General classes, you merely have to pass a test and pay your fee to get your Amateur Extra license. This class of license is more comprehensive than the lower license classes. The exam is longer – 50 questions – and the minimum passing score is higher – 37. However, once you get your Amateur Extra license, all ham frequencies, VHF, UHF and HF are available for your enjoyment. The Extra exam covers regulations, specialized operating practices, advanced electronics theory, and radio equipment design.

Like for the other license classes, the question pool for the Amateur Extra license is available online for downloading (http://www.ncvec.org/downloads/REVISED%202012-2016%20Extra%20Class%20Pool.doc). It is also available in print form in such publications as *The ARRL Extra Class License Manual Revised 9th Edition* (ISBN 978-0-87259-887-4).

Topics for the Extra License in Amateur Radio

Below is the syllabus for the Amateur Extra Class for July 1, 2012 to June 30, 2016.

Subelement E1 – Commission's Rules

[6 Exam Questions – 6 Groups]

E1A – Operating Standards: frequency privileges; emission standards; automatic message forwarding; frequency sharing; stations aboard ships or aircraft

E1B – Station restrictions and special operations: restrictions on station location; general operating restrictions, spurious emissions, control operator reimbursement; antenna structure restrictions; RACES operations

E1C – Station control: definitions and restrictions pertaining to local, automatic and remote control operation; control operator responsibilities for remote and automatically controlled stations

E1D – Amateur Satellite service: definitions and purpose; license requirements for space stations; available frequencies and bands; telecommand and telemetry operations; restrictions, and special provisions; notification requirements

E1E – Volunteer examiner program: definitions, qualifications, preparation and administration of exams; accreditation; question pools; documentation requirements

E1F – Miscellaneous rules: external RF power amplifiers; national quiet zone; business communications; compensated communications; spread spectrum; auxiliary stations; reciprocal operating privileges; IARP and CEPT licenses; third party communications with foreign countries; special temporary authority

Subelement E2 – Operating procedures

[5 Exam Questions – 5 Groups]

E2A – Amateur radio in space: amateur satellites; orbital mechanics; frequencies and modes; satellite hardware; satellite operations

E2B – Television practices: fast scan television standards and techniques; slow scan television standards and techniques

E2C – Operating methods: contest and DX operating; spread-spectrum transmissions; selecting an operating frequency

E2D – Operating methods: VHF and UHF digital modes; APRS

E2E – Operating methods: operating HF digital modes; error correction

Subelement E3 – Radio wave propagation

[3 Exam Questions – 3 Groups]

E3A – Propagation and technique, Earth-Moon-Earth communications; meteor scatter

E3B – Propagation and technique, trans-equatorial; long path; gray-line; multi-path propagation

E3C – Propagation and technique, Aurora propagation; selective fading; radio-path horizon; take-off angle over flat or sloping terrain; effects of ground on propagation; less common propagation modes

Subelement E4 – Amateur practices

[5 Exam Questions – 5 Groups]

E4A – Test equipment: analog and digital instruments; spectrum and network analyzers, antenna analyzers; oscilloscopes; testing transistors; RF measurements

E4B – Measurement technique and limitations: instrument accuracy and performance limitations; probes; techniques to minimize errors; measurement of "Q"; instrument calibration

E4C – Receiver performance characteristics, phase noise, capture effect, noise floor, image rejection, MDS, signal-to-noise-ratio; selectivity

E4D – Receiver performance characteristics, blocking dynamic range, intermodulation and cross-modulation interference; 3rd order intercept; desensitization; preselection

E4E – Noise suppression: system noise; electrical appliance noise; line noise; locating noise sources; DSP noise reduction; noise blankers

Subelement E5 – Electrical principles

[4 Exam Questions – 4 Groups]

E5A – Resonance and Q: characteristics of resonant circuits: series and parallel resonance; Q; half-power bandwidth; phase relationships in reactive circuits

E5B – Time constants and phase relationships: RLC time constants: definition; time constants in RL and RC circuits; phase angle between voltage and current; phase angles of series and parallel circuits

E5C – Impedance plots and coordinate systems: plotting impedances in polar coordinates; rectangular coordinates

E5D – AC and RF energy in real circuits: skin effect; electrostatic and electromagnetic fields; reactive power; power factor; coordinate systems

Subelement E6 – Circuit components

[6 Exam Questions – 6 Groups]

E6A – Semiconductor materials and devices: semiconductor materials germanium, silicon, P-type, N-type; transistor types: NPN, PNP, junction, field-effect transistors: enhancement mode; depletion mode; MOS; CMOS; N-channel; P-channel

E6B – Semiconductor diodes

E6C – Integrated circuits: TTL digital integrated circuits; CMOS digital integrated circuits; gates

E6D – Optical devices and toroids: cathode-ray tube devices; charge-coupled devices (CCDs); liquid crystal displays (LCDs); toroids: permeability, core material, selecting, winding

E6E – Piezoelectric crystals and MMICs: quartz crystals; crystal oscillators and filters; monolithic amplifiers

E6F – Optical components and power systems: photoconductive principles and effects, photovoltaic systems, optical couplers, optical sensors, and optoisolators

Subelement E7 – Practical circuits

[8 Exam Questions – 8 Groups]

E7A – Digital circuits: digital circuit principles and logic circuits: classes of logic elements; positive and negative logic; frequency dividers; truth tables

E7B – Amplifiers: Class of operation; vacuum tube and solid-state circuits; distortion and intermodulation; spurious and parasitic suppression; microwave amplifiers

E7C – Filters and matching networks: filters and impedance matching networks: types of networks; types of filters; filter applications; filter characteristics; impedance matching; DSP filtering

E7D – Power supplies and voltage regulators

E7E – Modulation and demodulation: reactance, phase and balanced modulators; detectors; mixer stages; DSP modulation and demodulation; software defined radio systems

E7F – Frequency markers and counters: frequency divider circuits; frequency marker generators; frequency counters

E7G – Active filters and op-amps: active audio filters; characteristics; basic circuit design; operational amplifiers

E7H – Oscillators and signal sources: types of oscillators; synthesizers and phase-locked loops; direct digital synthesizers

Subelement E8 – Signals and emissions

[4 Exam Questions – 4 Groups]

E8A – AC waveforms: sine, square, sawtooth and irregular waveforms; AC measurements; average and PEP of RF signals; pulse and digital signal waveforms

E8B – Modulation and demodulation: modulation methods; modulation index and deviation ratio; pulse modulation; frequency and time division multiplexing

E8C – Digital signals: digital communications modes; CW; information rate vs. bandwidth; spread-spectrum communications; modulation methods

E8D – Waves, measurements, and RF grounding: peak-to-peak values, polarization; RF grounding

Subelement E9 – Antennas and transmission lines

[8 Exam Questions – 8 Groups]

E9A – Isotropic and gain antennas: definition; used as a standard for comparison; radiation pattern; basic antenna parameters: radiation resistance and reactance, gain, beamwidth, efficiency

E9B – Antenna patterns: E and H plane patterns; gain as a function of pattern; antenna design; Yagi antennas

E9C – Wire and phased vertical antennas: beverage antennas; terminated and resonant rhombic antennas; elevation above real ground; ground effects as related to polarization; take-off angles

E9D – Directional antennas: gain; satellite antennas; antenna beamwidth; losses; SWR bandwidth; antenna efficiency; shortened and mobile antennas; grounding

E9E – Matching: matching antennas to feed lines; power dividers

E9F – Transmission lines: characteristics of open and shorted feed lines: 1/8 wavelength; 1/4 wavelength; 1/2 wavelength; feed lines: coax versus open-wire; velocity factor; electrical length; transformation characteristics of line terminated in impedance not equal to characteristic impedance

E9G – The Smith chart

E9H – Effective radiated power; system gains and losses; radio direction finding antennas

Subelement E0 – Safety

[1 exam question – 1 group]

E0A – Safety: amateur radio safety practices; RF radiation hazards; hazardous materials

Once your new call sign is listed in the FCC database, you are good to go. For an Amateur Extra license in Ohio, your call sign will consist of a prefix of K, N or W, the number eight (8), and a two-letter suffix, or a two-letter prefix beginning with A, N, K or W, the number eight (8), and a one-letter suffix, or a two-letter prefix beginning with A, the number eight (8), and a two-letter suffix.

Ham radio equipment can be expensive or you can do it "on the cheap." The cost will run from a couple hundred dollars to well in the thousands, depending on what you have available. eBay, and Craigslist are good places to start looking. Most ham clubs do some sort of hamfest annually wherein club members or others are willing to part with older equipment. See Appendix A for a list of clubs in Ohio.

Another excellent source of equipment, as well as advice on setting the equipment up and how to use it properly, is current ham operators. In Appendix B, the author has listed all the FCC licensed ham operators in Ohio, listed by city, and then sorted by street and house number on the street. Who knows, maybe someone who lives close to you is a ham operator. Be a good neighbor, stop by and have a chat with him/her.

Like CB radios, ham radios come in three formats – base, mobile, and handheld. They can use the electric company for power, or operate off a car battery. In the opinion of this author, in spite of the slightly higher cost of the equipment and having to take a test to legally use the equipment, ham radio is the way to go when concerned about communication during times of crisis.

Canadian Call Sign Prefixes

Because of our proximity to Canada, many times ham contact is made with our northern neighbors. Below is a chart showing the origin of Canadian call sign prefixes.

Call Sign Prefix	Provence or Territory
CY0	Sable Island
CY9	St. Paul Island
VA1, VE1	New Brunswick, Nova Scotia
VA2, VE2	Quebec
VA3, VE3	Ontario
VA4, VE4	Manitoba
VA5, VE5	Saskatchewan
VA6, VE6	Alberta
VA7, VE7	British Columbia
VE8	North West Territories
VE9	New Brunswick
VO1	Newfoundland
VO2	Labrador
VY0	Nunavut
VY1	Yukon
VY2	Prince Edward Island

Common Radio Bands in the United States

Certain radio bands are more popular with ham radio enthusiasts than others. Below is a chart showing these bands and when they are most popular.

	Band (meter)	Frequency (MHz)	Use
HF	160	1.8 – 2.0	Night
	80	3.5 – 4.0	Night and Local Day
	40	7.0 – 7.3	Night and Local Day
	30	10.1 – 10.15	CW and Digital
	20	14.0 – 14.350	World Wide Day and Night
	17	18.068 – 18.168	World Wide Day and Night
	15	21.0 – 21.450	Primarily Daytime
	12	24.890 – 24.990	Primarily Daytime
	10	28.0 – 29.70	Daytime during Sunspot highs
VHF	6	50 – 54	Local to World Wide
	2	144 – 148	Local to Medium Distance
UHF	70 cm	430 – 440	Local

Common Amateur Radio Bands in Canada

160 Meter Band - Maximum bandwidth 6 kHz

1.800 - 1.820 MHz - CW
1.820 - 1.830 MHz - Digital Modes
1 830 - 1.840 MHz - DX Window
1.840 - 2.000 MHz - SSB and other wide band modes

80 Meter Band - Maximum bandwidth 6 kHz

3.500 - 3.580 MHz - CW
3.580 - 3.620 MHz - Digital Modes
3.620 - 3.635 MHz - Packet/Digital Secondary
3.635 - 3.725 MHz - CW
3.725 - 3.790 MHz - SSB and other side band modes*
3.790 - 3.800 MHz - SSB DX Window
3.800 - 4.000 MHz - SSB and other wide band modes

40 Meter Band - Maximum bandwidth 6 kHz

7.000 - 7.035 MHz - CW
7.035 - 7.050 MHz - Digital Modes
7.040 - 7.050 MHz - International packet
7.050 - 7.100 MHz - SSB
7.100 - 7.120 MHz - Packet within Region 2
7.120 - 7.150 MHz - CW
7.150 - 7.300 MHz - SSB and other wide band modes

30 Meter Band - Maximum bandwidth 1 kHz

10.100 - 10.130 MHz - CW only
10.130 - 10.140 MHz - Digital Modes
10.140 - 10.150 MHz - Packet

20 Meter Band - Maximum bandwidth 6 kHz

14.000 - 14.070 MHz - CW only
14.070 - 14.095 MHz - Digital Mode
14.095 - 14.099 MHz - Packet
14.100 MHz - Beacons
14.101 - 14.112 MHz - CW, SSB, packet shared
14.112 - 14.350 MHz - SSB
14.225 - 14.235 MHz - SSTV

17 Meter Band - Maximum bandwidth 6 kHz

18.068 - 18.100 MHz - CW
18.100 - 18.105 MHz - Digital Modes
18.105 - 18.110 MHz - Packet
18.110 - 18.168 MHz - SSB and other wide band modes

15 Meter Band - maximum bandwidth 6 kHz

21.000 - 21.070 MHz - CW
21.070 - 21.090 MHz - Digital Modes
21.090 - 21.125 MHz - Packet
21.100 - 21.150 MHz - CW and SSB
21.150 - 21.335 MHz - SSB and other wide band modes
21.335 - 21.345 MHz - SSTV
21.345 - 21.450 MHz - SSB and other wide band modes

12 Meter Band - Maximum bandwidth 6 kHz

24.890 - 24.930 MHz - CW
24.920 - 24.925 MHz - Digital Modes
24.925 - 24.930 MHz - Packet
24.930 - 24.990 MHz - SSB and other wide band modes

10 Meter Band - Maximum band width 20 kHz

28.000 - 28.200 MHz - CW
28.070 - 28.120 MHz - Digital Modes
28.120 - 28.190 MHz - Packet
28.190 - 28.200 MHz - Beacons
28.200 - 29.300 MHz - SSB and other wide band modes
29.300 - 29.510 MHz - Satellite
29.510 - 29.700 MHz - SSB, FM and repeaters

160 Meters (1.8-2.0 MHz)

1.800 - 2.000 CW
1.800 - 1.810 Digital Modes
1.810 CW QRP
1.843-2.000 SSB, SSTV and other wideband modes
1.910 SSB QRP
1.995 - 2.000 Experimental
1.999 - 2.000 Beacons

80 Meters (3.5-4.0 MHz)

3.590 RTTY/Data DX
3.570-3.600 RTTY/Data
3.790-3.800 DX window
3.845 SSTV
3.885 AM calling frequency

40 Meters (7.0-7.3 MHz)

7.040 RTTY/Data DX
7.080-7.125 RTTY/Data
7.171 SSTV
7.290 AM calling frequency

30 Meters (10.1-10.15 MHz)

10.130-10.140 RTTY
10.140-10.150 Packet

20 Meters (14.0-14.35 MHz)

14.070-14.095 RTTY
14.095-14.0995 Packet
14.100 NCDXF Beacons
14.1005-14.112 Packet
14.230 SSTV
14.286 AM calling frequency

17 Meters (18.068-18.168 MHz)

18.100-18.105 RTTY
18.105-18.110 Packet

15 Meters (21.0-21.45 MHz)

21.070-21.110 RTTY/Data
21.340 SSTV

12 Meters (24.89-24.99 MHz)

24.920-24.925 RTTY
24.925-24.930 Packet

10 Meters (28-29.7 MHz)

28.000-28.070 CW
28.070-28.150 RTTY
28.150-28.190 CW
28.200-28.300 Beacons
28.300-29.300 Phone
28.680 SSTV
29.000-29.200 AM
29.300-29.510 Satellite Downlinks
29.520-29.590 Repeater Inputs
29.600 FM Simplex
29.610-29.700 Repeater Outputs

6 Meters (50-54 MHz)

50.0-50.1 CW, beacons
50.060-50.080 beacon subband
50.1-50.3 SSB, CW
50.10-50.125 DX window
50.125 SSB calling
50.3-50.6 All modes
50.6-50.8 Nonvoice communications
50.62 Digital (packet) calling
50.8-51.0 Radio remote control (20-kHz channels)
51.0-51.1 Pacific DX window
51.12-51.48 Repeater inputs (19 channels)
51.12-51.18 Digital repeater inputs
51.5-51.6 Simplex (six channels)
51.62-51.98 Repeater outputs (19 channels)
51.62-51.68 Digital repeater outputs
52.0 52.48 Repeater inputs (except as noted; 23 channels)
52.02, 52.04 FM simplex
52.2 TEST PAIR (input)
52.5-52.98 Repeater output (except as noted; 23 channels)
52.525 Primary FM simplex
52.54 Secondary FM simplex
52.7 TEST PAIR (output)
53.0-53.48 Repeater inputs (except as noted; 19 channels)
53.0 Remote base FM simplex
53.02 Simplex
53.1, 53.2, 53.3, 53.4 Radio remote control
53.5-53.98 Repeater outputs (except as noted; 19 channels)
53.5, 53.6, 53.7, 53.8 Radio remote control
53.52, 53.9 Simplex

2 Meters (144-148 MHz)

144.00-144.05 EME (CW)
144.05-144.10 General CW and weak signals
144.10-144.20 EME and weak-signal SSB
144.200 National calling frequency
144.200-144.275 General SSB operation
144.275-144.300 Propagation beacons
144.30-144.50 New OSCAR subband
144.50-144.60 Linear translator inputs
144.60-144.90 FM repeater inputs
144.90-145.10 Weak signal and FM simplex (145.01,03,05,07,09 are widely used for packet)
145.10-145.20 Linear translator outputs
145.20-145.50 FM repeater outputs
145.50-145.80 Miscellaneous and experimental modes
145.80-146.00 OSCAR subband
146.01-146.37 Repeater inputs
146.40-146.58 Simplex
146.52 National Simplex Calling Frequency
146.61-146.97 Repeater outputs
147.00-147.39 Repeater outputs
147.42-147.57 Simplex
147.60-147.99 Repeater inputs

1.25 Meters (222-225 MHz)

222.0-222.150 Weak-signal modes
222.0-222.025 EME
222.05-222.06 Propagation beacons
222.1 SSB & CW calling frequency
222.10-222.15 Weak-signal CW & SSB
222.15-222.25 Local coordinator's option; weak signal, ACSB, repeater inputs, control
222.25-223.38 FM repeater inputs only
223.40-223.52 FM simplex
223.52-223.64 Digital, packet
223.64-223.70 Links, control
223.71-223.85 Local coordinator's option; FM simplex, packet, repeater outputs
223.85-224.98 Repeater outputs only

70 Centimeters (420-450 MHz)

420.00-426.00 ATV repeater or simplex with 421.25 MHz video carrier control links and experimental
426.00-432.00 ATV simplex with 427.250-MHz video carrier frequency
432.00-432.07 EME (Earth-Moon-Earth)
432.07-432.10 Weak-signal CW
432.10 70-cm calling frequency

432.10-432.30 Mixed-mode and weak-signal work
432.30-432.40 Propagation beacons
432.40-433.00 Mixed-mode and weak-signal work
433.00-435.00 Auxiliary/repeater links
435.00-438.00 Satellite only (internationally)
438.00-444.00 ATV repeater input with 439.250-MHz video carrier frequency and repeater links
442.00-445.00 Repeater inputs and outputs (local option)
445.00-447.00 Shared by auxiliary and control links, repeaters and simplex (local option)
446.00 National simplex frequency
447.00-450.00 Repeater inputs and outputs (local option)

33 Centimeters (902-928 MHz)

902.0-903.0 Narrow-bandwidth, weak-signal communications
902.0-902.8 SSTV, FAX, ACSSB, experimental
902.1 Weak-signal calling frequency
902.8-903.0 Reserved for EME, CW expansion
903.1 Alternate calling frequency
903.0-906.0 Digital communications
906-909 FM repeater inputs
909-915 ATV
915-918 Digital communications
918-921 FM repeater outputs
921-927 ATV
927-928 FM simplex and links

23 Centimeters (1240-1300 MHz)

1240-1246 ATV #1
1246-1248 Narrow-bandwidth FM point-to-point links and digital, duplex with 1258-1260.
1248-1258 Digital Communications
1252-1258 ATV #2
1258-1260 Narrow-bandwidth FM point-to-point links digital, duplexed with 1246-1252
1260-1270 Satellite uplinks, reference WARC '79
1260-1270 Wide-bandwidth experimental, simplex ATV
1270-1276 Repeater inputs, FM and linear, paired with 1282-1288, 239 pairs every 25 kHz, e.g. 1270.025, .050, etc.
1271-1283 Non-coordinated test pair
1276-1282 ATV #3
1282-1288 Repeater outputs, paired with 1270-1276
1288-1294 Wide-bandwidth experimental, simplex ATV
1294-1295 Narrow-bandwidth FM simplex services, 25-kHz channels
1294.5 National FM simplex calling frequency
1295-1297 Narrow bandwidth weak-signal communications (no FM)
1295.0-1295.8 SSTV, FAX, ACSSB, experimental
1295.8-1296.0 Reserved for EME, CW expansion

1296.00-1296.05 EME-exclusive
1296.07-1296.08 CW beacons
1296.1 CW, SSB calling frequency
1296.4-1296.6 Crossband linear translator input
1296.6-1296.8 Crossband linear translator output
1296.8-1297.0 Experimental beacons (exclusive)
1297-1300 Digital Communications

2300-2310 and 2390-2450 MHz

2300.0-2303.0 High-rate data
2303.0-2303.5 Packet
2303.5-2303.8 TTY packet
2303.9-2303.9 Packet, TTY, CW, EME
2303.9-2304.1 CW, EME
2304.1 Calling frequency
2304.1-2304.2 CW, EME, SSB
2304.2-2304.3 SSB, SSTV, FAX, Packet AM, Amtor
2304.30-2304.32 Propagation beacon network
2304.32-2304.40 General propagation beacons
2304.4-2304.5 SSB, SSTV, ACSSB, FAX, Packet AM, Amtor experimental
2304.5-2304.7 Crossband linear translator input
2304.7-2304.9 Crossband linear translator output
2304.9-2305.0 Experimental beacons
2305.0-2305.2 FM simplex (25 kHz spacing)
2305.20 FM simplex calling frequency
2305.2-2306.0 FM simplex (25 kHz spacing)
2306.0-2309.0 FM Repeaters (25 kHz) input
2309.0-2310.0 Control and auxiliary links
2390.0-2396.0 Fast-scan TV
2396.0-2399.0 High-rate data
2399.0-2399.5 Packet
2399.5-2400.0 Control and auxiliary links
2400.0-2403.0 Satellite
2403.0-2408.0 Satellite high-rate data
2408.0-2410.0 Satellite
2410.0-2413.0 FM repeaters (25 kHz) output
2413.0-2418.0 High-rate data
2418.0-2430.0 Fast-scan TV
2430.0-2433.0 Satellite
2433.0-2438.0 Satellite high-rate data
2438.0-2450.0 WB FM, FSTV, FMTV, SS experimental

3300-3500 MHz

3456.3-3456.4 Propagation beacons

5650-5925 MHz
5760.3-5760.4 Propagation beacons

10.00-10.50 GHz
10.368 Narrow band calling frequency 10.3683-10.3684 Propagation beacons
10.3640 Calling frequency

Now that you have your license (you do, don't you?), and your equipment, you are ready to go live. Below is a suggested start.

1) Assuming you have the HT set up to the appropriate frequency, and offset, press the mic button on the HT and say, "KK4HWX listening." Replace the KK4HWX with your own call sign, the one assigned to you by the FCC (it's the law). If no one responds to your call, you may wish to try again. Hopefully someone will respond to your call.

2) Once you get a response, it will be in the form of something like, "KK4HWX this is ??1??? in Eastport returning. My name is Florence. Back to you. ??1???" then a tone. Let us examine the response more closely. She first acknowledged your call sign (KK4HWX), then identified hers (??1???). From the 1 in her call sign, you know that she first got her license in Region 1, meaning she got it while a resident of CT, ME, MA, NH, RI, or VT. She then told you where she's transmitting from (Eastport). The term "returning" means that she is returning your call. Her name is Florence. The phrase, "Back to you" indicates that she is turning over the conversation to you. She then repeats her call sign. The tone indicates to you that it is okay to proceed with your response. BTW if she had used the term "Over" instead of "Back to you," it would mean the same thing, just fewer words.

3) At this point, press the mic button and continue with the conversation. You should restate your call sign often during the conversation (perhaps every 10 minutes or less and whenever you begin transmitting). Don't forget to say, "Over" or "Back to you" whenever you are giving Florence control of the conversation again.

4) When you are ready to stop the conversation, you should say goodbye or use the phrase "73", meaning "best wishes." Your conversation would end something like, "??1??? 73, this is KK4HWX clear and monitoring." The "clear and monitoring" indicates that you are going to continue to monitor the frequency. If you are not going to continue monitoring, you may wish to end the conversation with Florence with, "clear and QRT" instead. The QRT means that you are stopping transmissions.

Call Sign Phonics

Because of different accents of various people, sometimes it is difficult to understand call sign letters when spoken. For this reason, most ham operators verbalize their call sign using phonics. Below is a table listing the accepted phonics for letters and numbers.

A = ALFA	S = SIERRA	
B = BRAVO	T = TANGO	
C = CHARLIE	U = UNIFORM	
D = DELTA	V = VICTOR	
E = ECHO	W = WHISKEY	
F = FOXTROT	X = X-RAY	
G = GOLF	Y = YANKEE	
H = HOTEL	Z = ZULU (ZED)	
I = INDIA	1 = ONE	
J = JULIETT	2 = TWO	
K = KILO	3 = THREE (TREE)	
L = LIMA	4 = FOUR	
M = MIKE	5 = FIVE (FIFE)	
N = NOVEMBER	6 = SIX	
O = OSCAR	7 = SEVEN	
P = PAPA (PA-PA')	8 = EIGHT	
Q = QUEBEC (KAY-BEK')	9 = NINE (NINER)	
R = ROMEO	0 = ZERO	

The words in parentheses are the pronunciation or the alternate pronunciations for the words or numbers, but you will hear both used. With the letter Z, (ZED) is by far the most commonly used. With the number 9, NINER is the most common and easiest to understand ON THE AIR.

If you wish to use Morse code (CW) instead of voice communication, the "conversation" would follow the same steps, with a few modifications. To type out each word would require a lot of typing and translating. If you are like this author, more means more, i.e., more typing means more typos are likely. To help with this situation, CW enthusiasts have developed a language all their own – they use abbreviations for common phrases. Below is a chart showing some of these abbreviations.

Abbreviation	Use
AR	Over
de	From or "this is"
ES	And
GM	Good Morning
K	Go
KN	Go only
NM	Name
QTH	Location
RPT	Report
R	Roger
SK	Clear
tnx	Thanks
UR	Your, you are
73	Best Wishes

Morse Code and Amateur Radio

If you wish to use CW, but are concerned about accuracy, you might consider purchasing a Morse code translator. This is an electronic device that you place in front of your speakers. It takes the CW sounds and translates them into English and displays the transmission on an LCD display. For the reverse, you can pick up a CW keyboard. With the keyboard, you type in your message and it converts the text to Morse code. The translator does not need to be attached to your ham equipment, whereas the keyboard would.

For your convenience, below is a table showing the Morse code signals and their meaning.

Character	Code
A	· —
B	— · · ·
C	— · — ·
D	— · ·
E	·
F	· · — ·
G	— — ·
H	· · · ·
I	· ·
J	· — — —
K	— · —
L	· — · ·
M	— —
N	— ·
O	— — —
P	· — — ·
Q	— — · —
R	· — ·
S	· · ·
T	—
U	· · —
V	· · · —
W	· — —
X	— · · —
Y	— · — —
Z	— — · ·
0	— — — — —
1	· — — — —
2	· · — — —
3	· · · — —
4	· · · · —
5	· · · · ·

6	— · · · ·
7	— — · · ·
8	— — — · ·
9	— — — — ·
Ampersand [&], Wait	· — · · ·
Apostrophe [']	· — — — — ·
At sign [@]	· — — · — ·
Colon [:]	— — — · · ·
Comma [,]	— — · · — —
Dollar sign [$]	· · · — · · —
Double dash [=]	— · · · —
Exclamation mark [!]	— · — · — —
Hyphen, Minus [-]	— · · · · —
Parenthesis closed [)]	— · — — · —
Parenthesis open [(]	— · — — ·
Period [.]	· — · — · —
Plus [+]	· — · — ·
Question mark [?]	· · — — · ·
Quotation mark ["]	· — · · — ·
Semicolon [;]	— · — · — ·
Slash [/], Fraction bar	— · · — ·
Underscore [_]	· · — — · —

An advantage of using Morse Code is that when broadcasting CW, you are using reduced power, thereby saving your battery. Your battery is used only while actually transmitting or receiving.

International Call Sign Prefixes

As was stated earlier, all ham radio call signs begin with letters (or numbers) taken from blocks assigned to each country of the world by the *ITU - International Telecommunications Union,* a body controlled by the United Nations. The following chart indicates which call sign series are allocated to which countries.

Call Sign Series	Allocated to
AAA-ALZ	**United States of America**
AMA-AOZ	Spain
APA-ASZ	Pakistan (Islamic Republic of)
ATA-AWZ	India (Republic of)
AXA-AXZ	Australia
AYA-AZZ	Argentine Republic
A2A-A2Z	Botswana (Republic of)
A3A-A3Z	Tonga (Kingdom of)
A4A-A4Z	Oman (Sultanate of)
A5A-A5Z	Bhutan (Kingdom of)

A6A-A6Z	United Arab Emirates
A7A-A7Z	Qatar (State of)
A8A-A8Z	Liberia (Republic of)
A9A-A9Z	Bahrain (State of)
BAA-BZZ	China (People's Republic of)
CAA-CEZ	Chile
CFA-CKZ	Canada
CLA-CMZ	Cuba
CNA-CNZ	Morocco (Kingdom of)
COA-COZ	Cuba
CPA-CPZ	Bolivia (Republic of)
CQA-CUZ	Portugal
CVA-CXZ	Uruguay (Eastern Republic of)
CYA-CZZ	Canada
C2A-C2Z	Nauru (Republic of)
C3A-C3Z	Andorra (Principality of)
C4A-C4Z	Cyprus (Republic of)
C5A-C5Z	Gambia (Republic of the)
C6A-C6Z	Bahamas (Commonwealth of the)
C7A-C7Z	World Meteorological Organization
C8A-C9Z	Mozambique (Republic of)
DAA-DRZ	Germany (Federal Republic of)
DSA-DTZ	Korea (Republic of)
DUA-DZZ	Philippines (Republic of the)
D2A-D3Z	Angola (Republic of)
D4A-D4Z	Cape Verde (Republic of)
D5A-D5Z	Liberia (Republic of)
D6A-D6Z	Comoros (Islamic Federal Republic of the)
D7A-D9Z	Korea (Republic of)
EAA-EHZ	Spain
EIA-EJZ	Ireland
EKA-EKZ	Armenia (Republic of)
ELA-ELZ	Liberia (Republic of)
EMA-EOZ	Ukraine
EPA-EQZ	Iran (Islamic Republic of)
ERA-ERZ	Moldova (Republic of)
ESA-ESZ	Estonia (Republic of)
ETA-ETZ	Ethiopia (Federal Democratic Republic of)
EUA-EWZ	Belarus (Republic of)
EXA-EXZ	Kyrgyz Republic
EYA-EYZ	Tajikistan (Republic of)
EZA-EZZ	Turkmenistan
E2A-E2Z	Thailand
E3A-E3Z	Eritrea
E4A-E4Z	Palestinian Authority

E5A-E5Z	New Zealand - Cook Islands (WRC-07)
E7A-E7Z	Bosnia and Herzegovina (Republic of) (WRC-07)
FAA-FZZ	France
GAA-GZZ	United Kingdom of Great Britain and Northern Ireland
HAA-HAZ	Hungary (Republic of)
HBA-HBZ	Switzerland (Confederation of)
HCA-HDZ	Ecuador
HEA-HEZ	Switzerland (Confederation of)
HFA-HFZ	Poland (Republic of)
HGA-HGZ	Hungary (Republic of)
HHA-HHZ	Haiti (Republic of)
HIA-HIZ	Dominican Republic
HJA-HKZ	Colombia (Republic of)
HLA-HLZ	Korea (Republic of)
HMA-HMZ	Democratic People's Republic of Korea
HNA-HNZ	Iraq (Republic of)
HOA-HPZ	Panama (Republic of)
HQA-HRZ	Honduras (Republic of)
HSA-HSZ	Thailand
HTA-HTZ	Nicaragua
HUA-HUZ	El Salvador (Republic of)
HVA-HVZ	Vatican City State
HWA-HYZ	France
HZA-HZZ	Saudi Arabia (Kingdom of)
H2A-H2Z	Cyprus (Republic of)
H3A-H3Z	Panama (Republic of)
H4A-H4Z	Solomon Islands
H6A-H7Z	Nicaragua
H8A-H9Z	Panama (Republic of)
IAA-IZZ	Italy
JAA-JSZ	Japan
JTA-JVZ	Mongolia
JWA-JXZ	Norway
JYA-JYZ	Jordan (Hashemite Kingdom of)
JZA-JZZ	Indonesia (Republic of)
J2A-J2Z	Djibouti (Republic of)
J3A-J3Z	Grenada
J4A-J4Z	Greece
J5A-J5Z	Guinea-Bissau (Republic of)
J6A-J6Z	Saint Lucia
J7A-J7Z	Dominica (Commonwealth of)
J8A-J8Z	Saint Vincent and the Grenadines
KAA-KZZ	**United States of America**
LAA-LNZ	Norway
LOA-LWZ	Argentine Republic

LXA-LXZ	Luxembourg
LYA-LYZ	Lithuania (Republic of)
LZA-LZZ	Bulgaria (Republic of)
L2A-L9Z	Argentine Republic
MAA-MZZ	United Kingdom of Great Britain and Northern Ireland
NAA-NZZ	**United States of America**
OAA-OCZ	Peru
ODA-ODZ	Lebanon
OEA-OEZ	Austria
OFA-OJZ	Finland
OKA-OLZ	Czech Republic
OMA-OMZ	Slovak Republic
ONA-OTZ	Belgium
OUA-OZZ	Denmark
PAA-PIZ	Netherlands (Kingdom of the)
PJA-PJZ	Netherlands (Kingdom of the) - Netherlands Antilles
PKA-POZ	Indonesia (Republic of)
PPA-PYZ	Brazil (Federative Republic of)
PZA-PZZ	Suriname (Republic of)
P2A-P2Z	Papua New Guinea
P3A-P3Z	Cyprus (Republic of)
P4A-P4Z	Netherlands (Kingdom of the) - Aruba
P5A-P9Z	Democratic People's Republic of Korea
RAA-RZZ	Russian Federation
SAA-SMZ	Sweden
SNA-SRZ	Poland (Republic of)
SSA-SSM	Egypt (Arab Republic of)
SSN-STZ	Sudan (Republic of the)
SUA-SUZ	Egypt (Arab Republic of)
SVA-SZZ	Greece
S2A-S3Z	Bangladesh (People's Republic of)
S5A-S5Z	Slovenia (Republic of)
S6A-S6Z	Singapore (Republic of)
S7A-S7Z	Seychelles (Republic of)
S8A-S8Z	South Africa (Republic of)
S9A-S9Z	Sao Tome and Principe (Democratic Republic of)
TAA-TCZ	Turkey
TDA-TDZ	Guatemala (Republic of)
TEA-TEZ	Costa Rica
TFA-TFZ	Iceland
TGA-TGZ	Guatemala (Republic of)
THA-THZ	France
TIA-TIZ	Costa Rica
TJA-TJZ	Cameroon (Republic of)
TKA-TKZ	France

TLA-TLZ	Central African Republic
TMA-TMZ	France
TNA-TNZ	Congo (Republic of the)
TOA-TQZ	France
TRA-TRZ	Gabonese Republic
TSA-TSZ	Tunisia
TTA-TTZ	Chad (Republic of)
TUA-TUZ	Côte d'Ivoire (Republic of)
TVA-TXZ	France
TYA-TYZ	Benin (Republic of)
TZA-TZZ	Mali (Republic of)
T2A-T2Z	Tuvalu
T3A-T3Z	Kiribati (Republic of)
T4A-T4Z	Cuba
T5A-T5Z	Somali Democratic Republic
T6A-T6Z	Afghanistan (Islamic State of)
T7A-T7Z	San Marino (Republic of)
T8A-T8Z	Palau (Republic of)
UAA-UIZ	Russian Federation
UJA-UMZ	Uzbekistan (Republic of)
UNA-UQZ	Kazakhstan (Republic of)
URA-UZZ	Ukraine
VAA-VGZ	Canada
VHA-VNZ	Australia
VOA-VOZ	Canada
VPA-VQZ	United Kingdom of Great Britain and Northern Ireland
VRA-VRZ	China (People's Republic of) - Hong Kong
VSA-VSZ	United Kingdom of Great Britain and Northern Ireland
VTA-VWZ	India (Republic of)
VXA-VYZ	Canada
VZA-VZZ	Australia
V2A-V2Z	Antigua and Barbuda
V3A-V3Z	Belize
V4A-V4Z	Saint Kitts and Nevis
V5A-V5Z	Namibia (Republic of)
V6A-V6Z	Micronesia (Federated States of)
V7A-V7Z	Marshall Islands (Republic of the)
V8A-V8Z	Brunei Darussalam
WAA-WZZ	**United States of America**
XAA-XIZ	Mexico
XJA-XOZ	Canada
XPA-XPZ	Denmark
XQA-XRZ	Chile
XSA-XSZ	China (People's Republic of)
XTA-XTZ	Burkina Faso

XUA-XUZ	Cambodia (Kingdom of)
XVA-XVZ	Viet Nam (Socialist Republic of)
XWA-XWZ	Lao People's Democratic Republic
XXA-XXZ	China (People's Republic of) - Macao (WRC-07)
XYA-XZZ	Myanmar (Union of)
YAA-YAZ	Afghanistan (Islamic State of)
YBA-YHZ	Indonesia (Republic of)
YIA-YIZ	Iraq (Republic of)
YJA-YJZ	Vanuatu (Republic of)
YKA-YKZ	Syrian Arab Republic
YLA-YLZ	Latvia (Republic of)
YMA-YMZ	Turkey
YNA-YNZ	Nicaragua
YOA-YRZ	Romania
YSA-YSZ	El Salvador (Republic of)
YTA-YUZ	Serbia (Republic of) (WRC-07)
YVA-YYZ	Venezuela (Republic of)
Y2A-Y9Z	Germany (Federal Republic of)
ZAA-ZAZ	Albania (Republic of)
ZBA-ZJZ	United Kingdom of Great Britain and Northern Ireland
ZKA-ZMZ	New Zealand
ZNA-ZOZ	United Kingdom of Great Britain and Northern Ireland
ZPA-ZPZ	Paraguay (Republic of)
ZQA-ZQZ	United Kingdom of Great Britain and Northern Ireland
ZRA-ZUZ	South Africa (Republic of)
ZVA-ZZZ	Brazil (Federative Republic of)
Z2A-Z2Z	Zimbabwe (Republic of)
Z3A-Z3Z	The Former Yugoslav Republic of Macedonia
2AA-2ZZ	United Kingdom of Great Britain and Northern Ireland
3AA-3AZ	Monaco (Principality of)
3BA-3BZ	Mauritius (Republic of)
3CA-3CZ	Equatorial Guinea (Republic of)
3DA-3DM	Swaziland (Kingdom of)
3DN-3DZ	Fiji (Republic of)
3EA-3FZ	Panama (Republic of)
3GA-3GZ	Chile
3HA-3UZ	China (People's Republic of)
3VA-3VZ	Tunisia
3WA-3WZ	Viet Nam (Socialist Republic of)
3XA-3XZ	Guinea (Republic of)
3YA-3YZ	Norway
3ZA-3ZZ	Poland (Republic of)
4AA-4CZ	Mexico
4DA-4IZ	Philippines (Republic of the)
4JA-4KZ	Azerbaijani Republic

4LA-4LZ	Georgia (Republic of)
4MA-4MZ	Venezuela (Republic of)
4OA-4OZ	Montenegro (Republic of) (WRC-07)
4PA-4SZ	Sri Lanka (Democratic Socialist Republic of)
4TA-4TZ	Peru
4UA-4UZ	United Nations
4VA-4VZ	Haiti (Republic of)
4WA-4WZ	Democratic Republic of Timor-Leste (WRC-03)
4XA-4XZ	Israel (State of)
4YA-4YZ	International Civil Aviation Organization
4ZA-4ZZ	Israel (State of)
5AA-5AZ	Libya (Socialist People's Libyan Arab Jamahiriya)
5BA-5BZ	Cyprus (Republic of)
5CA-5GZ	Morocco (Kingdom of)
5HA-5IZ	Tanzania (United Republic of)
5JA-5KZ	Colombia (Republic of)
5LA-5MZ	Liberia (Republic of)
5NA-5OZ	Nigeria (Federal Republic of)
5PA-5QZ	Denmark
5RA-5SZ	Madagascar (Republic of)
5TA-5TZ	Mauritania (Islamic Republic of)
5UA-5UZ	Niger (Republic of the)
5VA-5VZ	Togolese Republic
5WA-5WZ	Samoa (Independent State of)
5XA-5XZ	Uganda (Republic of)
5YA-5ZZ	Kenya (Republic of)
6AA-6BZ	Egypt (Arab Republic of)
6CA-6CZ	Syrian Arab Republic
6DA-6JZ	Mexico
6KA-6NZ	Korea (Republic of)
6OA-6OZ	Somali Democratic Republic
6PA-6SZ	Pakistan (Islamic Republic of)
6TA-6UZ	Sudan (Republic of the)
6VA-6WZ	Senegal (Republic of)
6XA-6XZ	Madagascar (Republic of)
6YA-6YZ	Jamaica
6ZA-6ZZ	Liberia (Republic of)
7AA-7IZ	Indonesia (Republic of)
7JA-7NZ	Japan
7OA-7OZ	Yemen (Republic of)
7PA-7PZ	Lesotho (Kingdom of)
7QA-7QZ	Malawi
7RA-7RZ	Algeria (People's Democratic Republic of)
7SA-7SZ	Sweden
7TA-7YZ	Algeria (People's Democratic Republic of)

7ZA-7ZZ	Saudi Arabia (Kingdom of)
8AA-8IZ	Indonesia (Republic of)
8JA-8NZ	Japan
8OA-8OZ	Botswana (Republic of)
8PA-8PZ	Barbados
8QA-8QZ	Maldives (Republic of)
8RA-8RZ	Guyana
8SA-8SZ	Sweden
8TA-8YZ	India (Republic of)
8ZA-8ZZ	Saudi Arabia (Kingdom of)
9AA-9AZ	Croatia (Republic of)
9BA-9DZ	Iran (Islamic Republic of)
9EA-9FZ	Ethiopia (Federal Democratic Republic of)
9GA-9GZ	Ghana
9HA-9HZ	Malta
9IA-9JZ	Zambia (Republic of)
9KA-9KZ	Kuwait (State of)
9LA-9LZ	Sierra Leone
9MA-9MZ	Malaysia
9NA-9NZ	Nepal
9OA-9TZ	Democratic Republic of the Congo
9UA-9UZ	Burundi (Republic of)
9VA-9VZ	Singapore (Republic of)
9WA-9WZ	Malaysia
9XA-9XZ	Rwandese Republic
9YA-9ZZ	Trinidad and Tobago

Third-Party Communications and Amateur Radio

If all of this information about ham radios is somewhat intimidating, do not despair. "You" can still use ham radios for communications without being a licensed operator. Yes, you do have to have a ham license in order to legally transmit by ham equipment (or be under the direct supervision of someone else who is licensed), but there is an alternative – third-party communication.

Third-party communications occur when a licensed operator sends either written or verbal messages on behalf of unlicensed persons or organizations. There are two "controls" on third-party communication.

First, the communication must be noncommercial and of a personal nature. Asking a ham operator to contact another ham operator located in an area just hit by tornados and, because of being without power, phones do not work in Grandma Sally's city so you can check up on her, is okay. Asking a ham to send a message out that you have an old Chevy for sale would not be okay.

Second, the message must be going to a permitted area. Transmitting from a US location to another US location is okay, but transmitting from the US to another country may not. Because third-party communications bypass a country's normal telephone and postal systems, many foreign governments forbid such communications. In order to transmit from one country to another, the other country must have signed a third-party agreement with the US. What follows is a list of those countries that do have third-party a communications agreement with the US.

V2	Antigua / Barbuda
LU	Argentina
VK	Australia
V3	Belize
CP	Bolivia
T9	Bosnia-Herzegovina
PY	Brazil
VE	Canada
CE	Chile
HK	Colombia
D6	Comoros (Federal Islamic Republic of)
TI	Costa Rica
CO	Cuba
HI	Dominican Republic
J7	Dominica
HC	Ecuador
YS	El Salvador
C5	Gambia, The
9G	Ghana
J3	Grenada
TG	Guatemala
8R	Guyana
HH	Haiti
HR	Honduras
4X	Israel
6Y	Jamaica
JY	Jordan
EL	Liberia
V7	Marshall Islands
XE	Mexico
V6	Micronesia, Federated States of
YN	Nicaragua
HP	Panama
ZP	Paraguay
OA	Peru
DU	Philippines
VR6	Pitcairn Island

V4	St. Christopher / Nevis
J6	St. Lucia
J8	St. Vincent and the Grenadines
9L	Sierra Leone
ZS	South Africa
3DA	Swaziland
9Y	Trinidad / Tobago
TA	Turkey
GB	United Kingdom
CX	Uruguay
YV	Venezuela
4U1ITUITU	Geneva
4U1VICVIC	Vienna

Remember, before TSHTF, keep your pantry well stocked, your powder dry, and your batteries fully charged. 73

APPENDIX A

American Radio Relay League

Affiliated Amateur Radio Clubs in

Ohio

ARRL Affiliated Club	Pioneer A R Fellowship
City:	Akron, OH
Call Sign:	W8CTT
Section:	OH
Links:	www.qsl.net/w8ctt

ARRL Affiliated Club	Goodyear Amateur Radio Club
City:	Akron, OH
Call Sign:	WA8UXP
Section:	OH

ARRL Affiliated Club	Alliance Amateur Radio Club
City:	Alliance, OH
Call Sign:	W8LKY
Section:	OH
Links:	www.w8lky.org

ARRL Special Service Club	Ashland Area Amateur Radio Club
City:	Ashland, OH
Call Sign:	N8IHI
Section:	OH

ARRL Affiliated Club	Athens County Amateur Radio Association
City:	Athens, OH
Call Sign:	W8UKE
Section:	OH
Links:	www.ac-ara.org

ARRL Affiliated Club	Northern Ohio Amateur Radio Society
City:	Avon Lake, OH
Call Sign:	K8KRG
Section:	OH
Links:	www.noars.net

ARRL Special Service Club	West Park Radiops Amateur Radio Club
City:	Bay Village, OH
Call Sign:	W8VM
Section:	OH
Links:	www.westparkradiops.org

ARRL Affiliated Club	Cleveland Wireless Assn. Inc.
City:	Bay Village, OH
Call Sign:	W8CWA
Section:	OH
Links:	www.hamfaqs.com/cwa/, members.core.com/~af8c/cwa

ARRL Affiliated Club
City:
Call Sign:
Section:
Links:

Lake Erie Amateur Radio Association
Beachwood, OH
WB8CQR
OH
www.leara.org

ARRL Affiliated Club
City:
Call Sign:
Section:
Links:

Bellbrook Amateur Radio Club
Bellbrook, OH
W8DGN
OH
barc.febo.com

ARRL Affiliated Club
City:
Call Sign:
Section:
Links:

Champaign Logan Amateur Radio Club Inc.
Bellefontaine, OH
W8EBG
OH
W8FTV.com

ARRL Affiliated Club
City:
Call Sign:
Section:
Links:

Wood County Amateur Club
Bowling Green, OH
K8TIH
OH
wcarc.bgsu.edu

ARRL Affiliated Club
City:
Call Sign:
Section:
Links:

Woodchuck Amateur Radio Club
Brook Park, OH
KC8KLU
OH
www.woodchuckradio.org

ARRL Special Service Club
City:
Call Sign:
Section:
Links:

Cambridge Amateur Radio Association
Cambridge, OH
W8VP
OH
www.w8vp.org

ARRL Affiliated Club
City:
Call Sign:
Section:
Links:

Canton Amateur Radio Club
Canton, OH
W8AL
OH
www.w8al.org/

ARRL Affiliated Club	North Coast Contesters
City:	Chesterland, OH
Call Sign:	NC8C
Section:	OH
Links:	www.northcoastcontesters.com
ARRL Special Service Club	OH-KY-IN Amateur Radio Society
City:	Cincinnati, OH
Call Sign:	K8SCH
Section:	OH
Links:	OH-KY-IN website
ARRL Affiliated Club	Queen City Emergency Net
City:	Cincinnati, OH
Call Sign:	W8VVL
Section:	OH
Links:	www.qcen.org
ARRL Affiliated Club	University of Cincinnati Amateur Radio Club
City:	Cincinnati, OH
Call Sign:	W8YX
Section:	OH
Links:	www.uc.edu/w8yx/, www.w8yx.org
ARRL Affiliated Club	Ohio Valley Amateur Radio Association
City:	Cincinnati, OH
Call Sign:	W4FU
Section:	OH
ARRL Affiliated Club	Greater Cincinnati Amateur Radio Association
City:	Cincinnati, OH
Call Sign:	W8DZ
Section:	OH
Links:	www.gcara.org
ARRL Affiliated Club	Parma Radio Club
City:	Cleveland, OH
Call Sign:	W8PRC
Section:	OH
Links:	www.freewebs.com/w8prc/
ARRL Affiliated Club	Caribbean Contesting Consortium
City:	Columbus, OH
Call Sign:	W0DX
Section:	OH
Links:	asgard.kent.edu/ccc

ARRL Affiliated Club   Capital City Repeater Assn.
City: Columbus, OH
Call Sign: K8DRE
Section: OH
Links: www.ohioccra.net

ARRL Affiliated Club   Central OH Severe Weather Net
City: Columbus, OH
Call Sign: N8WX
Section: OH
Links: www.coswn.org, www.severe-weather.org

ARRL Affiliated Club   Amateur Radio Club of Ohio State University
City: Columbus, OH
Call Sign: W8LT
Section: OH
Links: www.w8lt.org

ARRL Affiliated Club   Voice of Aladdin Amateur Radio Club
City: Columbus, OH
Call Sign: W8FEZ
Section: OH
Links: www.aladdinshrine.org/voa.htm

ARRL Special Service Club   Central Ohio ARES
City: Columbus, OH
Call Sign: K8DDG
Section: OH
Links: www.COARES.org

ARRL Affiliated Club   South West Columbus Ham Radio Club
City: Columbus, OH
Call Sign: W8RWR
Section: OH
Links: swchrc.com

ARRL Affiliated Club   Conneaut Amateur Radio Club
City: Conneaut, OH
Call Sign: W8BHZ
Section: OH
Links: www.qsl.net/w8bhz,
                              www.conneautamateurradioclub.com

ARRL Affiliated Club	Coshocton County Amateur Radio Association, Inc.
City:	Coshocton, OH
Call Sign:	W8CCA
Section:	OH
Links:	www.w8cca.org
ARRL Affiliated Club	Cuyahoga Falls Amateur Radio Club
City:	Cuyahoga Falls, OH
Call Sign:	W8VPV
Section:	OH
ARRL Affiliated Club	Huber Heights Amateur Radio Club
City:	Dayton, OH
Call Sign:	NO8I
Section:	OH
Links:	www.hharc.org
ARRL Special Service Club	Delaware Amateur Radio Association
City:	Delaware, OH
Call Sign:	K8ES
Section:	OH
Links:	www.k8es.org
ARRL Affiliated Club	Preble Amateur Radio Association
City:	Eaton, OH
Call Sign:	K8YR
Section:	OH
ARRL Affiliated Club	Lorain County Amateur Radio Association
City:	Elyria, OH
Call Sign:	KC8BED
Section:	OH
Links:	www.qsl.net/lcAmateur Radio Association
ARRL Affiliated Club	Butler County Amateur Radio Association
City:	Fairfield, OH
Call Sign:	W8WRK
Section:	OH
Links:	bcara.net
ARRL Special Service Club	FINDLAY RADIO CLUB
City:	Findlay, OH
Call Sign:	W8FT
Section:	OH
Links:	www.findlayradioclub.org

ARRL Affiliated Club   Crawford County Amateur Radio Club
City: Galion, OH
Call Sign: W8BAE
Section: OH

ARRL Affiliated Club   GRANT Amateur Radio Club
City: Georgetown, OH
Call Sign: W8STZ
Section: OH
Links: www.garcohio.net

ARRL Affiliated Club   U.S.S. Jurassic - Star Trek and Amateur Radio Club
City: Hamersville, OH
Call Sign: K8SSJ
Section: OH
Links: www.ussjurassic.com

ARRL Affiliated Club   Amateur Radio Public Service Corps of Hamilton
                              County, OH
City: Hamilton, OH
Call Sign: K8YOJ
Section: OH
Links: www.hamcoarpsc.org

ARRL Affiliated Club   Butler County VHF Association
City: Hamilton, OH
Call Sign: W8CCI
Section: OH
Links: www.mindspring.com/~bcvhfa/

ARRL Affiliated Club   Central OH Operators Klub Extra-Novice
City: Hebron, OH
Call Sign: W8TNX
Section: OH
Links: www.cooken.org

ARRL Affiliated Club   Highland Amateur Radio Association
City: Hillsboro, OH
Call Sign: K8HO
Section: OH
Links: groups.yahoo.com/group/highlandara/

ARRL Affiliated Club	Firelands Amateur Repeater Association
City:	Huron, OH
Call Sign:	WB8LLY
Section:	OH
Links:	wb8lly.org
ARRL Affiliated Club	Cuyahoga Amateur Radio Society
City:	Independence, OH
Call Sign:	K8ZFR
Section:	OH
Links:	www.2cars.org/
ARRL Affiliated Club	Jackson County Amateur Radio Club
City:	Jackson, OH
Call Sign:	KD8XL
Section:	OH
Links:	www.jacksoncountyarc.org
ARRL Affiliated Club	Lancaster & Fairfield City Amateur Radio Club
City:	Lancaster, OH
Call Sign:	K8QIK
Section:	OH
Links:	www.k8qik.org
ARRL Affiliated Club	Southwest Ohio DX Association
City:	Lebanon, OH
Call Sign:	W8EX
Section:	OH
Links:	www.swodxa.org/
ARRL Affiliated Club	Amateur Radio Club of Wally Byam Caravan Club
City:	Lebanon, OH
Call Sign:	WB8RC
Section:	OH
Links:	rvsvcnet.wbcci.net
ARRL Affiliated Club	Preble Amateur Radio Assn.
City:	Lewisburg, OH
Call Sign:	K8YR
Section:	OH
Links:	www.prebleara.org
ARRL Affiliated Club	Northwest Ohio Amateur Radio Club
City:	Lima, OH
Call Sign:	WB8ULC
Section:	OH
Links:	www.nwoarc.org

ARRL Affiliated Club	Madison County Amateur Radio Club
City:	London, OH
Call Sign:	KE8RV
Section:	OH
Links:	www.mcarcoh.org

ARRL Affiliated Club	Stark DX Assn.
City:	Louisville, OH
Call Sign:	N8TU
Section:	OH

ARRL Special Service Club	Intercity Amateur Radio Club
City:	Mansfield, OH
Call Sign:	W8WE
Section:	OH
Links:	www.iarc.ws

ARRL Special Service Club	Portage Amateur Radio Club Inc.
City:	Mantua, OH
Call Sign:	KB8ZHP
Section:	OH
Links:	www.portagearc.org

ARRL Affiliated Club	Morrow County Amateur Radio Service
City:	Marengo, OH
Call Sign:	W8NL
Section:	OH
Links:	www.morrowcountyares.org

ARRL Affiliated Club	Marrietta Amateur Radio Club, Inc.
City:	Marietta, OH
Call Sign:	W8HH
Section:	OH

ARRL Affiliated Club	Marion Amateur Radio Club
City:	Marion, OH
Call Sign:	W8GVB
Section:	OH
Links:	www.marionhamradio.org

ARRL Affiliated Club	Massillon Amateur Radio Club
City:	Massillon, OH
Call Sign:	W8NP
Section:	OH
Links:	www.w8np.org

ARRL Affiliated Club	Medina 2 Meter Group
City:	Medina, OH
Call Sign:	W8EOC
Section:	OH
Links:	www.w8eoc.org
ARRL Affiliated Club	Mound Amateur Radio Association
City:	Miamisburg, OH
Call Sign:	W8DYY
Section:	OH
Links:	www.w8dyy.org
ARRL Affiliated Club	Dial Radio Club
City:	Middletown, OH
Call Sign:	W8BLV
Section:	OH
Links:	www.qsl.net/w8blv, www.qsl.net/w8blv/
ARRL Affiliated Club	Milford Amateur Radio Club
City:	Milford, OH
Call Sign:	W8MRC
Section:	OH
Links:	www.w8mrc.com
ARRL Affiliated Club	Toledo Radio Amateur Club
City:	Monclova, OH
Call Sign:	W8RZM
Section:	OH
Links:	trac-online.org
ARRL Special Service Club	Mount Vernon Amateur Radio Club
City:	Mount Vernon, OH
Call Sign:	K8EEN
Section:	OH
Links:	www.mvarc.net
ARRL Affiliated Club	Tusco Amateur Radio Club Inc.
City:	New Philadelphia, OH
Call Sign:	W8ZX
Section:	OH
Links:	www.tuscoarc.org
ARRL Special Service Club	Western Reserve Amateur Radio Club
City:	New Springfield, OH
Call Sign:	W8WRC
Section:	OH
Links:	www.qsl.net/w8wrc/, www.wrarc.net

ARRL Affiliated Club	Newark Amateur Radio Assn.
City:	Newark, OH
Call Sign:	N8Amateur Radio Association
Section:	OH
Links:	www.n8ara.org
ARRL Special Service Club	Lake County Amateur Radio Association Inc.
City:	Painesville, OH
Call Sign:	N8BC
Section:	OH
Links:	www.lcara.org
ARRL Affiliated Club	CRES-Amateur Radio Club
City:	Pickerington, OH
Call Sign:	W8ZPF
Section:	OH
Links:	w8zpf.org
ARRL Affiliated Club	Ottawa County Amateur Radio Club
City:	Port Clinton, OH
Call Sign:	K8VXH
Section:	OH
ARRL Affiliated Club	Portsmouth Radio Club
City:	Portsmouth, OH
Call Sign:	N8QA
Section:	OH
Links:	www.portsmouthradioclub.com/
ARRL Affiliated Club	Portage County Amateur Radio Service Inc
City:	Ravenna, OH
Section:	OH
Links:	www.portcars.org/
ARRL Special Service Club	Salem Area Amateur Radio Association
City:	Salem, OH
Call Sign:	K8BTP
Section:	OH
Links:	www.qsl.net/saAmateur Radio Association
ARRL Affiliated Club	Sandusky Radio Exp. League
City:	Sandusky, OH
Call Sign:	W8LBZ
Section:	OH
Links:	www.w8lbz.org

ARRL Affiliated Club	Clark County Amateur Radio Association
City:	Springfield, OH
Call Sign:	W8OG
Section:	OH
Links:	www.claraw8og.org/
ARRL Affiliated Club	Independent Radio Assn. Inc.
City:	Springfield, OH
Call Sign:	K8IRA
Section:	OH
Links:	www.K8IRA.org
ARRL Affiliated Club	Steubenville-Weirton Amateur Radio Club
City:	Steubenville, OH
Call Sign:	W8CWO
Section:	OH
Links:	www.daytamark.com/swarc, www.swarc.net
ARRL Affiliated Club	Northern Ohio DX Assn.
City:	Strongsville, OH
Call Sign:	W8DXA
Section:	OH
Links:	www.papays.com/nodxa.html
ARRL Affiliated Club	Central Ohio Radio Club Inc.
City:	Sunbury, OH
Call Sign:	W8AIC
Section:	OH
Links:	www.corc.us
ARRL Affiliated Club	Seneca Radio Club
City:	Tiffin, OH
Call Sign:	W8ID
Section:	OH
Links:	www.w8id.com
ARRL Special Service Club	Toledo Mobile Radio Association
City:	Toledo, OH
Call Sign:	W8HHF
Section:	OH
Links:	www.tmrahamradio.org
ARRL Affiliated Club	Van Wert Amateur Radio Club, Inc.
City:	Van Wert, OH
Call Sign:	W8FY
Section:	OH
Links:	www.w8fy.org

ARRL Affiliated Club   Warren Amateur Radio Assn.
City: Warren, OH
Call Sign: W8VTD
Section: OH
Links: www.w8vtd.org/ or kc8pvb.com

ARRL Affiliated Club   Fulton County Amateur Radio Club
City: Wauseon, OH
Call Sign: K8BXQ
Section: OH
Links: k8bxq.org

ARRL Affiliated Club   Scioto Valley Amateur Radio Club
City: Waverly, OH
Call Sign: W8BAP
Section: OH

ARRL Affiliated Club   West Chester Amateur Radio Association
City: West Chester, OH
Call Sign: WC8VOA
Section: OH
Links: wc8voa.org

ARRL Affiliated Club   Buckeye DX Club
City: Westerville, OH
Call Sign: W8OS
Section: OH

ARRL Affiliated Club   Clinton County Amateur Radio Association
City: Wilmington, OH
Call Sign: W8GO
Section: OH

ARRL Affiliated Club   Wayne Amateur Radio Club
City: Wooster, OH
Call Sign: W8WOO
Section: OH
Links: www.w8woo.net

ARRL Special Service Club   Mahoning Valley Amateur Radio Association
City: Youngstown, OH
Call Sign: W8QLY
Section: OH
Links: www.mvara.org

ARRL Affiliated Club   20 Over 9 Radio Club Inc.
City: Youngstown, OH
Call Sign: K8TKA
Section: OH
Links: www.20over9.org, www.qsl.net/20over9/

ARRL Affiliated Club   Zanesville Amateur Radio Club
City: Zanesville, OH
Call Sign: W8ZZV
Section: OH
Links: zarc.eqth.org/

ARRL Affiliated Club   Muskingum Valley Ham Radio Club
City: Zanesville, OH
Call Sign: N8HR
Section: OH
Links: n8hr.bravehost.com/

APPENDIX B

Amateur Radio License Holders

in

Ohio: South East Region
(by City)

FCC Amateur Radio Licenses in Adams Mills

Call Sign: KD8ESS
Randy A Park
890 Raiders Rd
Adams Mills OH 43821

FCC Amateur Radio Licenses in Adamsville

Call Sign: KB8TAL
Tina L Baker
11185 Bethesda Church Rd
Adamsville OH 43802

Call Sign: KD8HWG
Walter J Kreis
7255 Knicely Rd
Adamsville OH 43802

FCC Amateur Radio Licenses in Adelphi

Call Sign: KC8NYT
Zachary L Johnston
11744 Main St
Adelphi OH 43101

Call Sign: KC8MIR
Jayme D Johnston
11744 Main St
Adelphi OH 431010461

Call Sign: KC8TVN
Harley M Wood
11802 Main St
Adelphi OH 43101

FCC Amateur Radio Licenses in Albany

Call Sign: N8MHM
Marvin E Parsons
2350 Baker Rd
Albany OH 45710

Call Sign: KA8ZYO
Vicky L Schlosser
4424 Baker Rd
Albany OH 45710

Call Sign: KA8ZYP
Michael F Schlosser
4424 Baker Rd
Albany OH 45710

Call Sign: KC8QKP
Beverly S Barnes
2460 Crabtree Rd
Albany OH 45710

Call Sign: KC8HXB
Earl E Barnes
2460 Crabtree Rd
Albany OH 457109213

Call Sign: W8NEO
Beverly S Barnes
2460 Crabtree Rd
Albany OH 457109213

Call Sign: K8WWV
William D Anderson Jr
2188 Ladd Ridge Rd
Albany OH 45710

Call Sign: KD8GFK
Deborah S Perry
39699 Mound Hill Rd
Albany OH 45710

Call Sign: KD8EAA
Milton L Perry
39699 Mound Hill Rd
Albany OH 45710

Call Sign: W8MLP
Milton L Perry
39699 Mound Hill Rd
Albany OH 45710

Call Sign: KD8DJE
Russell L Perry
39699 Mound Hill Rd
Albany OH 45710

Call Sign: KC8ZPJ
Dennis A Mcfarland
40090 Mound Hill Rd
Albany OH 45710

Call Sign: KC8YUO
Vinton County ARC
38797 Northrun Rd
Albany OH 45710

Call Sign: W8VCO
Vinton County ARC
38797 Northrun Rd
Albany OH 45710

Call Sign: KD8DJD
Kenneth J Coen
38797 Northrun Rd
Albany OH 45710

Call Sign: AB8XG
Kenneth J Coen
38797 Northrun Rd
Albany OH 45710

Call Sign: WB8VTP
Robert L Barnhart
28146 Old St Rt 346
Albany OH 45710

Call Sign: AC8EQ
Robert L Barnhart
28146 Old St Rt 346
Albany OH 45710

Call Sign: N8QPW
Donald A Ellis
40994 Pageville Rd
Albany OH 457109239

Call Sign: N8MZC
David W Ferguson
3115 Reynoldsburg New
Albany Rd
Albany OH 43054

Call Sign: KC8RHG
Evan L Dickinson
37248 Salem School Lot
Rd
Albany OH 45710

Call Sign: K8ELD
Evan L Dickinson
37248 Salem School Lot
Rd
Albany OH 45710

Call Sign: W8LNH
Frances L Davis
40516 Salem School Lot
Rd Rd3 B239C
Albany OH 45710

Call Sign: KC8UYL
Arlin Radekin
38115 School Lot Rd
Albany OH 45710

Call Sign: KC8UYK
Patricia Radekin
38115 School Lot Rd
Albany OH 45710

Call Sign: KC8VPP
Robert J Sparks
28660 St Rt 143
Albany OH 45710

Call Sign: W8VCD

Carl B Johnson
3787 St Rt 681
Albany OH 457109221

Call Sign: KF4YAC
Patricia B Tillis
35203 St Rt 681 S
Albany OH 457109120

Call Sign: KF4YAD
John W Tillis
35203 St Rt 681 S
Albany OH 457109120

Call Sign: NS8O
Greg L Weinfurtner
40192 St Rt 689
Albany OH 45710

Call Sign: NV5Z
Edwin S Thomas
3855 Tanager Pointe
Albany OH 45710

Call Sign: KA8YME
Robert Wachenschwanz
Jr
5248 W Clinton St
Albany OH 45710

Call Sign: KB8ZMP
Joseph M Hulcher
Albany OH 45710

**FCC Amateur Radio
Licenses in Amesville**

Call Sign: KC8IFD
John E O Donnell
11 Harrison St
Amesville OH
457110143

Call Sign: KD8PUI
Mike T Cunningham

14651 Jago Vly Rd
Amesville OH 45711

Call Sign: N8KZF
Charles A Hammer
12666 Parmiter Rd
Amesville OH 45711

Call Sign: W8HAW
Herbert A Whitlatch II
17080 Plantsville Rd
Amesville OH 45711

Call Sign: KD8LKI
Trish J Whitlatch
17080 Plantsville Rd
Amesville OH 45711

Call Sign: KB8TET
Robert W Dearth Sr
14688 Robinson Rd
Amesville OH 45711

Call Sign: WD8COU
Wesley D Dutiel
14722 SR 329 N
Amesville OH 45711

Call Sign: KC8ZHR
Kathy M Jacobson
Amesville OH 45711

Call Sign: KC8JXA
Constantine P Faller
Amesville OH
457110058

**FCC Amateur Radio
Licenses in Athens**

Call Sign: KC8AAK
Dan O Young
41 2nd St
Athens OH 45701

Call Sign: KD8KMZ
Lance J Groeneveld
105 2nd St
Athens OH 45701

Call Sign: KD8KNA
Linsey W Groeneveld
105 2nd St
Athens OH 45701

Call Sign: KC8JRV
Kirk A Groeneveld
105 2nd St
Athens OH 45701

Call Sign: WD8RIF
William E Mc Fadden
12600 Adeline Cir
Athens OH 45701

Call Sign: KD8KNB
Kate G Mcfadden
12600 Adeline Cir
Athens OH 45701

Call Sign: KD8KNC
Miles S Mcfadden
12600 Adeline Cir
Athens OH 45701

Call Sign: KC8MAJ
Victoria S Mc Fadden
12600 Adeline Cir
Athens OH 457019628

Call Sign: KC8AAV
 Sunday Creek Amateur
Radio Federation
5004 Angel Ridge Rd
Athens OH 45701

Call Sign: KC8QDP
Curtis M Duncan
5004 Angel Ridge Rd
Athens OH 45701

Call Sign: KC8QKL
Shonda D Duncan
5004 Angel Ridge Rd
Athens OH 45701

Call Sign: KA0GPR
Sean T O Malley
4724 Angel Ridge Rd
Athens OH 45701

Call Sign: K8TUT
William H Creighton
40 Angela St
Athens OH 45701

Call Sign: K8MMC
Marion M Crawley
21 Avon Pl
Athens OH 457011402

Call Sign: WB3LUC
Amerigo P Pallini
6401 Baker Rd
Athens OH 457019229

Call Sign: WB3LUD
Hazel L Pallini
6401 Baker Rd
Athens OH 457019229

Call Sign: KD8KZI
Jarrett M Bright
145 Beal Rd
Athens OH 45701

Call Sign: KC8ZUF
Brian D Shapiro
217 Beal Rd
Athens OH 457013443

Call Sign: WA8YVE
Franklyn Vargo
7947 Bennita Ln
Athens OH 457013510

Call Sign: KC8MAK
Karen S Jones
17 Berkley Dr
Athens OH 45701

Call Sign: WT8E
Walter H Jones
17 Berkley Dr
Athens OH 45701

Call Sign: KA8RWQ
Sarah N Graham
Box 16965 River Rd
Athens OH 45701

Call Sign: W8MHV
Drewrey O Mc Daniel
61 Briarwood Dr
Athens OH 45701

Call Sign: N8JJY
Frederick G Bush
6989 Cameron Rd
Athens OH 45701

Call Sign: KD8EXW
Raymond A Croxford
7343 Cameron Rd
Athens OH 45701

Call Sign: AK8V
Raymond A Croxford
7343 Cameron Rd
Athens OH 45701

Call Sign: KC8SKZ
Nasseef A Abukamail
12 Canterbury Dr
Athens OH 45701

Call Sign: AB8MZ
Nasseef A Abukamail
12 Canterbury Dr
Athens OH 45701

Call Sign: AC8K
Nasseef A Abukamail
12 Canterbury Dr
Athens OH 45701

Call Sign: N8JJX
Jack L Mathews
6 Cardiff Ln
Athens OH 45701

Call Sign: KD8AUM
Gobahams
45 Carol Ln
Athens OH 457013657

Call Sign: KG8OBA
Gobahams
45 Carol Ln
Athens OH 457013657

Call Sign: KD8LHQ
Athens County Red
Cross ARS
45 Carol Ln
Athens OH 45701

Call Sign: WA8ARC
Athens County Red
Cross ARS
45 Carol Ln
Athens OH 45701

Call Sign: KD8PUJ
Janet M Slattery
45 Carol Ln
Athens OH 45701

Call Sign: N8SUZ
Samuel J Slattery
45 Carol Ln
Athens OH 45701

Call Sign: W9AON
Joseph H Berman

52 Charles St
Athens OH 45701

Call Sign: KC8OVB
James E Crouse
47 Columbia Ave
Athens OH 45701

Call Sign: KD8KNE
Margaret W Pearce
66 Columbia Ave
Athens OH 45701

Call Sign: KD8KNF
Michael J Hermann
66 Columbia Ave
Athens OH 45701

Call Sign: W8KVK
Edward W Jacobson
97 Columbia Ave
Athens OH 457011308

Call Sign: KC8YAE
Emily C Bain
110 Columbia Ave
Athens OH 45701

Call Sign: KA8JXG
Carl J Denbow
17 Coventry Ln
Athens OH 457013718

Call Sign: N8VZ
Carl J Denbow
17 Coventry Ln
Athens OH 457013718

Call Sign: KD8RYJ
Christopher Howerth
101 Dudley Dr
Athens OH 45701

Call Sign: NC8V
John A Cornwell

15100 E Scatter Ridge
Rd
Athens OH 45701

Call Sign: N8EEG
Sally L Taylor Gardner
950 E State St Plaza Apt
6A
Athens OH 457012148

Call Sign: W8WG
William R Gardner
950 E State St Plaza Apt
6A
Athens OH 457012148

Call Sign: KC8QMO
Mark D Guda
8680 Elliotsville Rd
Athens OH 45701

Call Sign: KD8DKN
Robert M Mayer
42 Elmwood Pl
Athens OH 45701

Call Sign: KC8JWY
Gregory E Broadhurst
14 Granville Ave
Athens OH 45701

Call Sign: KB6JVX
Barbara A Grosh
139 Grosvenor
Athens OH 45701

Call Sign: KC8KNF
Patrick J Balding
6686 Gura Rd
Athens OH 45701

Call Sign: KD8PJD
Rodney E Haines
8960 Haines Ridge Rd
Athens OH 45701

Call Sign: N3GIS
Christopher M Cross
12851 Hawks Nest Rd
Athens OH 45701

Call Sign: KD8IMS
Gary L Hudson
3670 Hebbardsville Rd
Athens OH 45701

Call Sign: KC8SLA
Bruce R Tong
17 Home St
Athens OH 45701

Call Sign: KD8IDO
Eva M Bear
264 Hooper St
Athens OH 45701

Call Sign: WB8HWO
Kent Phillips
6549 Hudnall Rd
Athens OH 45701

Call Sign: KD8IIO
Lorraine Phillips
6549 Hudnall Rd
Athens OH 45701

Call Sign: KD8MNN
Charles E Williams
14400 Kincade Rd
Athens OH 45701

Call Sign: WD8SCV
Paul D Schulz
14400 Kincade Rd
Athens OH 45701

Call Sign: KB8VRR
Gregory M Hanek
128 La Mar Dr
Athens OH 457013731

Call Sign: KA8YMG
Murray R Chapman Jr
7074 Lemaster Rd
Athens OH 457019135

Call Sign: KB8DYF
Danny L Holley
7849 Long Run Rd
Athens OH 45701

Call Sign: KC8RRJ
Thomas G Moore
203 Longview Heights
Athens OH 45701

Call Sign: W8VKD
Robert L Shellman
215 Longview Heights
Athens OH 457013343

Call Sign: WB8RWK
Eurless L Shellman
471 Longview Heights
Athens OH 45701

Call Sign: WB8NMZ
Francis H Crane
493 Longview Heights
Athens OH 457013347

Call Sign: KB8LPS
Jeffery L Van Sickie
180 Louise Ln
Athens OH 45701

Call Sign: KB8DTX
James L Dillinger
16017 Mansfield Rd
Athens OH 45701

Call Sign: KD8BDG
Claire E Moore
13010 McDougal Rd
Athens OH 45701

Call Sign: KB8LPU
Joshua A Hodson
21 Meadow Ln
Athens OH 45701

Call Sign: N8JYK
Ted C Flood
6 Mulligan Rd
Athens OH 457013735

Call Sign: WD8LWC
William J Warthman
48 Mulligan Rd
Athens OH 457013737

Call Sign: K8WJW
William J Warthman
48 Mulligan Rd
Athens OH 457013737

Call Sign: K4GST
Lyle H Munn
62 Mulligan Rd
Athens OH 45701

Call Sign: N8KEV
Roy E Rankins
182 N Congress St
Athens OH 45701

Call Sign: KB8LPW
Jason D Licht
6272 N Coolville Ridge
Rd
Athens OH 45701

Call Sign: W8VCM
Jason D Licht
6272 N Coolville Ridge
Rd
Athens OH 45701

Call Sign: AC8BZ
Jason D Licht

6272 N Coolville Ridge
Rd
Athens OH 45701

Call Sign: KB8LPV
Scott D Mingus
9 N May
Athens OH 45701

Call Sign: WD8DMY
Earl S Stump
15 N May Ave
Athens OH 45701

Call Sign: KC8WMY
Michael B Cooper
12576 N Peach Ridge
Rd
Athens OH 45701

Call Sign: KD8BLY
Eileen M Sherman
45 N Shafer St B5
Athens OH 45701

Call Sign: N8XWO
John W Mccutcheon
18 Nottingham Dr
Athens OH 45701

Call Sign: KC8BUU
Stephen F West
23 Old Coach Rd
Athens OH 45701

Call Sign: W8CSH
Armond F Rist
4645 Pleasant Hill Rd
Athens OH 45701

Call Sign: KB8UVQ
Brian J Hedrick
12474 Pleasant Vly Ln
Athens OH 45701

Call Sign: KD8FRQ
Robert A Curtis
12475 Pleasanton Rd
Athens OH 45701

Call Sign: K8EYI
Roger E Wolfe
11 Pleasantview Dr
Athens OH 45701

Call Sign: WB8CEE
Charles G Bennett
3 Pleasantview Dr
Athens OH 45701

Call Sign: AB8JE
Clay C Bennett
3 Pleasantview Dr
Athens OH 45701

Call Sign: KC8GWE
Terry L Crabtree
4661 Radford
Athens OH 45701

Call Sign: KB8EVF
Thomas G Ferguson
5808 Radford Rd
Athens OH 457013436

Call Sign: KB8AYZ
Randall H Mace
5885 Radford Rd
Athens OH 457013437

Call Sign: WD8KKI
Marilyn J Snedden
7500 Radford Rd
Athens OH 45701

Call Sign: WD8KKJ
Robert S Snedden
7500 Radford Rd
Athens OH 45701

Call Sign: KB8PFD
Robert M Betz III
11940 Rainbow Lk Rd
Athens OH 457018998

Call Sign: W5XF
James L Mayer
6 Ransom Rd
Athens OH 457011835

Call Sign: KD8QHW
Alice G Tharp
366 Richland Ave Apt
4107
Athens OH 45701

Call Sign: N8JUF
John P Beale
13818 Robinson Ridge
Rd
Athens OH 45701

Call Sign: N8HEK
Murray R Chapman Sr
11049 Rosewood Ln
Athens OH 457019002

Call Sign: N8JRC
James B Mc Garvey
7 Roxbury Dr
Athens OH 45701

Call Sign: KA8NDC
Rodney G Holley
15267 S Canaan Rd
Athens OH 457018958

Call Sign: W3GYD
Henri C Zuber
29 Sandstone Ter Rd
Athens OH 457018765

Call Sign: W8DKP
David K Parks
54 Sandstone Ter Rd

Athens OH 45701

Call Sign: KD8CDK
Roger O Beal
12933 Scatter Ridge Rd
Athens OH 45701

Call Sign: W8PZS
 OH University ARC
313 Stocker Engineering
Ctr
Athens OH 45701

Call Sign: W8ADE
John R Anderson
7880 Stone Castle Rd
Athens OH 457018873

Call Sign: WA8HTC
Alma J Anderson
7880 Stone Castle Rd
Athens OH 457018873

Call Sign: KA8NID
William I Moorehead
61 Sunnyside Dr
Athens OH 45701

Call Sign: W8KMM
James C Gilfert
37 Sunsct Dr
Athens OH 457011610

Call Sign: N8EZE
Paul D Cook
37 Townsend Pl
Athens OH 45701

Call Sign: WB8BCO
Timothy H Cook
37 Townsend Pl
Athens OH 45701

Call Sign: KB8TAD
Richard Post

12 Virginia Ln
Athens OH 457013681

Call Sign: WB8SYW
Richard E Perry
7295 Vore Ridge Rd
Athens OH 45701

Call Sign: WB8TEP
Sharron R Perry
7295 Vore Ridge Rd
Athens OH 45701

Call Sign: KC8JHL
Richard F Perry
7303 Vore Ridge Rd
Athens OH 45701

Call Sign: AB8MY
Richard F Perry
7303 Vore Ridge Rd
Athens OH 45701

Call Sign: KB9LQN
Marc A Komperda
6106 Voreridge Rd
Athens OH 45701

Call Sign: WL7COS
Robert G Glover
35 Wolfe St Apt 29
Athens OH 45701

Call Sign: WD8JLM
John F Biddle
80 Wonder Hills Dr
Athens OH 45701

Call Sign: W8PG
John F Biddle
80 Wonder Hills Dr
Athens OH 45701

Call Sign: N8ATB
Joseph H Berman

Athens OH 45701

Call Sign: AA8SA
Howard M Fox
Athens OH 45701

Call Sign: KB8WWV
Richard L Wolfe
Athens OH 45701

Call Sign: KC8THI
Royce T Holliday
Athens OH 457010735

Call Sign: W8UKE
 Athens County ARA
Athens OH 457015714

Call Sign: KC8BHI
 Athens County ARA
Athens OH 457015714

FCC Amateur Radio Licenses in Ava

Call Sign: KD8CNL
Joshua C Woodworth
Ava OH 43711

FCC Amateur Radio Licenses in Bannock

Call Sign: KC8HYG
Gordon A Nagy
69561 Center St
Bannock OH 43972

Call Sign: KC8ONI
Emilie L Nagy
69561 Center St
Bannock OH 43972

Call Sign: N8PYQ
Wilfrid J Gallagher
36080 Bethesda St Ext

Barnesville OH 43713

Call Sign: KD8KOE
Karen S Gallagher
36080 Bethesda St Ext
Barnesville OH 43713

Call Sign: KA8REN
Karen S Gallagher
36080 Bethesda St Ext
Barnesville OH 43713

Call Sign: KC8ZQL
Thomas W Gallagher
36080 Bethesda St Ext
Barnesville OH 43713

Call Sign: W8KQA
Richard B Justice
132 Cherry St
Barnesville OH 43713

Call Sign: WB8WJT
Richard B Justice Jr
132 Cherry St
Barnesville OH 43713

Call Sign: KC8UJL
Theresa M Justice
132 Cherry St
Barnesville OH 43713

Call Sign: WD8DAZ
Robert D Gibson
139 Cherry St
Barnesville OH 43713

Call Sign: WD8OIT
Chester Kinney Jr
208 E Walnut St
Barnesville OH
437131239

Call Sign: N4SRW
Brian D Kinney
220 E Walnut St
Barnesville OH
437131239

Call Sign: WA8NFA
Paul L Medley
227 Laws St
Barnesville OH 43713

Call Sign: KD8GPN
Ronald J Mcconnell
516 Leggett Ave
Barnesville OH 43713

Call Sign: KC8OMW
Derek J Kistler
58604 Lower Sandy
Ridge Rd
Barnesville OH 43713

Call Sign: WB2HNT
Clarence A Van Dyne
62734 McMillan Rd
Barnesville OH
437139613

Call Sign: N8JXH
Steven D Whitacre
62944 McMillan Rd
Barnesville OH 43713

Call Sign: KD8AGR
David A Carroll
618.5 N Broadway
Barnesville OH 43713

Call Sign: KC8QNK
Larry R Kiddey Jr
522 N Broadway St
Barnesville OH 43713

Call Sign: K8XT

Ray L Ryman
602 N Chestnut St
Barnesville OH 43713

Call Sign: KG8JZ
Samuel A Allar
402 N Lincoln
Barnesville OH 43713

Call Sign: WD8BOR
Gilbert H Harris Sr
126 Ohio St
Barnesville OH 43713

Call Sign: KD8RAY
Raynard Merritt
303 Sycamore St
Barnesville OH 43713

Call Sign: N8VZL
Raynard Merritt
303 Sycamore St
Barnesville OH 43713

Call Sign: N8PWH
Mark A Meadows
137 Vine St
Barnesville OH
437130068

Call Sign: KD8QCZ
Brian W Sellers
302 W Church St
Barnesville OH 43713

Call Sign: KD8MSJ
Jeffery A Schanks
501 W Main St
Barnesville OH 43713

Call Sign: WD8DBZ
Jack O English
61895 W Tacoma Rd
Barnesville OH 43713

Call Sign: KA8HPW
Jean E English
61895 W Tacoma Rd
Barnesville OH
437139468

Call Sign: N8EQO
William B Miller
201 Walnut
Barnesville OH 43713

Call Sign: N8EAP
Polly D Collins
58230 Wright Rd
Barnesville OH 43713

Call Sign: WD8JOY
Richard L Collins Sr
58230 Wright Rd
Barnesville OH 43713

Call Sign: KC8SBC
Tina A Gyles
59265 Wright Rd
Barnesville OH 43713

Call Sign: KC8WBI
Brent A Heatherington
Barnesville OH 43713

FCC Amateur Radio Licenses in Barton

Call Sign: KB8EDX
Larry J Apicella Jr
Barton OH 43905

FCC Amateur Radio Licenses in Beallsville

Call Sign: K8UUO
Michael R Hanna
50100 Headley
Beallsville OH 43716

Call Sign: KD8LKY
Mark A Mellott
51975 Mellott Ridge Rd
Beallsville OH 43716

Call Sign: KD8LLB
Bettie J Mellott
44826 St Rt 556
Beallsville OH 47716

Call Sign: WD8JTG
David H Thurston
48457 St Rt 556
Beallsville OH 43716

Call Sign: KC8EUV
Clarence R Huntsman
43601 Washington St
Beallsville OH 43716

FCC Amateur Radio Licenses in Beaver

Call Sign: KD8KAK
Tim L Dean
311 Bliss Rd
Beaver OH 45613

Call Sign: WD8BKY
Caroline S Whitely
4344 Red Hollow Rd
Beaver OH 45613

Call Sign: WA8WIW
Norman Whitely
Redhollow Rd
Beaver OH 45613

Call Sign: KD8NSQ
Daniel S Stepp
940 Umblebee Rd
Beaver OH 45613

Call Sign: KA9MGF
Edmund P Taylor Jr

Beaver OH 45613

Call Sign: KE8T
Harold L Adams
Beaver OH 456130154

FCC Amateur Radio Licenses in Bellaire

Call Sign: N8DBS
David B Slie
616 32nd St
Bellaire OH 43906

Call Sign: N8VZL
Raynard Merritt
700 41st St Apt 38
Bellaire OH 439061181

Call Sign: WB8JHD
Jarrid D Day
1787 Belmont St
Bellaire OH 43719

Call Sign: WB6OGJ
Gary L Lappert
64960 Breezy Point Ln
Bellaire OH 43906

Call Sign: K8GSD
Gary L Lappert
64960 Breezy Point Ln
Bellaire OH 43906

Call Sign: KC8DKU
Carol A Smith
65184 Breezy Point Ln
Bellaire OH 439069746

Call Sign: W8ZQ
Northern Panhandle ARC
65184 Breezy Point Ln
Bellaire OH 439069746

Call Sign: WB8WRQ
John R Green
65184 Breezy Pt Ln
Bellaire OH 43906

Call Sign: K8JRG
John R Green
65184 Breezy Pt Ln
Bellaire OH 43906

Call Sign: KB3EZC
Carl S Noel
230 E 23rd St
Bellaire OH 43906

Call Sign: N8MUC
Lois J Wallace
4168 Franklin St
Bellaire OH 43906

Call Sign: WD8JIK
Lawrence D Wallace
4168 Franklin St
Bellaire OH 439061168

Call Sign: KD8JKR
Kevin M Sochor
4231 Franklin St
Bellaire OH 43906

Call Sign: K2CDS
Leonard J D Airo
55065 Fulton Hill Rd
Bellaire OH 43906

Call Sign: KC8IQR
Polly I Donohue
3662 Guernsey St
Bellaire OH 43906

Call Sign: WD8JIL
Joseph A Perrie
3111 Hamilton St
Bellaire OH 43906

Call Sign: N8ITC
Dennis F Pasz
1272 High St
Bellaire OH 43906

Call Sign: K8WDC
Charles R Sempirek
57680 Hospital Rd
Bellaire OH 43906

Call Sign: KF8OP
Joseph W Funkhouser
57020 Jordan Run
Bellaire OH 43906

Call Sign: KB8RJJ
Joseph W Funkhouser
III
57020 Jordan Run Rd
Bellaire OH 43906

Call Sign: K8EDG
John L Nowak
1326 Maple St
Bellaire OH 439061058

Call Sign: KC8GDY
Michael F Snively
65932 McGregor Rd
Bellaire OH 43906

Call Sign: KD8LYQ
Haven G Thompson
57300 Mehlman Rd
Bellaire OH 43906

Call Sign: N8GP
Haven G Thompson
57300 Mehlman Rd
Bellaire OH 43906

Call Sign: KB8FJS
Daniel J Alexander
65293 Nicole Ln
Bellaire OH 43906

Call Sign: KE8TD
Daniel R Alexander
65293 Nicole Ln
Bellaire OH 43906

Call Sign: WC8T
Frank J Nemeth
65975 Patterson Hill Rd
Bellaire OH 43906

Call Sign: N8WLX
Michael L Bilyeu
64691 Sand Hill Rd
Bellaire OH 43906

Call Sign: N8ZAG
William L Bilyeu
64691 Sand Hill Rd
Bellaire OH 43906

Call Sign: N8ZAJ
Patricia A Bilyeu
64691 Sand Hill Rd
Bellaire OH 43906

Call Sign: K8WDQ
Jack W Sechrest
57256 Spring Hill Rd
Bellaire OH 43906

Call Sign: N8TOE
Ralph J Hadley
57815 Spring Hill Rd
Bellaire OH 43906

Call Sign: KA8NWZ
Lawrence E Garloch Jr
54563 St Joe
Bellaire OH 43906

Call Sign: N8ZEY
Charles D Roman
3735 Stark St
Bellaire OH 43906

Call Sign: N8MXC
Bonnie S Ackermann
2368 W 23rd St
Bellaire OH 43906

Call Sign: WZ8F
Michael J Ackermann Sr
2368 W 23rd St
Bellaire OH 43906

Call Sign: N8MZD
Tabitha A Ackermann
2368 W 23rd St
Bellaire OH 43906

Call Sign: KA8SDZ
Mary W Ciancone
23101 W 23rd St
Bellaire OH 43906

Call Sign: KA8SEA
Nelson Ciancone
23101 W 23rd St
Bellaire OH 43906

Call Sign: N8WLV
James M Clark
3215 Washington St
Bellaire OH 43906

Call Sign: WF8A
James M Clark
3215 Washington St
Bellaire OH 43906

Call Sign: WB8TQI
Julius H Crumbaker
51287 Wegee Rd
Bellaire OH 43906

Call Sign: KB8RMI
Bernard L Hannum Sr
307 West St
Belle Valley OH 43717

Call Sign: KD8ARH
Kenneth D Hyland
309 West St
Belle Valley OH 43717

Call Sign: KA8JRV
Wayne A Oakes
Belle Valley OH 43717

Call Sign: KD8HMC
Robert A Sproul
42011 Horseshoe Bend
Rd
Belmont OH 43718

Call Sign: KD8LNX
Parnell S Metz
43905 Main St
Belmont OH 43718

Call Sign: KD8FWB
Jacob D Feisley
66565 Muller Rd
Belmont OH 43718

Call Sign: KD8AIU
Julie C Maidens
67380 New Laffery Rd
Belmont OH 43718

Call Sign: N8DBY
Paul E Scott
129 W Main St
Belmont OH 43718

Call Sign: WD8DIP
Paul E Scott

129 W Main St
Belmont OH 43718

Call Sign: KD8OBT
Randy B Watkins
708 4th St
Belpre OH 45714

Call Sign: W8KXQ
Lewis A Naylor
312 6th St
Belpre OH 45714

Call Sign: KB8WHK
Kenny D Sims
2206 Ames Ave
Belpre OH 45714

Call Sign: KB8WHL
Randall L Sims
2206 Ames Ave
Belpre OH 45714

Call Sign: KG8MD
Richard H Thorn
513 Barclay St
Belpre OH 45714

Call Sign: KC8YUS
John E Sink
504 Beach Dr
Belpre OH 45714

Call Sign: WD8LFP
Patrick E Mc Dole
917 Belrock Ave
Belpre OH 45714

Call Sign: KC8OVE
Mary E Kibble-Leu
901 Blvd Dr
Belpre OH 45714

Call Sign: N8YXX
Sandra M Ellenwood
Box 111
Belpre OH 45714

Call Sign: N8ZAP
John E Deleruyelle
762 George St
Belpre OH 45714

Call Sign: WA8MNE
David R Rodgers
2417 Norris Ave
Belpre OH 45714

Call Sign: WB8IFN
Paul E Sims
Box 374
Belpre OH 45714

Call Sign: WD8MPL
George H Norris
2404 Hanvey Ave
Belpre OH 45714

Call Sign: AC4OZ
Floyd E Pickens
711 Norway Ave
Belpre OH 45714

Call Sign: KB8EKQ
Patricia A Moore
Box 442
Belpre OH 45714

Call Sign: KB8GYU
Dana A Fouss
1015 Joe Skinner Rd
Belpre OH 45714

Call Sign: KA8UVZ
Joseph S Keesey
1809 Pennsylvania Ave
Belpre OH 45714

Call Sign: KB8EOY
Debbie A Moore
Box 442
Belpre OH 45714

Call Sign: WA8NTX
Gregory C Stone
1423 King St House
Belpre OH 45714

Call Sign: K8MVR
Walter H Buskirk
1210 Poplar St
Belpre OH 45714

Call Sign: N8SCV
Michael D Harris Sr
824 Campbell Dr
Belpre OH 45714

Call Sign: KC8YMQ
Larry A Lee
1573 Lois St
Belpre OH 45714

Call Sign: KB3HNY
Elmer G Zillier
6704 Ridge St
Belpre OH 457142491

Call Sign: KD8IND
Eugene D Boggs
809 Clement Ave Apt A
Belpre OH 45714

Call Sign: KA8FUG
Wheaton M Shearman
311 Maple St
Belpre OH 45714

Call Sign: W8OFB
James A Dukas
1808 Rockland Ave
Belpre OH 457141146

Call Sign: KC8MOY
Kimberly A Sampson
753 Covey Ct
Belpre OH 45714

Call Sign: KB8YAD
Charlotte L Jordan
325 Maple St
Belpre OH 45714

Call Sign: KA8FUE
Patrick E Milhoan
2409 Rockland Ave
Belpre OH 45714

Call Sign: N8ZNS
Steven B Pinkerman
122 Elm St
Belpre OH 45714

Call Sign: WD8RGZ
Ronald A Ferrell
738 Middle St
Belpre OH 45714

Call Sign: WD4AMB
Frederick B Sims
Rt 2
Belpre OH 45714

Call Sign: KA8QNK
Glen E Church
704 Elm St Apt 9
Belpre OH 45714

Call Sign: KA8NCX
Donald G Peck
60 Mill Branch Rd
Belpre OH 45714

Call Sign: WD8BWD
Robert L Mc Million
Rt 2
Belpre OH 45714

Call Sign: KE8TF
George F Kesterson
1 Sawgrass Cir
Belpre OH 45714

Call Sign: N8MMG
Bettie L Kesterson
1 Sawgrass Cir
Belpre OH 45714

Call Sign: N8PYD
Richard E Lucas
804 Seneca Dr
Belpre OH 45714

Call Sign: KB8OJA
Jonah D Fox
816 Seneca Dr
Belpre OH 45714

Call Sign: KB8EKO
Eloise Y Webb
107 Stone Rd
Belpre OH 45714

Call Sign: N8DZS
Karl L Webb
107 Stone Rd
Belpre OH 45714

Call Sign: WD8INS
Kenyon D Cox
2712 Underwood Dr
Belpre OH 457141949

Call Sign: KC8QJS
John N Gunsch
2529 Valley View Dr
Belpre OH 457141040

Call Sign: WA3IPC
Robert M Ackerman
7960 Veto Rd
Belpre OH 45714

Call Sign: KC8TUF
Denise L Magyarosi
9867 Veto Rd
Belpre OH 45714

Call Sign: WD8BXT
Evermont T Robinson
418 Walnut St
Belpre OH 45714

Call Sign: KB8IOZ
James P Logan
604 Walnut St
Belpre OH 45714

Call Sign: WR3A
Fred W Myers
707 Walnut St
Belpre OH 457141659

Call Sign: KD8PYD
Douglas P Hess Jr
813 Walnut St
Belpre OH 45314

Call Sign: N8BFE
Angela L Hess
813 Walnut St
Belpre OH 45714

Call Sign: KG8YH
Gary C Morrison
609 Walnut St
Belpre OH 45714

Call Sign: N8VWP
Amy J Mendenhall
810 Walnut St
Belpre OH 45714

Call Sign: K8VJP
Marion R Welch
713.5 Walnut St Apt A
Belpre OH 45714

Call Sign: N8XWQ
Kenneth E Reeder
115 Warren Ave
Belpre OH 45714

FCC Amateur Radio Licenses in Bethesda

Call Sign: N8VBF
Robert L Tush
61011 Hunter Bethesda Rd
Bethesda OH 437190483

Call Sign: KA8YEX
Belva M De Bolt
65979 McMillen Rd
Bethesda OH 43719

Call Sign: KC8TRT
Richard G Quinlin
302 N Main St
Bethesda OH 43719

Call Sign: W8DLB
Denny L Beardmore
306 N Main St
Bethesda OH 437190313

Call Sign: KA8AHY
Denny L Beardmore
306 N Main St Box 313
Bethesda OH 437190313

Call Sign: N8MHV
William C Burchette
301 Pear St
Bethesda OH 43719

Call Sign: KB8TFU
Carol B Burchette

301 Pear St Box 195
Bethesda OH 43719

Call Sign: KC8YCS
Jarrid D Day
309 Rice Ave
Bethesda OH 43719

Call Sign: KC8UJI
Donna L Gacek
59331 S 26 Rd
Bethesda OH 43719

Call Sign: NH6JE
James D Montgomery
305 S Main St
Bethesda OH 43719

Call Sign: KE8TC
Charles W Leisure
319 S Main St
Bethesda OH 43719

Call Sign: KC8IEH
John W Jenkins
211 Summit St
Bethesda OH 43719

FCC Amateur Radio Licenses in Beverly

Call Sign: KD8NRV
Thomas E Porter
2435 Big Run Rd
Beverly OH 45715

Call Sign: K8RED
James C Cline
504 Fairview Ave
Beverly OH 45715

Call Sign: KC8GBA
Paul L Wagner
425 Ray Harr Rd
Beverly OH 45715

Call Sign: KD8KN
Clifford R Martin
179 Riverview Dr
Beverly OH 457151415

Call Sign: KD8PYJ
James D Pool
20870 St Rt 60
Beverly OH 45715

Call Sign: WM8G
Mark E Grubb
59 Wilson St
Beverly OH 45715

Call Sign: KI8IP
Mark E Grubb
59 Wilson St
Beverly OH 457150336

Call Sign: WT8D
Gregory B Ferguson
Beverly OH 45715

Call Sign: AB8EY
Mark E Grubb
Beverly OH 45715

Call Sign: KD8RRH
Dayna L Ferguson
Beverly OH 45715

Call Sign: KC8NNJ
Larry E Webb
Beverly OH 457150111

FCC Amateur Radio Licenses in Blaine

Call Sign: KA8NXA
Kenneth E Garloch
54431 Farr Rd
Blaine OH 439090021

Call Sign: KC8CIW
Charles E Rufer
Blaine OH 43909

Call Sign: WB8CTC
Joe T Mc Cready
Blaine OH 43909

FCC Amateur Radio Licenses in Blue Rock

Call Sign: KC8NPM
Les Chancey
10595 Center Rd
Blue Rock OH 43720

Call Sign: KD8MWD
Caitlyn Tanner
5476 Cutler Lk Rd
Blue Rock OH 43720

Call Sign: KD8RIZ
Bobby J Vaughn
1535 Moody Hollow Rd
Blue Rock OH 43720

Call Sign: KD8ESQ
Jeff E Shook
8390 Poverty Ridge Rd
Blue Rock OH 43720

Call Sign: KD8PEF
Jesse J Rayner
10905 Rayner Ln
Blue Rock OH 43720

Call Sign: KB8SHS
John R England
7000 S River Rd
Blue Rock OH 43720

Call Sign: KD8ETF
Shawn V Van Meter
9820 Union Hill Rd
Blue Rock OH 43720

FCC Amateur Radio Licenses in Bridgeport

Call Sign: N8SGJ
Thomas E Mc Elfresh
105.5 6th St
Bridgeport OH 43912

Call Sign: WD8PPR
Harry H Trumpie
154 Bench St
Bridgeport OH
439121303

Call Sign: KB8PJJ
Stanley L Galownia
69500 Blaine Chermont
Rd
Bridgeport OH 43912

Call Sign: KD8LNW
Rose M Mccready
68275 Blaine Chermont
Rd
Bridgeport OH 43912

Call Sign: N8EVY
Joseph J Orzolek
25 Elm St
Bridgeport OH 43912

Call Sign: KD8EVM
A Michael Kenenske
53340 Farmington Rd
Bridgeport OH 43912

Call Sign: KD8RMV
Michele R Hill
1 Gould Park Rd Apt
315
Bridgeport OH 43912

Call Sign: KD8LKU
James D Janos

400 Jacquette St
Bridgeport OH 43912

Call Sign: W8GBH
Norman R Russell
67471 Kirkwood
Heights Rd
Bridgeport OH
439129730

Call Sign: N8SMA
Kathy J Fish
70738 Lollini Rd
Bridgeport OH 43912

Call Sign: WD8BSA
Robby L Fish
70738 Lollini Rd
Bridgeport OH 43912

Call Sign: N5KJF
Kathy J Fish
70738 Lollini Rd
Bridgeport OH 43912

Call Sign: KC8PQP
Robert A Barricklow
606 Main St
Bridgeport OH 43912

Call Sign: KB8PJK
Jonathan R Thomas
70370 Pine Hollow Rd
Bridgeport OH 43912

Call Sign: N8EGQ
Robbie J Davis
55520 Poplar Ave
Bridgeport OH 43912

Call Sign: WB8WHJ
William R Davis Jr
55520 Poplar Ave
Bridgeport OH 43912

Call Sign: KC8UGS
William E Goff Jr
510 Spring Heights
Bridgeport OH 43912

Call Sign: KC8IG
Daniel R Perko
522 Spring Heights
Bridgeport OH 43912

Call Sign: KB8DNI
Richard S Jackson
69410 Starlight Dr
Bridgeport OH 43912

Call Sign: KB8DNJ
Eleane R Jackson
69410 Starlight Dr
Bridgeport OH 43912

Call Sign: WD8MTT
Chester W Bondzeleske
70405 Sunset Hgts Rd
Bridgeport OH 43912

Call Sign: KD8BWZ
Charles R Bell
404 Whitely St
Bridgeport OH 43912

Call Sign: AB8VC
Charles R Bell
404 Whitely St
Bridgeport OH 43912

Call Sign: KA8TSP
Mary E Ellison
69024 Woods Rd
Bridgeport OH 43912

Call Sign: KA8TSR
John W Ellison Jr
69024 Woods Rd
Bridgeport OH 43912

Call Sign: KC8ONR
Daniel Dawson
69955 Woods Rd
Bridgeport OH 43912

FCC Amateur Radio Licenses in Buchtel

Call Sign: N8VOU
Jerrold E Sullivan
17616 S Akron Ave
Buchtel OH 45716

Call Sign: KB8UUD
Bobby L Harris
5645 SR 78
Buchtel OH 457160147

Call Sign: KD8CWG
Jeff R Addis
17473 Wilson Ave
Buchtel OH 45716

Call Sign: KD8FRR
Michael Holbrook
Buchtel OH 45716

FCC Amateur Radio Licenses in Byesville

Call Sign: KD8MPZ
Bryon G Lowry
13682 Catbird Rd
Byesville OH 43723

Call Sign: KC8SBD
Susan K Stuebe
59002 Cherry Hill Rd
Byesville OH 43723

Call Sign: KB8SUZ
Susan K Stuebe
59002 Cherry Hill Rd
Byesville OH 43723

Call Sign: KB8PYK
Herbert D Ailing
209 Euclid Ave
Byesville OH 43723

Call Sign: K8TER
Michael D Mesarchik
210 Euclid Ave
Byesville OH 43723

Call Sign: KD8HKJ
Ted R Fehrman
249 Euclid Ave
Byesville OH 43723

Call Sign: WA8NRR
Joseph Ellwood Jr
45 Greenwood Mob Park
Byesville OH 43723

Call Sign: KD8OUL
Randolph L Van Kirk
12088 Ideal Rd
Byesville OH 43723

Call Sign: KI8KD
David C Dilbeck
12663 Ideal Rd
Byesville OH 43723

Call Sign: KD8JVO
Matthew A Mallett
9153 Indian Lk Rd
Byesville OH 43723

Call Sign: KD8ETG
Matthew W Norris
402 Jacqueline Dr
Byesville OH 43723

Call Sign: KC8AAM
Glen D Logan
114 Jeniffer Dr
Byesville OH 43723

Call Sign: WD8KPI
Cleveland L Beatty Jr
8821 Lucasburg Rd
Byesville OH 43723

Call Sign: KC8SFB
Harold J Milner
9078 Lucasburg Rd
Byesville OH 43723

Call Sign: KA8LFI
Harold J Milner
9078 Lucasburg Rd
Byesville OH 43723

Call Sign: KC8MLT
Benjamin J Baker
204 McLaughlin Ave
Byesville OH 43723

Call Sign: KC8WDN
Benjamin J Baker
204 McLaughlin Ave
Byesville OH 43723

Call Sign: KD8PDW
Patrick J Gadd
9606 Pioneer Rd
Byesville OH 43723

Call Sign: W8MZP
Myron E Larrick
211 Race Ave
Byesville OH
437231262

Call Sign: KD8CNC
Aaron F Long
280 S 5th St
Byesville OH 43723

Call Sign: KD8MPE
Cassandra N Anker
215 S 9th St Lot 41

Byesville OH 43723

Call Sign: KC8WXC
Donald D Towner Jr
202 Seneca Ave Apt 3
Byesville OH 43723

Call Sign: KD8MQT
Todd W Stone
101 Sequoia Dr
Byesville OH 43723

Call Sign: KD8HWE
Vern L Johnson
10215 Sycamore St
Byesville OH 43723

Call Sign: WA8MOS
Harry A Bowman Sr
59246 Trailrun Rd
Byesville OH 43723

Call Sign: K8IOX
Robert M Geese
112 Walnut St Apt D
Byesville OH 43723

Call Sign: KD8JVE
Ethan A Kirkman
10337 Washington St
Byesville OH 43723

**FCC Amateur Radio
Licenses in Caldwell**

Call Sign: KA8VLR
Mary E Coyle
13586 Chapel Dr
Caldwell OH 43724

Call Sign: KC8HDN
Ramon B Postel
48780 CR 128
Caldwell OH 43724

Call Sign: WD8KFL
Norman F Still
14286 CR 13
Caldwell OH 43724

Call Sign: K8LTH
Virginia B Wilkos
16547 CR 132
Caldwell OH 43724

Call Sign: KB8RQV
Daniel K Mote
40361 CR 15
Caldwell OH 43724

Call Sign: N8YGK
Richard G Rutherford
44731 CR 66
Caldwell OH 43724

Call Sign: WA8TBY
Charles S Evilsizer
113 Cumberland St Apt
1
Caldwell OH 43724

Call Sign: KD8RIS
Mark A Massaro
19155 Harl Weiller Rd
Caldwell OH 43724

Call Sign: W8REX
Rex E Theobald
18844 Harl Weiller Rd
297
Caldwell OH 43724

Call Sign: KD8JVX
Chad A Haga
17443 Industrial Hw
Caldwell OH 43724

Call Sign: KD8RJC
Jorge E Wilkjos
606 Main St

Caldwell OH 43724

Call Sign: KB8PZQ
Paul D Wallace
816 Main St
Caldwell OH 43724

Call Sign: KC8OII
Joyce L Johnson
816 Main St
Caldwell OH 43724

Call Sign: KD8MQP
Karli J Niswonger
16286 McConnellsville
Rd
Caldwell OH 43724

Call Sign: K8WYG
Myron E Merry
430 North St
Caldwell OH 43724

Call Sign: N8YGE
Steven L Campbell
1315 North St
Caldwell OH 43724

Call Sign: KA8GMQ
Alvin F Vavrek
45746 Old SR 21
Caldwell OH 43724

Call Sign: KD8SAJ
Laura A Coyle
47825 Outback Ln
Caldwell OH 43724

Call Sign: N2LC
Charles L Coyle
47825 Outback Ln
Caldwell OH 43724

Call Sign: KD8MPQ
Ricky E Vincent

13815 Rayner Rd
Caldwell OH 43724

Call Sign: KD8JVT
Paul T Siddle
20060 Salt Run Rd
Caldwell OH 43724

Call Sign: KB8WBI
Timothy L Overly
19068 SR 78
Caldwell OH 43724

Call Sign: KB8PYL
Jerry B Porter
48 Sunset Dr
Caldwell OH
437249714

Call Sign: K8YLR
Richard R Miller
41142 TR 298A
Caldwell OH 43724

Call Sign: KC8UXH
Meredythe L Wilkinson
48181 TR 41
Caldwell OH 43724

Call Sign: NC8OH
 Noble County ARC
18844 Twp 297
Caldwell OH 43724

Call Sign: KF8XK
Rex E Theobald
18844 Twp Rd 297
Caldwell OH 43724

Call Sign: KD8OSI
Gary J Oliver
48697 Wargo Rd
Caldwell OH 43724

Call Sign: KD8RZP

Pamela S Oliver
48697 Wargo Rd
Caldwell OH 43724

Call Sign: KC8WOZ
Nicolas C Stiers
Wolfrun Rd
Caldwell OH 43724

FCC Amateur Radio Licenses in Cambridge

Call Sign: KA8NZS
Evelyn F Barton
62810 1st Ave
Cambridge OH 43725

Call Sign: KB8MGI
Clarence F Barton Jr
62810 1st Ave
Cambridge OH 43725

Call Sign: KC8WOT
Caleb J Barton
62810 1st Ave
Cambridge OH 43725

Call Sign: AB8XI
Robert D Baird
64346 Arrowhead Rd
Cambridge OH 43725

Call Sign: KC8LQ
Joseph J Zaleski
904 Avon Dr
Cambridge OH 43725

Call Sign: KD8RRG
Gilbert J Barczak
66756 Barret Hill Rd
Cambridge OH 43725

Call Sign: KD8MPJ
Chad S Gardner
920 Beatty Ave

Cambridge OH 43725

Call Sign: WD8LGJ
James H Koch
1406 Beatty Ave
Cambridge OH 43725

Call Sign: WV8Z
William F Wagner
62131 Beech Cir Rd
Cambridge OH 43725

Call Sign: WD8JKH
John P Schoendorff
65736 Beeham Run Rd
Cambridge OH
437258829

Call Sign: KC8OQW
David M Thompson
65935 Beeham Run Rd
Cambridge OH 43725

Call Sign: KD8MQE
Zachary T Warehime
2895 Best Rd
Cambridge OH 43725

Call Sign: N8NTI
William M Belknap
1824 Brenton Rd
Cambridge OH 43725

Call Sign: N8XAY
Joshua E Boyd
5805 Brick Church Rd
Cambridge OH 43725

Call Sign: KD8GKK
Jamie L Boyd
5805 Brick Church Rd
Cambridge OH 43725

Call Sign: N7XGR
Bruce E Mc Kim

2476 Broad St
Cambridge OH
437259326

Call Sign: KB8MBZ
Albert S Mc Intire
6992 Brushrun Rd
Cambridge OH 43725

Call Sign: KA8MSL
Earl B Detrick
10536 Cadiz Rd
Cambridge OH 43725

Call Sign: KD8CNK
Randy Wissler
230 Cambridge St
Cambridge OH 43725

Call Sign: N8TRH
David A Gregg
60201 Christian Hill Rd
Cambridge OH 43725

Call Sign: N8YGL
Joseph R Boyd
60399 Christian Hill Rd
Cambridge OH 43725

Call Sign: KD8AJQ
Leah M Welch
330 Clark St
Cambridge OH 43725

Call Sign: KD8HWF
Michael A Price
409 Clark St
Cambridge OH 43725

Call Sign: WB8YHU
Charles L Melanko
802 Clark St
Cambridge OH 43725

Call Sign: N8ZVO

Roger L Albaugh
112 Clay Ave
Cambridge OH 43725

Call Sign: KD8HLD
Matthew A Warehime
4391 Clay Pike Rd
Cambridge OH 43725

Call Sign: KD8JVI
Brent D Fogg
5593 Clay Pike Rd
Cambridge OH 43725

Call Sign: KD8EIQ
Shelba J Watson
6474 Clay Pike Rd
Cambridge OH 43725

Call Sign: KD8HLA
Harold Z Marlatt
58298 Coleman Rd
Cambridge OH 43725

Call Sign: K8LYM
Galen V Howard
19 Coventry Dr
Cambridge OH 43725

Call Sign: KE8NI
Robert B Gray
5358 Covered Bridge
Rd
Cambridge OH
437259463

Call Sign: KB7EIU
Dan J Edmunds
8000 Dozer Rd
Cambridge OH 43725

Call Sign: KB7RXV
Julie A Edmunds
8000 Dozer Rd
Cambridge OH 43725

Call Sign: KC8NRX
Roger L Davis
12172 E Pike Rd
Cambridge OH 43725

Call Sign: AB8JH
Roger L Davis
12172 E Pike Rd
Cambridge OH 43725

Call Sign: KD8RIK
Timothy M Bryan
6063 Fairdale Dr
Cambridge OH 43725

Call Sign: KD8MQI
Kenneth A Applegate
6373 Fairdale Rd
Cambridge OH 43725

Call Sign: KB8UQB
Michael R Mitchell
1306 Foste Ave
Cambridge OH 43725

Call Sign: KD8PGQ
Brent T Clark
621 Foster Ave
Cambridge OH 43725

Call Sign: N8YGM
Richard R Evilsizor Jr
8897 Francis Pl
Cambridge OH 43725

Call Sign: KD8RIO
Dustin M Hannahs
1122 Gomber Ave
Cambridge OH 43725

Call Sign: WD8SDH
Richard W Wayt
605 Halbar Dr
Cambridge OH 43725

Call Sign: KC8HRW
Greg G Childs
64806 Hidden Acres Ln
Cambridge OH 43725

Call Sign: K8BD
Raymond Howard
61951 High Hill Rd
Cambridge OH 43725

Call Sign: KA8SYH
Lois M Howard
61951 High Hill Rd
Cambridge OH 43725

Call Sign: KD8JYQ
Sherri L Hinnant
62341 High Hill Rd
Cambridge OH 43725

Call Sign: KD8JFW
Bruce E Ady
598 Highland Ave
Cambridge OH 43725

Call Sign: KD8JFX
Mary K Ady
598 Highland Ave
Cambridge OH 43725

Call Sign: KD8PEL
Daniel L Stein
468 Huston Hills Dr
Cambridge OH 43725

Call Sign: KB8QPD
Dale M Baker
62969 James Rd
Cambridge OH 43725

Call Sign: KB8PRV
Billie L Brown
550 Jefferson Ave
Cambridge OH 43725

Call Sign: KC8SBB
Mark S Jenei
61266 Kent Ln
Cambridge OH 43725

Call Sign: WD8LED
Barry K Ramsay
64021 Larrick Ridge Rd
Cambridge OH 43725

Call Sign: KC8AJP
Beth A Cole
9463 Liberty Rd
Cambridge OH 43725

Call Sign: KB8PSR
Robert L Cole
9463 Liberty Rd
Cambridge OH
437259023

Call Sign: N8TRG
William L Goodman
4059 Mantua Rd
Cambridge OH 43725

Call Sign: KD8LYI
Shellie M Brown
1828 Maple Rd 2A
Cambridge OH 43725

Call Sign: KC8JTO
William L Brown
1828 Maple Rd Apt 1B
Cambridge OH 43725

Call Sign: KD8JFV
Harold M Thompson
7650 Marysville Rd
Cambridge OH 43725

Call Sign: N8INB
Troy J Simmons
3268 Meadow Rd

Cambridge OH 43725

Call Sign: N8NTH
Stephen C Pierson
124 Merrick Rd
Cambridge OH 43725

Call Sign: N8YGJ
Kelly A Gordon
1327 Morton Ave
Cambridge OH 43725

Call Sign: KD8HKX
Trent L Nethers
168819 Mt Hermon Rd
Cambridge OH 43725

Call Sign: N8JMK
Bruce A Homer
64062 Mulberry St
Cambridge OH 43725

Call Sign: K8PSM
James O Green
602 N 10th St
Cambridge OH
437251524

Call Sign: WB4PXD
James O Green
602 N 10th St
Cambridge OH
437251524

Call Sign: W8JKQ
Wilford J Funk
817 N 12th St
Cambridge OH 43725

Call Sign: N8PGX
Wilmer E Cochran III
1430 N 12th St
Cambridge OH 43725

Call Sign: N4JDP

James K Sims Sr
1470 N 13th St
Cambridge OH 43725

Call Sign: KD8HWJ
Lucinda F Hill
987 N 18th St
Cambridge OH 43725

Call Sign: KA8GNK
Stanley F Rogers
409 N 5th St
Cambridge OH 43725

Call Sign: W8BMS
Albert D Blancett
425 N 6th St
Cambridge OH 43735

Call Sign: W8KNZ
Brooks H Eakin
615 N 6th St
Cambridge OH 43725

Call Sign: KD8LYH
Gene C Greenwalt
627 N 8th St
Cambridge OH 43725

Call Sign: K8LTN
Gene C Greenwalt
627 N 8th St
Cambridge OH 43725

Call Sign: WA8ZSH
Jewett E Richardson Jr
226 N 9th
Cambridge OH 43725

Call Sign: KD8JWA
Donald R Chesler Jr
619 N 9th St
Cambridge OH 43725

Call Sign: KD8CND

Jeremy A Hager
62319 N Westover Ln
Cambridge OH 43725

Call Sign: AC8DH
Danny L Hogan
12780 Narrows Rd
Cambridge OH 43725

Call Sign: N8MPT
Christopher J
Wittensoldner
8214 Oldham Rd
Cambridge OH 43725

Call Sign: W8IIN
Louis E Coury
1206 Portland Ave
Cambridge OH
437251037

Call Sign: KD8PDY
Kristen M Gilcher
65671 Rabbit Rd
Cambridge OH 43725

Call Sign: KC8BEY
Aaron B Yerian
67876 Read Rd
Cambridge OH 43725

Call Sign: K8ZWF
Richard L Huston
62834 Ridgewood Dr
Cambridge OH
437258974

Call Sign: KD8ETN
Kurt D Smith
9270 Ruth Ln
Cambridge OH 43725

Call Sign: KC8DUG
Debi L Leanza
744 S 8th St

Cambridge OH 43725

Call Sign: KD8MQL
Joshua R Butles
61384 Savage Rd
Cambridge OH 43725

Call Sign: N8RAI
Thomas S Mc Vicker II
440 Sherman Ave
Cambridge OH 43725

Call Sign: KD8EIR
Mary J Rhodes-Ellis
5855 Sherrard Rd
Cambridge OH 43725

Call Sign: KA8GLP
Bryce K Simmons
6100 Simmons Rd
Cambridge OH 43725

Call Sign: N8GUW
Jack D Carpenter
5026 Skyline Dr
Cambridge OH 43725

Call Sign: KA8MWI
Robert A Fair
6050 Skyline Dr
Cambridge OH 43725

Call Sign: WA8KRK
John T Fair Jr
6050 Skyline Dr
Cambridge OH 43725

Call Sign: KC8ZWS
Timothy E Honkus
4472 Sugar Grove Rd
Cambridge OH 43725

Call Sign: AB8P
James L Shaw
4473 Sugar Grove Rd

Cambridge OH 43725

Call Sign: KD8MFD
Leslie M Canning Jr
618 Taylor Ave
Cambridge OH 43725

Call Sign: N8STK
Sarah D Carpenter
1025 Taylor Ave
Cambridge OH 43725

Call Sign: N8MNY
Dorothy D Leanza
318 Wall Ave
Cambridge OH 43725

Call Sign: KD8MPO
Flora J Schneider
301 Water St
Cambridge OH 43725

Call Sign: WA8BMP
John W Vance
1032 Wheeling Ave
Cambridge OH 43725

Call Sign: WA8MLX
Stephen J Best
6380 William Ave
Cambridge OH
437259204

Call Sign: KB8PYG
Kenneth R Warehime
1480 Wills Crk Dr Apt
101 B
Cambridge OH 43725

Call Sign: KD8MHB
Guernsey County Ares
Cambridge OH 43725

Call Sign: K8AL
Alan E Day

Cambridge OH
437250303

Call Sign: W8VP
Cambridge ARC
Cambridge OH
437250303

FCC Amateur Radio Licenses in Carbon Hill

Call Sign: KC8HKL
Frank S Stufflebeam
41882 Front St
Carbon Hill OH 43111

Call Sign: WD8CIT
Michael S Coe
Carbon Hill OH 43111

Call Sign: AB8EZ
Frank S Stufflebeam
Carbon Hill OH 43111

Call Sign: KB8YPU
Don C Koon Sr
Carbon Hill OH
431110022

FCC Amateur Radio Licenses in Chandlersville

Call Sign: KD8ESX
Wesley J Shook
4845 Chandlersville Rd
Chandlersville OH
43727

Call Sign: KD8PEA
Gregory R Hamill
7655 Chandlersville Rd
Chandlersville OH
43727

Call Sign: KC8HFT
Duane L Sears
10605 Chandlersville Rd
Chandlersville OH
43727

Call Sign: KC8IXT
Jeffrey S Meadows
8672 Ridgeview Rd
Chandlersville OH
43727

Call Sign: K8WXV
Donald J Janicki
8645 Sugargrove Rd
Chandlersville OH
43727

Call Sign: KD8BUD
James R Davis
5295 Taylor Ln
Chandlersville OH
43727

Call Sign: KD8JUZ
Chase W Spillman
8825 Tumblin Rd
Chandlersville OH
43727

FCC Amateur Radio Licenses in Chaucey

Call Sign: KA8YMI
John H Johnson
52 Jacobs
Chauncey OH 45719

Call Sign: KC8MZD
Carl H Moody
12 Lexington Ave
Chauncey OH 45719

Call Sign: KB8NPM
Margaret H Gerberich
419 2nd Ave
Chesapeake OH 45619

Call Sign: WB8IGA
Wesley J Gerberich
419 2nd Ave
Chesapeake OH 45619

Call Sign: KD8LCM
Ronald M Musser
623 3rd Ave
Chesapeake OH 45619

Call Sign: KB8HXE
Ronald K Dillon
Box 234
Chesapeake OH 45619

Call Sign: KB8KTN
George C Hall
Box 251
Chesapeake OH 45619

Call Sign: N8YQE
Stanley M Diehl
Box 27
Chesapeake OH 45619

Call Sign: KB8MOO
Bryan R Gilpin
Box 550
Chesapeake OH 45619

Call Sign: KB8GWF
Jimmy R Mc Cown
Box 663
Chesapeake OH 45619

Call Sign: N8XZW

David M Sites
930 Brown St
Chesapeake OH 45689

Call Sign: KC8ERN
Robert J Murray
2 Candy Ln
Chesapeake OH 45619

Call Sign: KD8FPX
Joseph P Thompson
2951 Cord 59
Chesapeake OH 45619

Call Sign: KB8PLF
Kevin J Hennessy Dr
10652 CR 1
Chesapeake OH 45619

Call Sign: KB8RZZ
Charles E Worrell
10727 CR 1
Chesapeake OH 45619

Call Sign: KB8RZY
Belinda L Worrell
10727 CR 1
Chesapeake OH 45619

Call Sign: KD8FPW
Mary K Thompson
2951 CR 59
Chesapeake OH 45619

Call Sign: KC8VYE
Chad M Thompson
2951 CR 59
Chesapeake OH 45619

Call Sign: KD8IVA
Steven D Lynch
102 Overlook Dr
Chesapeake OH 45619

Call Sign: KD8ECS

Joe M Blazer
48 Private Dr 10657
Chesapeake OH
456196905

Call Sign: AB8ZK
Joe M Blazer
48 Private Dr 10657
Chesapeake OH
456196905

Call Sign: KC8GYP
Charles E Riley
47 Private Dr 1335 Co
Rd 124
Chesapeake OH 45619

Call Sign: WB8YKS
Michael L Love
109 Private Dr 633
Chesapeake OH 45619

Call Sign: N8QCY
Sally J Love
109 Private Dr 633
Chesapeake OH 45619

Call Sign: KC8DXR
Murrill L Napier
483 TR 1093
Chesapeake OH 45619

Call Sign: KD8RRZ
Kenny R Fields Jr
1734 TR 156
Chesapeake OH 45619

Call Sign: WA8GAD
David H Thomas
250 Twp 1097
Chesapeake OH 45619

Call Sign: N8WJT
Richard W Mc Fann
527 Grover Rd
Cheshire OH 45620

Call Sign: AB8WE
Ronald K Parcell
77 Honeysuckle Dr
Cheshire OH 45620

Call Sign: KB8UUC
Fredrick D Thomas
27799 SR 7
Cheshire OH 45620

Call Sign: KD8CSM
Teresa L Nance
2308 St Rt 554
Cheshire OH 45620

Call Sign: N8QDE
John R Davidson
27400 St Rt 7
Cheshire OH 45620

Call Sign: KC8UYM
Amanda S Morris
9342.5 St Rt 7 N
Cheshire OH 45620

FCC Amateur Radio Licenses in Chesterhill

Call Sign: KC8GFF
Paul Arvidson
801 Fischer Howard Rd
Chesterhill OH 43728

Call Sign: N8WXT
Steven L Lacy
5282 St Rt 377
Chesterhill OH 43728

Call Sign: N4RNT
Keith E Green

3238 W Goshen Run Rd
Chesterhill OH 43728

Call Sign: KD8IDQ
Matthew J Pepper
5055 Wogan Rd
Chesterhill OH 43728

FCC Amateur Radio Licenses in Chillicothe

Call Sign: KA8JMC
Harold R Miller
645 Adena Rd
Chillicothe OH 45601

Call Sign: N8ZOO
Charles R Van De Carr
IV
713 Allen Ave
Chillicothe OH 45601

Call Sign: N8SJO
Sarah C Rozell
1307 Andersonville Rd
Chillicothe OH 45601

Call Sign: WB8YEL
Robert D Rozell Sr
1307 Andersonville Rd
Chillicothe OH
456018263

Call Sign: WB8MJW
Donald H Lyons
275 Annis Ct
Chillicothe OH 45601

Call Sign: WD8OLP
Philip F Hopper
14 Applewood Dr
Chillicothe OH 45601

Call Sign: N8ITO
Hal J Adcock

468 Arch St
Chillicothe OH 45601

Call Sign: N1VXP
Richard A Mc Clure
506 Arch St
Chillicothe OH 45601

Call Sign: KF4TAO
Stephen R Meschke
48 Barnhart Dr
Chillicothe OH 45601

Call Sign: WA8NWY
Larry J Unger
330 Baum Hill Rd
Chillicothe OH 45601

Call Sign: N8XLM
Linda J Severson
589 Belleview Ave
Chillicothe OH 45601

Call Sign: WU8R
Roger E Severson
589 Belleview Ave
Chillicothe OH 45601

Call Sign: KC8FTQ
Roger W Smith
1448 Biers Run Rd
Chillicothe OH 45601

Call Sign: KB8ZGS
Connie S Mathuews
221 Black Run Rd
Chillicothe OH 45601

Call Sign: WA8ZVN
Willard H Mathuews
221 Black Run Rd
Chillicothe OH 45601

Call Sign: N8EYK
Scott R Cunningham

8505 Blain Hwy
Chillicothe OH
456018644

Call Sign: WD8NAD
Brookie J Diehl
1261 Bowdle Rd
Chillicothe OH 45601

Call Sign: KB8SSD
Ronald W Boring II
415 Bowdle Rd
Chillicothe OH 45601

Call Sign: KB8JTR
William B Adams Sr
111 Brown Hollow Rd
Chillicothe OH 45601

Call Sign: KA8PUN
Harold G Harper
11 Cahill Dr
Chillicothe OH 45601

Call Sign: WD8OTS
Wilby A Nelson
80 Cameo Ln
Chillicothe OH 45601

Call Sign: AA8YN
Richard R Miller
279 Carmel Dr
Chillicothe OH 45601

Call Sign: KB8RNC
Ora J Donaldson
3136 Cattail Rd
Chillicothe OH 45601

Call Sign: KB8TKS
Beverly A Donaldson
3136 Cattail Rd
Chillicothe OH 45601

Call Sign: KM8Q

Jerry H Rymer
95 Cedarwood Dr
Chillicothe OH 45601

Call Sign: WD8AUS
Harriet E Rymer
95 Cedarwood Dr
Chillicothe OH 45601

Call Sign: KC8DYB
Jack L Clark
159 Cedarwood Dr
Chillicothe OH 45601

Call Sign: KB8YSN
Gerald R Mitten
6054 Charleston Pike
Chillicothe OH 45601

Call Sign: WD8BGG
Roger L Burggraf
7849 Charleston Pike
Chillicothe OH 45601

Call Sign: N8ZON
Ethel P Taylor
18 Cheyenne Dr
Chillicothe OH 45601

Call Sign: N8ZOX
Richard D Taylor
18 Cheyenne Dr
Chillicothe OH 45601

Call Sign: N8UKO
Robert L Chemas
346 Chris Ct
Chillicothe OH 45601

Call Sign: KD8JSM
John A Debrosse
179 Church St
Chillicothe OH
456012406

Call Sign: N8ZOM
Timothy C Brooks
348 Clay St
Chillicothe OH 45601

Call Sign: WB0PIF
Harry M Hatmaker
340 Constitution Dr
Chillicothe OH 45601

Call Sign: KC8VNG
Rebecca L Pentecost
35 Courtland Dr
Chillicothe OH 45601

Call Sign: W4NOD
Howard F De Long Jr
93 Courtland Dr
Chillicothe OH 45601

Call Sign: K8SUB
Paul F Kysor
1174 Crouse Chapel Rd
Chillicothe OH
456019011

Call Sign: N8KAJ
James M Pratt
22 Cypress Rd
Chillicothe OH 45601

Call Sign: KA8EGX
George R Rhude
139 Cypress Rd
Chillicothe OH
456018484

Call Sign: N8VIE
Glenneth H Hutt
2255 Debord Rd
Chillicothe OH 45601

Call Sign: KC8IXI
Woodrow De Borde
38 Deerpath Rd

Chillicothe OH 45601

Call Sign: KC8TSF
Daniel L Ratliff
310 Devon Rd
Chillicothe OH 45601

Call Sign: K8ZWW
Daniel L Ratliff
310 Devon Rd
Chillicothe OH 45601

Call Sign: WB8GSI
Donald R Hunter
657 E 2nd St
Chillicothe OH 45601

Call Sign: NS8R
Warren E Dowler Sr
695 E 2nd St
Chillicothe OH 45601

Call Sign: WA8LRR
Robert L Bishop
173 E 2nd St Apt 3
Chillicothe OH 45601

Call Sign: N8NTZ
Bruce A Oyer
625 E 4th St
Chillicothe OH 45601

Call Sign: KI8HU
Gary L Nelson
397 E 7th St
Chillicothe OH 45601

Call Sign: KC8VOK
Norma M Nelson
397 E 7th St
Chillicothe OH 45601

Call Sign: KD8BWW
Tyler J Nelson
397 E 7th St

Chillicothe OH 45601

Call Sign: WW8A
Richard C Brown Sr
694 E Main St
Chillicothe OH 45601

Call Sign: KB8TKL
Sarah M Cade
711 E Main St
Chillicothe OH 45601

Call Sign: KA8OJJ
Noah M Porter Jr
20 E Riehle Rd
Chillicothe OH 45601

Call Sign: KD8EJX
Robert W Atwood
176 E Water St
Chillicothe OH 45601

Call Sign: KG8RY
Howard E Leach
62 Eagle Ct
Chillicothe OH
456018133

Call Sign: KB8OWL
Thomas L Beatty
1159 Easterday Rd
Chillicothe OH 45601

Call Sign: WD8CPW
Willard G Long
1098 Edgewood Dr
Chillicothe OH 45601

Call Sign: N8OUG
William G Wood
179 Emerald Ln
Chillicothe OH 45601

Call Sign: KC8CAP
Michael D Sherron

119 Forest Edge Dr
Chillicothe OH
456019551

Call Sign: N8MGO
Thomas E Blazer
174 Franklin Cir
Chillicothe OH 45601

Call Sign: K8GWM
Charles F Lawhorn
42 Fruithill Dr
Chillicothe OH
456011132

Call Sign: N8ULS
Paul D Martin
514 Golfview Dr
Chillicothe OH 45601

Call Sign: KD8LDO
Jeffery L Ling
450 Grubb Rd
Chillicothe OH 45601

Call Sign: KB8SBA
Glendon R Powell
612 Half High St Apt 2
Chillicothe OH 45601

Call Sign: KC8BPT
Daniel R Mathuews
2541 Hartwood Rd
Chillicothe OH 45601

Call Sign: WA8ZVN
Connie S Mathuews
2541 Hartwood Rd
Chillicothe OH 45601

Call Sign: KG8NQ
Otto L Tuttle
21 Harvestwood Dr
Chillicothe OH
456017058

Call Sign: KB8HF
Arthur L Vorhies
683 Hilltop Ct
Chillicothe OH 45601

Call Sign: WB8PPH
Leonard L Campbell
320 Hough Rd
Chillicothe OH
456019343

Call Sign: KA8YTE
Melissa A Hellen
694 Jefferson Ave
Chillicothe OH 45601

Call Sign: KJ3I
Donald W Hellen Jr
694 Jefferson Ave
Chillicothe OH 45601

Call Sign: WB8EEC
Charles L Drummond
785 Jefferson Ave
Chillicothe OH
456013541

Call Sign: W8JQK
Marion F Kepp
587 Johnson Rd
Chillicothe OH 45601

Call Sign: K8ZW
Mark S Floyd
96 King St
Chillicothe OH 45601

Call Sign: WK8M
Thomas E Hartley
593 Laurel St
Chillicothe OH
456011447

Call Sign: KC8OFQ

John A Mand
33 Ledgewood Dr
Chillicothe OH 45601

Call Sign: KD8KJD
Bryan K Largent
3622 Liberty Hill Rd
Chillicothe OH 45601

Call Sign: KD8QCX
Malcom L Porter
1990 Lick Run Rd
Chillicothe OH 45601

Call Sign: KC8MQM
Ronald J Simantel
24 Limestone Blvd
Chillicothe OH
456011157

Call Sign: N8EWL
H R Grimm
33 Limestone Blvd
Chillicothe OH 45601

Call Sign: WA8WZE
Charles V Brooks
48 Limestone Blvd
Chillicothe OH 45601

Call Sign: W8NBK
Earl M Reichman
71 Limestone Blvd
Chillicothe OH 45601

Call Sign: KA8JYC
Mark R Busch
226 Logan View Dr
Chillicothe OH 45601

Call Sign: WA8ZYV
Robert L Busch
226 Loganview Rd
Chillicothe OH 45601

Call Sign: WA8LHJ
Albert G Beeler Sr
403 Lunbeck Rd
Chillicothe OH 45601

Call Sign: K8CLJ
Richard C Hopper
411 Lunbeck Rd
Chillicothe OH 45601

Call Sign: WA8PZJ
Wilbur G Cartwright
270 Madeira Ave
Chillicothe OH 45601

Call Sign: WA8PBZ
Phillip R Beeler
931 Malone Rd
Chillicothe OH 45601

Call Sign: WA8RMF
Edward E Tuvell
145 Maple Grove Rd
Chillicothe OH 45601

Call Sign: K8OLK
Paul W Bethel Sr
270 Maple Grove Rd
Chillicothe OH 45601

Call Sign: W8BBW
Paul J Schumann
5418 Marietta Rd
Chillicothe OH 45601

Call Sign: N8ZOU
Rocky A Detty
2528 Massicville
Chillicothe OH 45601

Call Sign: WD8MDS
Robert J May Jr
4 May Ave
Chillicothe OH 45601

Call Sign: N8LPK
Larry J Mc Whorter
329 Midland Rd
Chillicothe OH 45601

Call Sign: KB8TKO
Billie W Myers
330 Midland Rd
Chillicothe OH
456011870

Call Sign: WB8LNZ
Steven L Streitenberger
460 Mill St
Chillicothe OH 45601

Call Sign: KD8EMR
Paul S Lapczynski
1529 Mingo Rd
Chillicothe OH 45601

Call Sign: N8ZOW
Wesley A Tull
716 Moss Hollow Rd
Chillicothe OH 45601

Call Sign: WB8MQV
Richard W Basye
2587 Moss Hollow Rd
Chillicothe OH 45601

Call Sign: WB8MQW
Connie S Basye
2587 Moss Hollow Rd
Chillicothe OH 45601

Call Sign: KB8ODN
James A Hart
6226 Mt Tabor Rd
Chillicothe OH 45601

Call Sign: KC8FWK
Richard A Cockrell
625 Mt Zion Rd
Chillicothe OH 45601

Call Sign: KD8LWX
Darian Dunn
1530 N Bridge St
Chillicothe OH 45601

Call Sign: KC8WEB
David C Pentecost
35 N Courtland Dr
Chillicothe OH 45601

Call Sign: KC8VNF
Deborah H Pentecost
35 N Courtland Dr
Chillicothe OH
456012841

Call Sign: KB8ZGQ
David O Harding
120 N High St
Chillicothe OH 45601

Call Sign: N8SJB
Maurice L Wilson
131 N Sugar St
Chillicothe OH
456012646

Call Sign: KC8GCN
Mary R Webb
121 N Watt St
Chillicothe OH 45601

Call Sign: WD8NUR
Robert A Peck
1231 Nelson Dr
Chillicothe OH 45601

Call Sign: KA8HGI
Steven G Miner
242 North St
Chillicothe OH 45601

Call Sign: N8KPM
Robert L Faulkner

3219 Patton Hill Rd
Chillicothe OH 45601

Call Sign: WB8TRA
Charles E Hafner
751 Philclaire Rd
Chillicothe OH 45601

Call Sign: W8CUO
William H Counts
310 Piatt Ave
Chillicothe OH 45601

Call Sign: K8MGA
Jerry T Larabee
12247 Pleasant Vly Rd
Chillicothe OH 45601

Call Sign: KB8USX
James F Anderson Jr
12346 Pleasant Vly Rd
Chillicothe OH 45601

Call Sign: WD8BGI
Leo F Brown
481 Pohlman Rd
Chillicothe OH 45601

Call Sign: WD8BGJ
Elizabeth L Brown
481 Pohlman Rd
Chillicothe OH 45601

Call Sign: WB8NNJ
James V Anzelmo
1304 Randall Ct
Chillicothe OH 45601

Call Sign: W9NYL
Richard M Sandy
1228 Randall Dr
Chillicothe OH
456011934

Call Sign: KC8SPO

Andrew J Peters
202 Reo Dr
Chillicothe OH 45601

Call Sign: KB8PMP
Lynn R Park
173 Rosewood Ct
Chillicothe OH 45601

Call Sign: WB8JOJ
James D Fairchild
2705 Rozelle Crk Rd
Chillicothe OH 45601

Call Sign: KA8SHV
Harley L Milligan
15802 Rt 104
Chillicothe OH 45601

Call Sign: W8LXJ
Robert A Blue
1650 Rt 207
Chillicothe OH 45601

Call Sign: W8JUD
John A Robertson
20702 Rt 23 N
Chillicothe OH 45601

Call Sign: N8XTW
Gerald F Michaels
3168 S Bridge St 28
Chillicothe OH 45601

Call Sign: N8SJL
Walsh L Walsh
197 S Mullberry St
Chillicothe OH 45601

Call Sign: KD8MNK
Christopher N Pazsint
245 S Paint St
Chillicothe OH 45601

Call Sign: KC8VTP

William D Lorenzo
79 S Watt St
Chillicothe OH 45601

Call Sign: KC8BBT
Bruce G Copeland
932 Schrake Rd
Chillicothe OH 45601

Call Sign: WB8GOT
Robert P Cutright Sr
860 Sherman Rd
Chillicothe OH
456011362

Call Sign: WB8NGD
Sondra A Cutright
860 Sherman Rd
Chillicothe OH
456011362

Call Sign: KC8WEA
Ronald W Stiltner Jr
805 Snyder Rd
Chillicothe OH 45601

Call Sign: KD8KBW
John R Gillow
99 Snyder Rd
Chillicothe OH
456019189

Call Sign: KB8OWK
Margaret E Grimes
1963 Spud Run Rd
Chillicothe OH 45601

Call Sign: WB8MCV
Michael H Grimes
1963 Spud Run Rd
Chillicothe OH
456018948

Call Sign: K8QOO
Grover E Bowen

20493 St Rt 104
Chillicothe OH 45601

Call Sign: W8ATE
VA Chi ARC
17273 St Rt 104 VA
Med Cntr
Chillicothe OH 45601

Call Sign: KB8TKT
Doris M Linehan Ms
5641 St Rt 159
Chillicothe OH 45601

Call Sign: KB8HLK
David L Fairchild
50 St Rt 180
Chillicothe OH 45601

Call Sign: KG8ET
Jacqueline A Berry
50 St Rt 180
Chillicothe OH 45601

Call Sign: N8LSV
Donald L Berry
50 St Rt 180
Chillicothe OH 45601

Call Sign: KF8GI
Douglas A Blue
2151 St Rt 207
Chillicothe OH 45601

Call Sign: KD8CHP
Jesse J Stanley
16153 St Rt 28
Chillicothe OH 45601

Call Sign: KC8FOJ
Gary J Doberstyn
7091 St Rt 772
Chillicothe OH 45601

Call Sign: KC8FOL

Kathy L Doberstyn
7091 St Rt 772
Chillicothe OH 45601

Call Sign: WB8LFR
Russell J Ingham
479 Stanley St
Chillicothe OH
456013458

Call Sign: N8XSV
John L Snyder
19 Tecumseh Dr
Chillicothe OH 45601

Call Sign: NY8U
James R Stafford Jr
238 Terrace Dr
Chillicothe OH 45601

Call Sign: AA8D
James R Stafford Jr
238 Terrace Dr
Chillicothe OH 45601

Call Sign: KC8PFN
Gary L Newman
73 Timberlane Dr
Chillicothe OH 45601

Call Sign: KA8BUF
Michael R Mathuews
934 Trego Crk Rd
Chillicothe OH 45601

Call Sign: N8SIZ
James A Routt
20544 US 23 N 20
Chillicothe OH 45601

Call Sign: KC8AMP
Nancy A Hawkins
27204 US 35
Chillicothe OH 45601

Call Sign: KB8OWM
Carl W Jones
32198 US 50
Chillicothe OH 45601

Call Sign: N8ULQ
Thomas M Smith
18795 US Rt 23
Chillicothe OH 45601

Call Sign: KB8OAT
Ralph E Shoemaker
16209 US Rt 50
Chillicothe OH 45601

Call Sign: AA8IZ
Deane E Hawkins Jr
27204 USR 35
Chillicothe OH 45601

Call Sign: N8ULR
Robert F Dempsey
29317 USR 50 10
Chillicothe OH 45601

Call Sign: KB8TNH
Royce E Davis
1259 Vigo Rd
Chillicothe OH 45601

Call Sign: KC8DYE
Alan W Cook
1265 Vigo Rd
Chillicothe OH
456015869

Call Sign: N8WJU
Val B Sigler
618 Vine St
Chillicothe OH 45601

Call Sign: KE8TE
Lee H Rowley
152 W 2nd St Apt 2
Chillicothe OH 45601

Call Sign: N8ZTD
Dan F Toth Jr
330 W 4th St
Chillicothe OH 45601

Call Sign: KD8BWV
James R Boyce
604 W 5th St
Chillicothe OH 45601

Call Sign: W8UVB
Cornell C Hunter
355 W Main St
Chillicothe OH 45601

Call Sign: KA8TJD
Judy K Rowley
447 W Main St
Chillicothe OH 45601

Call Sign: WA8FTT
Charles E Bishop
172 W Water St
Chillicothe OH 45601

Call Sign: KC8DYC
James B Sykes
742 Washington Ave
Chillicothe OH 45601

Call Sign: N8ZOS
Douglas E Thompson
309 Western Ave
Chillicothe OH 45601

Call Sign: W8KHE
Pete Stearos
1355 Western Ave Apt
16
Chillicothe OH 45601

Call Sign: N8SIY
Donald G Tinch
13264 Westfall Rd

Chillicothe OH 45601

Call Sign: KC8JDY
Teays ARC
13264 Westfall Rd
Chillicothe OH
456019418

Call Sign: N8MGN
Nicholas S Franklin
165 Whaley Pl
Chillicothe OH 45601

Call Sign: KC8EFV
Linda M Holdren
100 Whaley Pl Apt L
Chillicothe OH 45647

Call Sign: WA8GUG
Ross A Hatfield
47 Wildflower Ln
Chillicothe OH
456014094

Call Sign: KB8ZMF
Michael T Thomas
2258 Windy Ridge Rd
Chillicothe OH 45601

Call Sign: KB8RNB
Nicole M S Van Rengscl
156 Woodland Way
Chillicothe OH 45601

Call Sign: KC8LGL
Paul D Besimer
368 Woodview Dr
Chillicothe OH
456019722

Call Sign: N8JVL
Peter P Scott
93 Wright St
Chillicothe OH 45601

Call Sign: KB8TKN
Ratana Thompson
352 Zane Rd
Chillicothe OH 45601

Call Sign: N8ZOQ
Jack D Thompson
352 Zane Rd
Chillicothe OH 45601

Call Sign: N8ZOP
Roberta S Noble
Chillicothe OH 45601

Call Sign: N8ZOZ
Penny S Noble
Chillicothe OH 45601

Call Sign: KB8KCY
John D Mathers
Chillicothe OH 45601

Call Sign: KB8TKQ
Malcolm D Lewis
Chillicothe OH 45601

Call Sign: KB8WSC
Randall P Davies
Chillicothe OH 45601

Call Sign: KA8LJS
Earl F Bronkar Jr
Chillicothe OH
456010990

Call Sign: KC8WIX
Kevin G Matthews
176 Sullivan Rd
Chillilothe OH 45601

Call Sign: KC8WIW
Michael R Matthews
176 Sullivan Rd
Chillilothe OH 45601

FCC Amateur Radio Licenses in Clarington

Call Sign: WD8PAX
Lenzy R Darrah
51780 Boltz Hill Rd
Clarington OH 43915

Call Sign: K8HS
Highland R Smith
51260 SR 536
Clarington OH 43915

Call Sign: KG8VX
James A Henning
47810 Sykes Ridge Rd
Clarington OH 43915

FCC Amateur Radio Licenses in Clarksburg

Call Sign: KB8SFB
Terry L Dinkler
15222 Egypt Pike
Clarksburg OH 43115

Call Sign: KC8PAB
Richard J Caddell
17254 High St
Clarksburg OH 43115

Call Sign: KC8DPC
Roger L Wood
11063 N Main St
Clarksburg OH 43115

FCC Amateur Radio Licenses in Coal Grove

Call Sign: KB8PIE
Carolyn S Hunley
705 Lane St
Coal Grove OH 45638

Call Sign: KB8OIL

Jeffery A Young Jr
119 North St
Coal Grove OH 45638

Call Sign: KB8PID
Cynthia M Caskey
120 Steece Rd
Coal Grove OH 45638

Call Sign: KB8VHG
Ernest R Caskey
120 Steece Rd
Coal Grove OH 45638

FCC Amateur Radio Licenses in Coal Run

Call Sign: KB8WN
Joe C Faires
 Maple
Coal Run OH
457210127

Call Sign: KC8EEP
Donald N Barton
 Twp 117
Coal Run OH 45721

FCC Amateur Radio Licenses in Coalton

Call Sign: KB8YSO
Harley T Woltz Jr
20 Foster St
Coalton OH 45621

Call Sign: KC8FXM
Greg A Shook
91 Main St
Coalton OH 45621

Call Sign: KC8DFM
Margaret A Shook
8 Wells St
Coalton OH 45621

Call Sign: KC8DFP
Gerald A Shook
8 Wells St
Coalton OH 45621

Call Sign: WA6TGM
Bert L Bird
7400 Woodside Dr
Coalton OH 456215534

Call Sign: N8AJD
Stephen C Grant
Coalton OH 45621

Call Sign: KD8GSP
Darrell D Tilley Jr
Coalton OH 45621

FCC Amateur Radio Licenses in Coolville

Call Sign: KB8ZAJ
Charles W Rupe
1 8th St
Coolville OH 45723

Call Sign: KB8WQF
John R Pauley
43335 Bearwallow
Ridge Rd
Coolville OH 45723

Call Sign: KB8WQG
Roberta J Pauley
43335 Bearwallow
Ridge Rd
Coolville OH 45723

Call Sign: KB8ZVR
Wendy S Rupe
4525 Brandeberry Rd
Coolville OH 45723

Call Sign: KC8QGL

Sue E Eshelman
45100 Carr Rd
Coolville OH 45723

Call Sign: K8BEE
Sue E Eshelman
45100 Carr Rd
Coolville OH 45723

Call Sign: KD8NLH
Charles H Tholin
28221 Cincinnati Ridge
Coolville OH 45723

Call Sign: KC8TYY
Frank X Purcell Jr
28420 Cincinnati Ridge
Rd
Coolville OH 45723

Call Sign: KA4VNK
Robert G Riordan Jr
22750 Clark Rd
Coolville OH 45723

Call Sign: KB8JDH
Brynn E Riordan
27550 Clark Rd
Coolville OH 45723

Call Sign: KD8CAD
Elizabeth A Riordan
27750 Clark Rd
Coolville OH 45723

Call Sign: N8TGH
Karl A Arvidsson
27550 Clark Rd
Coolville OH 45723

Call Sign: WB8ZZK
Nina M James
5285 Federal Rd
Coolville OH 45723

Call Sign: KC8QMI
Dan E Swartz
5679 Ireland Rd
Coolville OH 45723

Call Sign: N8WJH
Larry F Ball
5590 Ireland Rd
Coolville OH 45723

Call Sign: KC8QMJ
Molly J Swartz
5679 Ireland Rd
Coolville OH 45723

Call Sign: WD8BBW
William H Arnott
26200 Main St
Coolville OH 45723

Call Sign: W8WHA
William H Arnott
26200 Main St
Coolville OH 45723

Call Sign: KD8WR
Ralph D Kinney
25960 Meadow Ln
Coolville OH 45723

Call Sign: KD8AUE
Cecil D James III
28877 Murphy Rd
Coolville OH 45723

Call Sign: KA8NJT
Kenneth L Fought Sr
605 Old 7 Rd
Coolville OH 45723

Call Sign: KC8MOU
Dianna K Fogle
1005 Old 7 Rd
Coolville OH 45723

Call Sign: KB8ROK
Bryan C Fogle
1005 Old 7 Rd
Coolville OH 48723

Call Sign: WD8OYH
Robert O Miller
27026 Rock Run Rd
Coolville OH 45723

Call Sign: KB8OZO
Juanita V Hedges
110 Rock St
Coolville OH 45723

Call Sign: KB8QQC
Charles W Hedges
110 Rock St
Coolville OH 45723

Call Sign: KB8ZTA
Alain P Robideaux
39 SR 7
Coolville OH 45723

Call Sign: N8LVX
Glenn D Easterling
886 SR 7
Coolville OH 45723

Call Sign: K8PSK
Glenn D Easterling
886 St Rt
Coolville OH 45723

Call Sign: KB8ZSK
Charles D Robideaux
39 St Rt 7
Coolville OH
457239774

Call Sign: W8DUX
Charles D Robideaux
39 St Rt 7

Coolville OH
457239774

Call Sign: KD8GMA
Kaye W Hamilton
42145 St Rt 7
Coolville OH 45723

Call Sign: KC8OXZ
Teresa L Maurath
617 Vanderhoof Rd
Coolville OH 45723

Call Sign: K8CFI
Kevyn J Maurath
617 Vanderhoof Rd
Coolville OH 45723

Call Sign: KC8LFF
Jason B Hager
42980 Vanderhoof Rd
Coolville OH 45723

FCC Amateur Radio Licenses in Corning

Call Sign: KD8PDX
Clyde S Garey
2370 Bearfield Twp Rd
318
Corning OH 43730

Call Sign: N8CKP
John J Dawson Sr
125 Comly St
Corning OH 437300016

Call Sign: N8DDA
Thomas A Gaitten
103 Graf St
Corning OH 43730

Call Sign: KC8FXL
Vern O Riley
Marshall St

Corning OH 43730

Crooksville OH 43731

**FCC Amateur Radio
Licenses in Creola**

Call Sign: KD8HJG
Nathan R Riffle
237 McKeever St
Crooksville OH 43731

Call Sign: N8NGZ
James M Thrasher
24939 Potter Ridge Rd
Creola OH 45622

Call Sign: KA8HMS
Richard L Cady
419 North St
Crooksville OH 43731

Call Sign: KD8MRW
Ronald E Ward
752 Barcus Hollow Rd
Crown City OH 45623

**FCC Amateur Radio
Licenses in Crooksville**

Call Sign: KD8HKM
Robert K Foster
6720 Old State Rd
Crooksville OH 43731

Call Sign: WW8RON
Ronald E Ward
752 Barcus Hollow Rd
Crown City OH 45623

Call Sign: KB8SLQ
Daniel S Beal
46 Brown Cir Dr
Crooksville OH 43731

Call Sign: KD8ETQ
Joe M Misuraca
445 S State St
Crooksville OH 43731

Call Sign: KC5THI
Arline G Wirtz
807 CR 72
Crown City OH 45623

Call Sign: KD8HWI
James W Dykes
11900 Buzzard Glory
Rd
Crooksville OH 43731

Call Sign: K7SXJ
Eugene F Loro
2457 SR 93 NE
Crooksville OH 43731

Call Sign: KK5ZP
Clarence D Wirtz
807 CR 72
Crown City OH 45623

Call Sign: KC8QXC
Joseph V Agriesti Jr
231 Cemetery St
Crooksville OH
437311016

Call Sign: KC7YK
Donald L Fox
3706 St Rt 13 SE
Crooksville OH 43731

Call Sign: KC8KTZ
Raymond L Rice
3324 CR 73
Crown City OH 45623

Call Sign: NG8B
John E Dalrymple
4588 Ceramic Rd NE
Crooksville OH 43731

Call Sign: KC8KGM
Janie M Knerr
217 W Main St
Crooksville OH 43731

Call Sign: KC8KYA
Kevin M Rice
3326 CR 73
Crown City OH 45623

Call Sign: KA8NOO
Ralph H Landerman
8601 Deavertown Rd
NW
Crooksville OH 43731

Call Sign: KD8MPF
Tony R Ansel
302 Whitehouse St
Crooksville OH 43731

Call Sign: KC8WDR
Harry L Rice Jr
3330 CR 73
Crown City OH 45623

Call Sign: WA8WNI
Billy J Colbert
12875 Harrison Twp 8
NE

Call Sign: KD8HLC
Thomas D Lucas Jr
Crooksville OH 43731

Call Sign: KC8JXI
Robert A Plybon Jr
422 Double Crk Rd
Crown City OH 45623

Call Sign: KA8VGM

Candy S Lee
15290 Hannan Trace Rd
Crown City OH 45623

Call Sign: KC8JH
Gregory Lee
15290 Hannan Trace Rd
Crown City OH 45623

Call Sign: W8GG
Gregory Lee
15290 Hannan Trace Rd
Crown City OH 45623

Call Sign: KA8YOX
Teresa L Cardwell
15422 Hannan Trace Rd
Crown City OH 45623

Call Sign: KD8ZU
Lester E Cardwell
15422 Hannan Trace Rd
Crown City OH 45623

Call Sign: N8QCX
Joshua L Cardwell
15422 Hannan Trace Rd
Crown City OH 45623

Call Sign: KE6NGH
Ronald E Traurig
189 Private Dr 123
Crown City OH 45623

Call Sign: KD8RXU
Larry L Sawyers
22688 St Rt 7
Crown City OH 45623

Call Sign: K8SUS
Stephen E Hutchison
28 TR 1352
Crown City OH 45623

Call Sign: KA8MZU

S Todd Hutchison
28 TR 1352
Crown City OH 45623

Call Sign: KD8MWJ
Mark L Bradshaw
115 TR 600
Crown City OH 45623

Call Sign: N8AOK
Mark L Bradshaw
115 TR 600
Crown City OH 45623

Call Sign: KC8NGL
Theresa E Moore
56 Twp Rd 1284
Crown City OH 45623

Call Sign: WD8PKP
Kermit T Adkins
43 Walnut St
Crown City OH
456230103

Call Sign: K8AQO
Kermit T Adkins
43 Walnut St
Crown City OH
456230103

FCC Amateur Radio Licenses in Cumberland

Call Sign: KC8BEU
Kenneth E Crawford
5998 Conner Rd
Cumberland OH 43732

Call Sign: KG8CZ
Richard D Clifton
55176 Iowa Rd
Cumberland OH 43732

Call Sign: W8CII
Larry E Brooks
10800 Oak Grove Rd
Cumberland OH 43732

Call Sign: KD8PEG
Joseph R Roberts
54765 Red Ln Rd
Cumberland OH 43732

Call Sign: KD8JVS
Kyle R Weingart
54048 Singer Rd
Cumberland OH 43732

FCC Amateur Radio Licenses in Cutler

Call Sign: KB8LQQ
Harold W Rhodes
Box 160A
Cutler OH 45724

Call Sign: KA8QMJ
Michelle L Kellar
Box 171F
Cutler OH 45724

Call Sign: W8FUS
Harold L Ferguson
Box 28A
Cutler OH 45724

Call Sign: WB8DRJ
Joseph B Malone
75 Patten Mills Rd
Cutler OH 45724

Call Sign: KD8MFV
Cameron W Bennett
15108 St Rt 555
Cutler OH 45724

Call Sign: KD8IRD
David K Bennett

15108 St Rt 555
Cutler OH 45724

FCC Amateur Radio Licenses in Deadman

Call Sign: KC8IDD
Daniel R Evans
1525 Moores Rd
Deadman OH 45679

FCC Amateur Radio Licenses in Dexter

Call Sign: KA8QWH
John C Welsh
Dexter OH 45726

FCC Amateur Radio Licenses in Dexter City

Call Sign: KB8FYL
James P Stack
16486 St Rt 339
Dexter City OH 45727

FCC Amateur Radio Licenses in Dresden

Call Sign: KD8HHS
James Kerr
12025 Bottom Rd
Dresden OH 43821

Call Sign: KD8MPY
Tyler R Lacy
13090 Bottom Rd
Dresden OH 43821

Call Sign: KB8DHG
L Bradford Dailey
14619 CR 14
Dresden OH 43821

Call Sign: KD8HKV
Steven M Ward
17117 CR 4
Dresden OH 43821

Call Sign: KD8RIY
Matthew B Shepherd
14976 CR 439
Dresden OH 43821

Call Sign: KD8JVH
Logan D Lacy
14922 CR 6
Dresden OH 43821

Call Sign: N8TRI
Charles E Todd
8120 Green Rd
Dresden OH 43821

Call Sign: KC8ENI
Karl F Wilson
63 Jody Dr Apt 1
Dresden OH 438219700

Call Sign: N2AFV
Karl F Wilson
63 Jody Dr Apt 1
Dresden OH 438219700

Call Sign: KD8HKP
Matthew D Jenkins
819.5 Main St
Dresden OH 43821

Call Sign: KD8NOM
 Dresden Elementary
Amateur Radio Station
1318 Main St
Dresden OH 43821

Call Sign: W8RSB
Bernard F Fisher
1390 Main St
Dresden OH 43821

Call Sign: KD8PGP
Nevin L Weekley
1740 Mollies Rock Rd
Dresden OH 43821

Call Sign: KD8RJB
Corry I White II
1900 N Branch Rd
Dresden OH 43821

Call Sign: KD8RJA
Seth R Wagner
3515 New Riley Rd
Dresden OH 43821

Call Sign: KA8DJR
Ella L Mullinnex
910 W 10th St
Dresden OH 43821

Call Sign: KD8RIP
Dwayne K Jenkins
41 W 6th St
Dresden OH 43821

Call Sign: N8GIX
Robert L Ruebush
18 W 8th
Dresden OH 43821

Call Sign: KC8YV
Glenn W Mitchell
98 W Dave Longaberger
Ave
Dresden OH 43821

Call Sign: N8SJR
Earl E Starner Jr
Dresden OH 43821

Call Sign: KC8PVY
Jeffrey N Wilbur
Dresden OH 43821

FCC Amateur Radio Licenses in Duncan Falls

Call Sign: N8RNZ
Jerry L Henderson
228 Mill St
Duncan Falls OH 43734

Call Sign: KB8NQ
Richard N Callihan
3260 Millers Ln
Duncan Falls OH
437349721

Call Sign: KD8RIT
Dakota A Mcconaha
2680 Red Fox
Duncan Falls OH 43734

Call Sign: KB8UVU
Carl E Smith Jr
3955 Salt Crk Dr
Duncan Falls OH 43734

FCC Amateur Radio Licenses in Ewing

Call Sign: W8KVR
Don E Casey
18309 SR 160
Ewington OH
456869190

FCC Amateur Radio Licenses in Fairpoint

Call Sign: KC8WBJ
Thomas C Ault
St Rt 9 N
Fairpoint OH 43927

FCC Amateur Radio Licenses in Fleming

Call Sign: KB8WHJ
Steve N Shotwell
1015 Rocky Point Rd
Fleming OH 45729

Call Sign: KA8ZRT
Douglas W Needham
13333 St Rt 550
Fleming OH 45729

FCC Amateur Radio Licenses in Flushing

Call Sign: KA8VAM
John Ciesielka
710 32 Flsg Mstwn Rd
Flushing OH 43977

Call Sign: KG8CB
Clyde L Porter
Box 42B
Flushing OH 43977

Call Sign: KD8QXO
Michael J Roddy
43295 County Line Rd
Flushing OH 43977

Call Sign: NE0C
Kenneth E Burrough
70260 Morristown
Flushing Rd
Flushing OH 43977

Call Sign: W8KEB
Kenneth E Burrough
70260 Morristown
Flushing Rd
Flushing OH 43977

Call Sign: KC8QBF
Harold J Vigoffi
40910 Mt Hope Rd
Flushing OH 43977

Call Sign: N8KGR
Russell Neitzelt
42460 Mt Hope Rd
Flushing OH 43977

Call Sign: K8YA
William T Alvis III
Flushing OH 43977

Call Sign: WC8P
Sandra K Williams
Flushing OH 43977

Call Sign: KA8ZWP
Donald G Gibas
Flushing OH 43977

FCC Amateur Radio Licenses in Frankfort

Call Sign: KB8QHN
Ernest E Morris
1371 Bushmill Rd
Frankfort OH 45628

Call Sign: W8EEM
Ernest E Morris
1371 Bushmill Rd
Frankfort OH 45628

Call Sign: KC8JDU
Wanda S Pierce
607 Clark Ln
Frankfort OH 45628

Call Sign: KG8UU
James E Pierce
607 Clark Ln
Frankfort OH 45628

Call Sign: W2OHD
Albert O Weasner
922 Davis Hill Rd
Frankfort OH 45628

Call Sign: KC8FAO
John W Peters
29 Jessica Dr
Frankfort OH 45628

Call Sign: W8JKS
John K Smart
1344 McDonald Hill Rd
Frankfort OH 45628

Call Sign: N8ZOV
Mindy J Hartmus
69 Musselman Station Rd
Frankfort OH 45628

Call Sign: WB8GRX
John R Hartmus II
69 Musselman Station Rd
Frankfort OH
456289712

Call Sign: N8ZEU
Carl R Henderson Jr
2803 Poplar Ridge
Frankfort OH 45628

Call Sign: KD8KJC
Trisha L Krueger
2803 Poplar Ridge
Frankfort OH 45628

Call Sign: KD8KJA
Henderson R David
2803 Poplar Ridge Rd
Frankfort OH 45628

Call Sign: KD8KJB
Theresa E Henderson
2803 Poplar Ridge Rd
Frankfort OH 45628

Call Sign: W8TZ

Ross A Hatfield
2127 Ragged Ridge Rd
Frankfort OH 45628

Call Sign: KD8DRJ
William S Schneider
278 Shawnee Trl
Frankfort OH 45628

Call Sign: KG8UN
Larry B Williams
283 Shiloh Rd
Frankfort OH 45628

Call Sign: W8KV
David Birnbaum
13131 St Rt 28
Frankfort OH 45628

Call Sign: N8RQK
Ronald L Gilmore
21 Sulphur Lick Rd
Frankfort OH 45628

Call Sign: N8OUI
Kevin L Pancake
10169 Westfall Rd
Frankfort OH 45628

Call Sign: W8OVP
John D Warth
Frankfort OH 45628

FCC Amateur Radio Licenses in Franklin Furnace

Call Sign: N8YN
Jerry L Huffman
2057 Apel Rd
Franklin Furnace OH 45629

Call Sign: KI8WW
Jerry L Huffman

2057 Aple Rd
Franklin Furnace OH 45629

Call Sign: KC8CXI
Landon W Brickey
338 Bihl Rd
Franklin Furnace OH 45629

Call Sign: KC8YTY
Michael A Holtzapfel
278 Camp St
Franklin Furnace OH 45629

Call Sign: KC8KS
Curtis D Tackett
58 Collingwood Ave
Franklin Furnace OH 45629

Call Sign: KB8VCT
Eddie D Burton
Gervais Rd
Franklin Furnace OH 45629

Call Sign: KB8FL
Ronald P Nichols
100 Scott Ave
Franklin Furnace OH 45629

FCC Amateur Radio Licenses in Frazeysburg

Call Sign: KD8ETK
William D Buzzard
68 4th St
Frazeysburg OH 43822

Call Sign: KD8PEM
Christopher C Untied

8495 Ashcraft Rd
Frazeysburg OH 43822

Call Sign: N8KBR
Earl L Paazig
10660 Black Run Rd
Frazeysburg OH 43822

Call Sign: N8RNB
Sondra J Paazig
10660 Black Run Rd
Frazeysburg OH 43822

Call Sign: N8ARA
Newark ARA
10660 Black Run Rd
Frazeysburg OH
438229771

Call Sign: KD8MSU
Joel T Randall
10905 Cannon Rd
Frazeysburg OH 43822

Call Sign: KD8MSO
John B Singleton
11080 Cannon Rd
Frazeysburg OH 43822

Call Sign: KD8MPK
John W Graham
13776 Hamby Hill Rd
Frazeysburg OH 43822

Call Sign: KD8HKL
Matt M Graham
13776 Hamby Hill Rd
Frazeysburg OH 43822

Call Sign: KC8PVW
Joshua R Lentz
9224 Lentz Rd
Frazeysburg OH 43822

Call Sign: KD8HKY

Stephen D Moore
121 Maple St
Frazeysburg OH 43822

Call Sign: N9DWP
David R Terborg
65 N State St
Frazeysburg OH 43822

Call Sign: N9EBQ
Kathy F Terborg
65 N State St
Frazeysburg OH 43822

Call Sign: KA8G
David R Terborg
65 N State St
Frazeysburg OH 43822

Call Sign: N8KFT
Kathy F Terborg
65 N State St
Frazeysburg OH 43822

Call Sign: KD8LTC
Patricia A Myers
12186 Pleasant Vly Rd
Frazeysburg OH 43822

Call Sign: KD8RIQ
Tanner J Kilpatrick
8785 Raiders Rd
Frazeysburg OH 43822

Call Sign: KB8UVT
Daniel G Osborn
12355 Scout Rd
Frazeysburg OH 43822

Call Sign: K8KLW
Rick E Gilson
23 State St
Frazeysburg OH 43822

Call Sign: KD8NSB

Rick E Gilson
23 State St Box 295
Frazeysburg OH 43822

Call Sign: KD8GSM
Timothy P Russell
15329 TR 4
Frazeysburg OH 43822

Call Sign: KD8IXG
Brian D Wolfe
35993 TR 72
Frazeysburg OH 43822

Call Sign: KD8IXF
Regina E Wolfe
35993 TR 72
Frazeysburg OH 43822

Call Sign: KD8ETA
Matt W L Summerfield
95 W 4th St
Frazeysburg OH 43822

FCC Amateur Radio Licenses in Friendship

Call Sign: WD8AJS
Beverly J Friend
Friendship OH 45630

Call Sign: KE8YD
Candice D Shively
Friendship OH 45630

Call Sign: WD8QOE
Chester V Shively
Friendship OH
456301455

FCC Amateur Radio Licenses in Gallipolis

Call Sign: N8FQY
Richard A Moore

747 2nd Ave
Gallipolis OH 45631

Call Sign: KD8DCZ
Brandon M Moore
749 2nd Ave
Gallipolis OH 45631

Call Sign: KD8EQN
Jeff E Johnson
1150 2nd Ave
Gallipolis OH 45631

Call Sign: KB8FAR
Stephen L Wilson
117 3rd Ave
Gallipolis OH 45631

Call Sign: KB8TNG
E V Clarke Jr
360 3rd Ave
Gallipolis OH 45631

Call Sign: KA8AUZ
Bryson R Carter
194 Brentwood Dr
Gallipolis OH 45631

Call Sign: KB8CDR
Jessie K Mullen
374 Bulaville Pike
Gallipolis OH
456318201

Call Sign: KB8WB
John F Mullen
374 Bulaville Pike
Gallipolis OH
456318201

Call Sign: KD8DDB
Gary L Perkins
727 Bunce Rd
Gallipolis OH 45631

Call Sign: WB8RFV
Dale L Salisbury
86 Cedarwood Ln
Gallipolis OH 45631

Call Sign: K8NDM
Dale L Salisbury
86 Cedarwood Ln
Gallipolis OH 45631

Call Sign: N8PRX
Michael E Mc Kean
54 Chillicothe Rd
Gallipolis OH 45631

Call Sign: KD8OHQ
Michael J Mcginnis
253 Chris Ln
Gallipolis OH 45631

Call Sign: K8MOR
Michael J Mcginnis
253 Chris Ln
Gallipolis OH 45631

Call Sign: KC8UFO
Ernest L Young
19 Debbie Dr
Gallipolis OH 45631

Call Sign: KD8DCY
Terry L Reed
220 Debbie Dr
Gallipolis OH 45631

Call Sign: N8XJF
Lyle C Shillington
1374 E Bethel Church
Rd
Gallipolis OH 45631

Call Sign: KD8LWS
Mark S Mccoy
111 Garfield Ave
Gallipolis OH 45631

Call Sign: KC0IZC
Mark D Moore
107 Garfield Ave
Gallipolis OH 45631

Call Sign: KD8BFF
Jayson L Tillis
80 Georges Crk Rd
Gallipolis OH 45631

Call Sign: W8OSP
Jayson L Tillis
80 Georges Crk Rd
Gallipolis OH 45631

Call Sign: KB8HQO
Paul D Parsons
171 Herman Rd
Gallipolis OH 45631

Call Sign: WD8MCD
William A Callicoat
1322 Jackson Pike
Gallipolis OH
456312601

Call Sign: W8KNM
Charles O Gilfilen
1420 Jackson Pike
Gallipolis OH 45631

Call Sign: KC8KPW
Erich L Philson
598 Jay Dr
Gallipolis OH 45631

Call Sign: N8PRV
Robert J Grubb
1552 Kemper Hollow
Rd
Gallipolis OH 45631

Call Sign: N8XJE
Robert J Grubb II

1552 Kemper Hollow Rd
Gallipolis OH 45631

Wilbur T Woodyard
1008 Neighborhood Rd
Gallipolis OH 45631

Paul S Koch
144 Sanders Dr
Gallipolis OH 45631

Call Sign: KD8DCW
James W Siders
1759 Kriner Rd
Gallipolis OH 45631

Call Sign: KB9QHW
Bruce M Huron
44 Neil Ave B
Gallipolis OH 45631

Call Sign: KB8LYK
Denise A Null
200 Sanders Dr
Gallipolis OH 45631

Call Sign: KC8AWA
Peter A Elmore
193 Lariat Dr
Gallipolis OH 45631

Call Sign: N8DCX
Brian Wood
38 Opal St
Gallipolis OH 45631

Call Sign: N8HPR
Charles M Null
200 Sanders Dr
Gallipolis OH 45631

Call Sign: N8PSA
Randy D Friend
119 Lincoln Pike
Gallipolis OH 45631

Call Sign: KD8DCX
Brian L Wood
38 Opal St
Gallipolis OH 45631

Call Sign: KD8DCS
Anthony R Haner
260 Sanders Dr
Gallipolis OH 45631

Call Sign: W8PA
James M Kiskis
258 Magnolia Dr
Gallipolis OH 45631

Call Sign: KB8CTP
Thomas C Beaver
883 Orchard Hill Rd
Gallipolis OH 45631

Call Sign: KD8EQP
Marlin E Jones
174 Saunders Dr
Gallipolis OH 45631

Call Sign: W8RRQ
Thomas L Crossen
263 Maple Dr
Gallipolis OH 45631

Call Sign: KB8CTQ
Shirley L Beaver
883 Orchard Hill Rd
Gallipolis OH 45631

Call Sign: KC8FOI
Ronald K Parcell
Spruce St
Gallipolis OH 45631

Call Sign: W8TFV
Nancy E Crossen
263 Maple Dr
Gallipolis OH 45631

Call Sign: KD8GI
Thomas R Beaver
883 Orchard Hill Rd
Gallipolis OH 45631

Call Sign: KF8ZM
Martha R Edelmann
4478 St Rt 141
Gallipolis OH 45631

Call Sign: N8ZET
Duane A Hively
361 Martin Dr
Gallipolis OH 45631

Call Sign: KD8DDS
Matthew T Beaver
883 Orchard Hill Rd
Gallipolis OH 45631

Call Sign: KA8ZBC
Daniel S Salisbury
4573 St Rt 141
Gallipolis OH 45631

Call Sign: KC8BEQ
Joseph R Mingus
414 McCully Rd
Gallipolis OH 45631

Call Sign: KC8POT
Patrick T Bailey
170 Pinecrest Dr
Gallipolis OH 45631

Call Sign: KC8JE
Louis M Mc Cormick
6023 St Rt 141
Gallipolis OH 45631

Call Sign: KD8DDA

Call Sign: KD8EQM

Call Sign: KC0IIG

Harry W Steele
14142 St Rt 7 S
Gallipolis OH 45631

Call Sign: W8FCF
Gilbert B Bush
6 State St
Gallipolis OH 45631

Call Sign: KD8CSO
David E Mcdonald
1092 Sunset Dr
Gallipolis OH 45631

Call Sign: KC8JFM
Howard E Linder
760 Vanco Rd
Gallipolis OH 45631

Call Sign: KD8DCV
Judith A Linder
760 Vanco Rd
Gallipolis OH 45631

Call Sign: W8HRB
H Patrick Lynch
Gallipolis OH 45631

Call Sign: W8QVT
Gerald L Bryan
Gallipolis OH 45631

Call Sign: KC5IND
William E Davis
Gallipolis OH 45631

Call Sign: KE4FZX
Lee A Holman
Gallipolis OH 45631

Call Sign: WD8NUY
Steve G Little
Gallipolis OH 45631

Call Sign: KD8DCU

William H Shaw
Gallipolis OH 45631

FCC Amateur Radio Licenses in Garfield

Call Sign: KD8PXD
Barbara Graves
13616 Bangor Ave
Garfield OH 44125

Call Sign: KD8BWH
Steve A Spisak
5100 Donovan Dr
Garfield OH 44125

Call Sign: N8WHB
Delbert M Pardue
4873 E 90
Garfield OH 44125

Call Sign: KC8CAO
Gerald L Witte
6213 Firestone Dr
Garfield OH 45014

Call Sign: N8PKX
Robert E Foley
9104 Park Hts Ave
Garfield OH 44125

Call Sign: KB8YLZ
William H Jeffers
9602 Plymouth Ave
Garfield OH 44125

FCC Amateur Radio Licenses in Glenford

Call Sign: KD8FHV
Major W Henry
7666 Brownsville Rd
Glenford OH 43739

Call Sign: N8TCE

Lewis S Henry
7666 Brownsville Rd
Glenford OH 43739

Call Sign: N8VWR
Michele R Henry
7666 Brownsville Rd
Glenford OH 43739

Call Sign: WA8ATF
Emmett R Mc Donald
14120 Flint Ridge Rd
SE
Glenford OH 43739

Call Sign: KD8RIG
William C Rensi
11234 Midland Oil Rd
Glenford OH 43739

Call Sign: KY8OTE
William H Ulmer
4355 St Rt 204
Glenford OH 43739

Call Sign: KC8HZ
Roger W Kissel
5555 Twp Td 22
Glenford OH 43739

FCC Amateur Radio Licenses in Glouster

Call Sign: W8CRS
Fred C Heffken
67 Rd
Glouster OH 45732

Call Sign: KC8YML
Heidi S Mender
8 Barbour St
Glouster OH 45732

Call Sign: KA8IVJ
Kenneth R Stump

4979 Beach Rd
Glouster OH 457329077

Call Sign: N8QLE
James A Dew
11744 Capos Rd
Glouster OH 45732

Call Sign: KB8ROW
Terry G Moody Sr
21150 Cemetery Rd
Hollister
Glouster OH 45732

Call Sign: KC8NES
Thomas E
Echstenkamper
25 Cherry
Glouster OH 45732

Call Sign: KF8TD
Ellis B Dew
20 Cherry St
Glouster OH 45732

Call Sign: K8EIQ
James R Wolfe
13224 Concord Ch Rd
Glouster OH 45732

Call Sign: KB8TCE
Yeshua Moser
13177 Concord Church
Rd
Glouster OH 45732

Call Sign: KI8CA
Peter Morris
11096 Congress Run Rd
Glouster OH 45732

Call Sign: KD8KZG
Scott E Green
8945 Cox Kolbe Rd
Glouster OH 45732

Call Sign: KC8UWZ
John P Byers
9265 Derthick Rd
Glouster OH 45732

Call Sign: W8BGS
Gilbert D Bingman
20530 Highland Ave
Glouster OH 45732

Call Sign: KC8BZW
Candice S Withem
11045 Hooper Ridge Rd
Glouster OH 45732

Call Sign: KC8VR
Allan R Withem
11045 Hooper Ridge Rd
Glouster OH 45732

Call Sign: KB8LV
Charles E Evans
8219 Hunterdon Rd
Glouster OH 45732

Call Sign: KA8JAY
Robert J Cooper
8221 Hunterdon Rd
Glouster OH 45732

Call Sign: N8MWK
Russell G Ellis
8051 Kochis Rd
Glouster OH 45732

Call Sign: KC8DLZ
Dana P Buckley
26 Maple St
Glouster OH 45732

Call Sign: N8MN
Dana P Buckley
26 Maple St
Glouster OH 45732

Call Sign: KC8JWZ
John D Thomas
19797 Skinner Rd
Glouster OH 45732

Call Sign: KD8FRP
Twila R Thomas
19797 Skinner Rd
Glouster OH 45732

Call Sign: KC8AIC
Anthony W Richards Sr
Smith Rn Rd
Glouster OH 45732

Call Sign: KD8IMR
Cheryl L Byers
18 Spring St
Glouster OH 45732

Call Sign: W8ZZO
William S Masters
8896 SR 329
Glouster OH 457329286

Call Sign: WA8EBE
John Dillon Sr
11609 St Rt 329
Glouster OH 45732

Call Sign: KD8FRM
David D Parks
5650 St Rt 685
Glouster OH 45732

Call Sign: KC8HXY
Gilbert D Bingman
19 Summit St
Glouster OH 45732

Call Sign: KC8HXR
Jeffrey L Schall
36 Town St
Glouster OH 45732

Call Sign: KC8VPQ
Andy L Mccloud
10821 Walnut St
Glouster OH 45732

Call Sign: KC8QDQ
Jeramy G Duncan
10847 Walnut St
Glouster OH 45732

Call Sign: KC8WZE
Barbara I Kamento
10847 Walnut St
Glouster OH 45732

Call Sign: KA6WIS
Kennith L Simerly
21282 Waterworks Hill
Rd
Glouster OH 45732

**FCC Amateur Radio
Licenses in Gratis**

Call Sign: KC8ECQ
Dennis W Lohrey
505 E South St
Gratis OH 45330

Call Sign: KC8CQV
George G Miller
2933 Enterprise Rd
Gratis OH 45330

Call Sign: W8YMK
Burhl S Apple
5 South St
Gratis OH 45330

Call Sign: KC8CHG
Kathryn A Wiggington
121 W South St
Gratis OH 45330

Call Sign: KD8BCF
Levi J Sheley
216 W South St
Gratis OH 45330

Call Sign: KD8BCC
Sherry C Sheley
216 W South St
Gratis OH 45330

Call Sign: KB8PFU
Johnny K Cassidy
Gratis OH 45330

**FCC Amateur Radio
Licenses in Graysville**

Call Sign: KC8OPN
April D Weckbacher
38555 Winland Ln
Graysville OH 45734

**FCC Amateur Radio
Licenses in Guysville**

Call Sign: KA8AJC
Patricia M Snedden
6747 Bethany Ridge
Guysville OH 45735

Call Sign: WD8KKH
Dennis L Snedden
6747 Bethany Ridge Rd
Guysville OH 45735

Call Sign: KD8LS
Dennis L Snedden
6747 Bethany Ridge Rd
Guysville OH 45735

Call Sign: WD8KKH
Dennis L Snedden
6747 Bethany Ridge Rd
Guysville OH 45735

Call Sign: KC8AAO
Ruth A Dudding
17940 Bucks Lk Rd
Guysville OH 45735

Call Sign: KK8X
Sidney A Grimes
3500 Greiner Rd
Guysville OH 45735

Call Sign: KD8MZC
Benjamin S Weibel
22376 Jordan Run Rd
Guysville OH 45735

Call Sign: KC8RYL
David B Underwood
22395 Jordan Run Rd
Guysville OH
457359594

Call Sign: KD8IDP
Thomas W Kelly
17500 Mill School Rd
Guysville OH 45735

Call Sign: KC8WNB
Rick D Manderick
3751 Roadside Park Rd
Guysville OH 45735

**FCC Amateur Radio
Licenses in Hamden**

Call Sign: KB8TNI
Robert E Jenkins
150 Central Ave
Hamden OH 45634

Call Sign: KD8GZZ
Donald W Staten
62249 Chillicothe St
Hamden OH 45634

Call Sign: KB8VSF

Charles E Boyer
111 E Miller Ave
Hamden OH 45634

Call Sign: KB8NPR
Lewis R Rodgers
175 Miller Ave
Hamden OH 45634

Call Sign: KC8CXP
William C Bowden
512 S Main St
Hamden OH 45634

Call Sign: KD8IIA
Daniel A Fulton
38728 St Rt 160
Hamden OH 45634

Call Sign: KV8N
James F Boring
223 Stanton Ave Box 67
Hamden OH 45634

Call Sign: KC8LJI
Stanley A Bartkowiak Jr
38118 Zion Rd
Hamden OH 45634

Call Sign: KC8CXQ
Sean J Fraley
Hamden OH 45634

Call Sign: AB8AX
Gary C Bowden
Hamden OH 45634

Call Sign: KB8TNN
Leisa K Leigh
Hamden OH 45634

Call Sign: KB8VSH
Rogene A Leigh
Hamden OH 45634

FCC Amateur Radio Licenses in Hannibal

Call Sign: KC8KLD
Jack L Throckmorton
Box 36
Hannibal OH 43931

Call Sign: KB8NDO
Frank M Bottcher
40671 Srf Box 243
Hannibal OH 43931

Call Sign: KB8NXK
John E Anzak
52479 Union St
Hannibal OH 43931

Call Sign: KB8TAX
Darren L Cook
Hannibal OH 43931

Call Sign: K8JLT
Jack L Throckmorton
Hannibal OH 43931

FCC Amateur Radio Licenses in Haverhill

Call Sign: KB8FMH
Mary M Palmer
Haverhill OH 45636

Call Sign: KD8YO
Charles D Palmer
Haverhill OH 45636

FCC Amateur Radio Licenses in Haydenville

Call Sign: AA8BJ
Melvin Myers
37518 Greasy Ridge Rd
Haydenville OH 43127

Call Sign: KC8RYM
Christopher D Boch
37398 Patton St
Haydenville OH 43127

Call Sign: KD8HHY
Kim J Myers
Haydenville OH 43127

FCC Amateur Radio Licenses in Hide-A-Way Hills

Call Sign: W8VNF
Bernard J Downs
Box 9
Hide-A-Way Hills OH
431079100

FCC Amateur Radio Licenses in Ironton

Call Sign: K8TVQ
Gary L Rambacher
1208 Apache Trl
Ironton OH 45638

Call Sign: KB8PBW
Larry R Sark
Box 270
Ironton OH 45638

Call Sign: N8VIG
James B King
Box 372
Ironton OH 45638

Call Sign: K8LC
Walter E Bess Jr
1527 Charlotte St
Ironton OH 456381145

Call Sign: WB8YQV
Donna G Bess

1527 Charlotte St
Ironton OH 456381145

1791 CR 44 S
Ironton OH 45638

415 Karin St
Ironton OH 45638

Call Sign: WB8ESU
Ronald P Gannon
731 CR 119
Ironton OH 456388113

Call Sign: KA8MPD
Donald E Hill
167 CR 44S
Ironton OH 456388439

Call Sign: K8ABD
Larry L Riedel
1507 Karin St
Ironton OH 45638

Call Sign: KI8AN
Jane A Jackson
3073 CR 181
Ironton OH 45638

Call Sign: KC8NNI
Charles L Johnson
556 CR 52
Ironton OH 45638

Call Sign: N8GDZ
Donna G Bess
1525 Karin St
Ironton OH 45638

Call Sign: KI8AO
Stephanie L Jackson
3073 CR 181
Ironton OH 45638

Call Sign: KC8GCQ
Jeffrey D Anson
4194 CR 52
Ironton OH 45638

Call Sign: N8KTB
Raymond H Eicher
1611 Karin St
Ironton OH 45638

Call Sign: KI8CN
Samantha A Jackson
3073 CR 181
Ironton OH 45638

Call Sign: KC8FEK
Clyde D Wood
4199 CR 52
Ironton OH 45638

Call Sign: K8VSH
Joseph Walters
713 Kemp Ave
Ironton OH 456382427

Call Sign: WB8OR
Jane A Jackson
3073 CR 181
Ironton OH 45638

Call Sign: KC8FIW
Pauline L Wood
4199 CR 52
Ironton OH 45638

Call Sign: KD8LBG
Christopher L Dishman
1923 Liberty Ave
Ironton OH 45638

Call Sign: KB8LVK
Lloyd E Webb
3073 CR 181
Ironton OH 45638

Call Sign: N8LNO
Diane R Curry Stockton
2310 Geswein Blvd
Ironton OH 45638

Call Sign: K8URQ
Robert J Goldcamp
1844 N 2nd St
Ironton OH 45638

Call Sign: W8OR
Clarence L Jackson
3073 CR 181
Ironton OH 45638

Call Sign: N8EGG
Carole A Goldcamp
2310 Geswein Blvd
Ironton OH 456380613

Call Sign: KD8OER
Matthew P Delong
1230 N 3rd St
Ironton OH 45638

Call Sign: KA8JPP
Judith A Sturgill
1791 CR 44 S
Ironton OH 45638

Call Sign: KB8LXA
John A Justice
819 Heplar St
Ironton OH 45638

Call Sign: AC8JV
Matthew P Delong
1230 N 3rd St
Ironton OH 45638

Call Sign: KB8KSA
Edward Sturgill

Call Sign: N8LRO
Arthur J Pierson

Call Sign: K8VEW
Vincel E Willis

2016 N 3rd St
Ironton OH 45638

Call Sign: N8YPY
William J Hitchcock
37 Private Dr 1635
Ironton OH 45638

Call Sign: N8KVR
Mary A Hitchcock
87 Private Dr 1635 St Rt
243
Ironton OH 456386031

Call Sign: WA8ESQ
Rodney D Hitchcock
87 Private Dr 1635 St Rt
243
Ironton OH 456386031

Call Sign: N8KVQ
Jesse W Hitchcock
87 Private Dr 1635 St Rt
243
Ironton OH 456386031

Call Sign: N8TVO
James A Rowe
92 Private Rd 723
Ironton OH 456388129

Call Sign: WA8NS
Lee I Mullins Sr
225 Rose St
Ironton OH 45638

Call Sign: KB8PWV
Connie S Lowe
2423 S 10th St
Ironton OH 45638

Call Sign: KI8FE
James E Hedge
223.5 S 2nd St
Ironton OH 45638

Call Sign: WA8BLI
Joyce R Lawless
1024 S 4th St
Ironton OH 45638

Call Sign: WA8JCO
William Lawless
1024 S 4th St
Ironton OH 45638

Call Sign: KC8MAG
Charles D Herrell
1550 S 4th St
Ironton OH 45638

Call Sign: KC8SNH
Margaret L Herrell
1550 S 4th St
Ironton OH 45638

Call Sign: KD8PTN
Kenneth R Bailey
2825 S 4th St
Ironton OH 45638

Call Sign: KB8UWN
Charlie B Craft
3023 S 5th
Ironton OH 45638

Call Sign: WA8NRJ
Martin L Smith
2007 S 5th St
Ironton OH 45638

Call Sign: KB8UDK
Kenneth H Koerper
625 S 6th St
Ironton OH 456381828

Call Sign: K8UNN
Ed R Rambacher
719 S 6th St
Ironton OH 45638

Call Sign: WB8RED
William Moore Jr
2824 S 6th St
Ironton OH 45638

Call Sign: WB8RHN
Margaret M Moore
2824 S 6th St
Ironton OH 456382811

Call Sign: W8UYO
Paul M Bierley
2118 S 7th St
Ironton OH 45638

Call Sign: N7VPD
Charles R Crockrell
1124 S 8th St
Ironton OH 45638

Call Sign: AB8AF
Matthew D Massie
2319 S 8th St
Ironton OH 45638

Call Sign: KC8GLF
Lisa D Massie
2319 S 8th St
Ironton OH 45638

Call Sign: KA8UFS
Michael L Reynolds
2552 S 8th St
Ironton OH 45638

Call Sign: KB8GWL
Larry Jewell
2726 S 8th St
Ironton OH 45638

Call Sign: W4LAS
Mabel P Banks
315 Susan Ct
Ironton OH 45638

Call Sign: KA8VWS
Norma J Ackison
1714 Thomas St
Ironton OH 45638

Call Sign: N8DPV
Odell Ackison
1714 Thomas St
Ironton OH 45638

Call Sign: KC8POV
Charles W Kettel
74 TR 1185
Ironton OH 45638

Call Sign: N8VBB
Helen D Shore
225 TR 136 N
Ironton OH 456388921

Call Sign: KD8LBF
Michael R Douglas
48 TR 332
Ironton OH 45638

Call Sign: KD8NYN
David L Bruce
287 TR 372
Ironton OH 45638

Call Sign: KD8ELD
Bernard E Nance
114 Twp Rd 1126
Ironton OH 45638

Call Sign: KC8ELB
Nicholas G Hoffman
851 Twp Rd 208
Ironton OH 45638

Call Sign: KC8ERO
Dawn E Hoffman
851 Twp Rd 208
Ironton OH 45638

Call Sign: WW8O
John E Stewart
1213 Vine St
Ironton OH 45638

Call Sign: WN8F
Kenneth N Massie
115 Woodlawn Dr
Ironton OH 45638

Call Sign: KA8MZW
Emery J Payton
Ironton OH 45638

Call Sign: KB8OUC
Paul E Turner
Ironton OH 45638

Call Sign: K8LCL
Robert M Goldcamp
Ironton OH 45638

Call Sign: KB8CHJ
Violet M Mullins
Ironton OH 45638

Call Sign: KD8BXN
Inc Southern OH ARA
Ironton OH 45638

Call Sign: W8SOE
Inc Southern OH ARA
Ironton OH 45638

Call Sign: N8LCA
William T Parsons
586 TR 111
Ironton OH 45680

FCC Amateur Radio Licenses in Jacksonville

Call Sign: KC8VPM

John W Ice
44 E Main St
Jacksonville OH
457400089

Call Sign: KC8HXQ
Frank W Dunlevy Jr
1 N 6th St
Jacksonville OH 45740

Call Sign: KC8LZY
Stephanie A Schall
22 S 6th St
Jacksonville OH 45740

Call Sign: AA8UX
Carol A Johnson
2 S 7th St
Jacksonville OH 45740

Call Sign: W8VIC
Victor V Johnson
2 S 7th St
Jacksonville OH 45740

Call Sign: KC8IEA
David L Conkey
34 S 7th St
Jacksonville OH
457400277

Call Sign: KC8IFE
Vanessa S Henry
Jacksonville OH
457400252

FCC Amateur Radio Licenses in Jacobsburg

Call Sign: KD8LNY
Patricia F Phillips
49359 Or W Station Rd
Jacobsburg OH 43933

Call Sign: KA8CDG

Kenneth J Melanko
62210 Ray Ramsey Rd
Jacobsburg OH 43933

Call Sign: AB5XG
Virginia L Wright
58625 Redstone Rd
Jacobsburg OH 43933

Call Sign: AB5XH
David C Wright
58625 Redstone Rd
Jacobsburg OH 43933

FCC Amateur Radio Licenses in Jerusalem

Call Sign: WD8COB
George E Chappell
53491 Boston Rd
Jerusalem OH 43747

Call Sign: KD8LOA
Derek A Stewart
52039 Church St
Jerusalem OH 43747

Call Sign: W8WLG
Wanda L Gallatin
49901 Grizzle Rdg Rd
Jerusalem OH 43747

Call Sign: K8VG
Vernon A Gallatin
49901 Grizzle Ridge Rd
Jerusalem OH 43747

Call Sign: WD8KBM
Terry W Groves
37941 Skinner Grimes
Rd
Jerusalem OH 43747

Call Sign: WB8J
Rodger A Groves

37991 Skinner Grimes
Rd
Jerusalem OH
437479627

Call Sign: N8TAK
Jodie R Ward
38240 Skinner Grimes
Rd
Jerusalem OH 43747

Call Sign: KD8JOX
Jerald L Phillips
52191 St Rt 26
Jerusalem OH 43747

Call Sign: KC8MPJ
Delbert E Britton
55021 St Rt 26
Jerusalem OH 43747

Call Sign: KC8HAM
Nathan R Book
52367 Stephens Rd
Jerusalem OH 43747

Call Sign: N8TZ
Stephen R Book
52367 Stephens Rd
Jerusalem OH 43747

Call Sign: KC8MPK
Sharon S Engler
48675 Twp Rd 112
Jerusalem OH 43747

FCC Amateur Radio Licenses in Junction City

Call Sign: KD8ETJ
Dustin R Binion
415 E Main St
Junction City OH 43748

Call Sign: KC8ZUE
Joshua C Sims
208 E Poplar St
Junction City OH 43748

Call Sign: KB8OWG
Sally J Wyrick
111 Iron St
Junction City OH 43748

Call Sign: N8RQA
Wayne D Bauer
2885 Mainesville Rd
Junction City OH 43748

Call Sign: KB8WNN
Kevin E Neal
2895 Mainesville Rd
Junction City OH 43748

Call Sign: WA4NIH
James C Schneider
203 W Poplar
Junction City OH 43748

FCC Amateur Radio Licenses in Kerr

Call Sign: KD8CYN
Southeast OH Ems
District ARA
Kerr OH 456430527

Call Sign: W8EMS
Southeast OH Ems
District ARA
Kerr OH 456430527

FCC Amateur Radio Licenses in Kimbolton

Call Sign: KD8AAX
Milo C Ball
72851 8th St Rd
Kimbolton OH 43749

Call Sign: KD8HWL
Jennifer L Brown
73475 Broadhead Rd
Kimbolton OH 43749

Call Sign: KF8MH
James R Booth
13223 Egress Rd
Kimbolton OH 43749

Call Sign: K8UGO
George H Booth
13397 Egress Rd
Kimbolton OH 43749

Call Sign: K8ANA
Marvin D Denison
11030 Freedom Rd
Kimbolton OH 43749

Call Sign: AA8RS
Michael J Gorman
72785 Hopewell Rd
Kimbolton OH
437499530

Call Sign: AB8DM
Joann Gorman
72785 Hopewell Rd
Kimbolton OH
437499530

Call Sign: KB8ZN
Michael J Gorman
72785 Hopewell Rd
Kimbolton OH
437499530

Call Sign: KD8MSL
Beverly M Bunn
4996 Little Indian Rd
Kimbolton OH 43749

Call Sign: KD8MFC

Steven G Bunn
4996 Little Indian Rd
Kimbolton OH 43749

Call Sign: KC8IXS
Michael A Casteel
73928 Mill Rd
Kimbolton OH 43749

Call Sign: N8RAG
Gerald R Kuthy Jr
75041 Old 21 Rd
Kimbolton OH 43749

Call Sign: KC8MBF
Paula R Kuthy
75041 Old 21 Rd
Kimbolton OH
437499115

Call Sign: WB8RVI
David J Reddick
75146 Old 21 Rd
Kimbolton OH 43749

Call Sign: KG8ZZ
Hazel P Reddick
75146 Old 21 Rd Rt 2
Kimbolton OH 43749

Call Sign: KB8GTG
Michael R Cihon
9474 Plainfield Rd
Kimbolton OH 43749

Call Sign: KD8PDP
Gene E Baumgardner
76150 Science Hill Rd
Kimbolton OH 43749

Call Sign: N8ICE
Raymond L Mc Cune
2390 Swan Rd
Kimbolton OH 43749

Call Sign: KC8CJI
Anthony W Mitchell
2580 Dearth Rd
Kingston OH
456449526

Call Sign: KC8UQZ
Joel M Vaughn
7392 Dry Run Rd
Kingston OH
456449711

Call Sign: KA8CSM
Ann W Huff
9541 Dry Run Rd
Kingston OH 45644

Call Sign: KA8WWI
David E Huff
9541 Dry Run Rd
Kingston OH 45644

Call Sign: WX8Q
Forrest E Weaver
10 Lynette Dr
Kingston OH 45644

Call Sign: N8TUW
Steve L Newland
400 Roe Ln
Kingston OH 45644

Call Sign: KC8VOL
Donald S Proehl
1595 Snyder Rd
Kingston OH 45644

Call Sign: W8OTO
Donald S Proehl
1595 Snyder Rd
Kingston OH 45644

Call Sign: W8YFK
Fred L Fetherolf
13716 SR 56 E
Kingston OH 45644

Call Sign: KC8YVP
William V Wetzel
2821 St Rt 180
Kingston OH
456449709

FCC Amateur Radio
Licenses in Kitts Hill

Call Sign: KB8RLY
Donald Lewis
475 CR 5
Kitts Hill OH 45645

Call Sign: KB8RRI
Maxine C Lewis
475 CR 5
Kitts Hill OH 45645

Call Sign: KA8RIS
Jackie L Hall
13562 St Rt 141
Kitts Hill OH 45645

Call Sign: KC8CWM
Diane Hall
13562 St Rt 141
Kitts Hill OH 45645

Call Sign: KC8GLG
Cheryle A Hall
13562 St Rt 141
Kitts Hill OH 45645

Call Sign: KC8HLS
Carl D Stapleton
1175 TR 256
Kitts Hill OH 45645

Call Sign: KD8LEQ

Patsy J Little
168 TR 337
Kitts Hill OH 45645

Call Sign: KD8LAT
Boyd C Little
168 TR 337
Kitts Hill OH 45645

Call Sign: KC8FVD
Georgene R Stapleton
1329 Twp Rd 256
Kitts Hill OH 45645

Call Sign: W8DOC
James O Stapleton
1329 Twp Rd 256
Kitts Hill OH 45645

Call Sign: KD8OMC
Patty A Little
194 Twp Rd 337
Kitts Hill OH 45645

Call Sign: KC8OBV
Donald W Mootz
Kitts Hill OH 45645

FCC Amateur Radio
Licenses in Lafferty

Call Sign: K8VB
Virgil J Beal Jr
70180 Beal Rd Box 147
Lafferty OH 439510147

Call Sign: N8NFH
Theodore Stoica
70204 Jordan St Bx 117
Lafferty OH 43951

Call Sign: KD8CZZ
Jay R Greenwood
43639 Lafferty Rd
Lafferty OH 43951

Call Sign: WD8PPX
Odas Arno
43650 Lafferty Rd
Lafferty OH 43951

Call Sign: W6OJB
Stanley J Sulek
43200 Mt Hope
Lafferty OH 43951

Call Sign: KA8WYE
Thomas E Travis
43038 Mt Hope Rd
Lafferty OH 43951

Call Sign: W8WLB
Frank Sulek
43200 Mt Hope Rd
Lafferty OH 43951

Call Sign: WD8PPY
Susan R Travis
Lafferty OH 43951

FCC Amateur Radio
Licenses in Langsville

Call Sign: KC8KPD
Bbarc
30720 Bowles Rd
Langsville OH 45741

Call Sign: KB8NUR
Kenneth S Brooks Sr
30720 Bowles Rd
Langsville OH
457419505

Call Sign: N8TWU
Kenneth S Brooks III
30720 Bowles Rd
Langsville OH
457419505

Call Sign: KB8QOG
Joseph B Argabright
Langsville OH 45741

FCC Amateur Radio Licenses in Lansing

Call Sign: KC8UYV
David L Ivan
55260 Poplar
Lansing OH 43934

FCC Amateur Radio Licenses in Latham

Call Sign: KC8TLM
Jerry E Cummings
440 Dogwood Ln
Latham OH 45646

Call Sign: KA8MID
William E Dean
Latham OH 45646

FCC Amateur Radio Licenses in Laurelville

Call Sign: KC8OZP
Gregory F Shires
26554 Armstrong Rd
Laurelville OH 43135

Call Sign: KO8D
Paul E Bowman
16174 Bailor Rd
Laurelville OH 43135

Call Sign: N8CXJ
Joan E Bowman
16174 Bailor Rd
Laurelville OH 43135

Call Sign: NW8I
Delbert E Anderson
16140 Creamery Hill Rd

Laurelville OH 43135

Call Sign: N8HV
 Hocking Valley
Amateur Radio Assn
19264 Keifel
Laurelville OH 43135

Call Sign: KC8DPB
Elwood R Smith
19264 Keifel Rd
Laurelville OH 43135

Call Sign: KB8AVL
John P Sharp
19309 Keifel Rd
Laurelville OH 43135

Call Sign: WD8T
Merwin W Mc Clelland
18576 Laurel St
Laurelville OH
431350246

Call Sign: KA8GDK
Shirley M Hanes
26518 Moccasin Rd
Laurelville OH 43135

Call Sign: WA8GLV
Charles H Hanes Sr
26518 Moccasin Rd
Laurelville OH 43135

Call Sign: KC8DTN
Gordon H Fossett Jr
16700 North St
Laurelville OH 43135

Call Sign: KD8ODZ
Benjamin J Brown
18918 Shriner St
Laurelville OH 43135

Call Sign: N8RQL

James E Reed
16076 Stump Run Rd
Laurelville OH 43135

Call Sign: KD8GNJ
Leroy C Truesdell
18755 Thompson Ridge
Rd
Laurelville OH 43135

Call Sign: K8LGN
 Hocking Valley ARC
19608 Thompson Ridge
Rd
Laurelville OH 43135

Call Sign: N8TWH
Theodore M Hayes
22494 Thompson Ridge
Rd
Laurelville OH 43135

Call Sign: KB8GUN
Raymond K Webb
19608 Thompson Ridge
Rd
Laurelville OH 43135

Call Sign: KC8GUN
Mary R Webb
19608 Thompson Ridge
Rd
Laurelville OH 43135

FCC Amateur Radio Licenses in Lewisville

Call Sign: KD8MTK
Jeremey C Taylor
36375 St Rt 78
Lewisville OH 43754

Call Sign: KC8ECV
Vera B Roth
35790 TH 50

Lewisville OH 43754

Call Sign: KD8ZA
John A Roth
35790 TH 50
Lewisville OH 43754

Call Sign: K8UGR
John W Bruce
48953 TR 68
Lewisville OH 43754

Call Sign: KD8GEL
John Seymour
31870 TR 7G
Lewisville OH 43754

FCC Amateur Radio Licenses in Little Hocking

Call Sign: KD8LKP
Dennis R Bennett Jr
46 1st Ave
Little Hocking OH
45742

Call Sign: N8BUB
Dennis R Bennett Jr
46 1st Ave
Little Hocking OH
45742

Call Sign: KB8SRK
Timothy A Grubb
378 Arrowhead Rd
Little Hocking OH
45742

Call Sign: W8RWS
Ernest R Evans
195 Baker Rd
Little Hocking OH
457425136

Call Sign: N8CIL
Clarence V Owens
Box 169
Little Hocking OH
45742

Call Sign: KC8LTH
Bernard E Muiznieks
Box 256
Little Hocking OH
457429795

Call Sign: N8RKS
Jeremy A Hamilton
Box 289
Little Hocking OH
45742

Call Sign: WB8YIF
William F White
Box 344
Little Hocking OH
45742

Call Sign: N8JNG
Brian E Lynch
Box 78A
Little Hocking OH
45742

Call Sign: N8NUT
Trekkers Club
Box 78A
Little Hocking OH
45742

Call Sign: KB8KNY
Michael N Fisher
3155 Federal Rd
Little Hocking OH
45742

Call Sign: KC8AGY
Mark H Krugman
1091 Hocking Rd

Little Hocking OH
45742

Call Sign: KC8NVS
Darren R Johnson
30 Pine Dr
Little Hocking OH
45742

Call Sign: WA8LVE
George T Belyus
85 Summitview Rd
Little Hocking OH
45742

Call Sign: W8LVE
George T Belyus
85 Summitview Rd
Little Hocking OH
45742

Call Sign: KC8HPO
Vernon S Snell
34 Suzanne St
Little Hocking OH
45742

Call Sign: K8VRN
Vernon S Snell
34 Suzanne St
Little Hocking OH
45742

Call Sign: N8ZVC
Paul F Foster
68 Teri Ln
Little Hocking OH
45742

Call Sign: N8PYF
Richard M Van Dyke
99 Wood Dr
Little Hocking OH
45742

Call Sign: KB8AJA
David K Davis
Little Hocking OH
45742

Call Sign: N8RNP
James R Snider
Little Hocking OH
45742

Call Sign: N8KVU
Karen C Stump
Little Hocking OH
45742

**FCC Amateur Radio
Licenses in Logan**

Call Sign: KD8LPX
Ricky L Burns
28890 Black Jack Rd
Logan OH 43138

Call Sign: N8TXJ
Helen M Dickey
29435 Blosser Rd
Logan OH 43138

Call Sign: W8HT
Frederick P Dickey
29435 Blosser Rd
Logan OH 43138

Call Sign: KB8TKX
Roger D Starner
50 Bowers Ct
Logan OH 43138

Call Sign: W8RDS
Roger D Starner
50 Bowers Ct
Logan OH 43138

Call Sign: W8FE
Jerry R Carmean

16341 Calico Ridge
Logan OH 43138

Call Sign: KD8DOC
Dave B Cosper
1115 Charles St
Logan OH 43138

Call Sign: KB8VML
Michael W Reeves
1324 Church St
Logan OH 43138

Call Sign: KB8VMM
Ginny L Reeves
1324 Church St
Logan OH 43138

Call Sign: KB8PPW
Robert L Naylor Sr
1500 Clay Bank Rd
Logan OH 43138

Call Sign: N8TXK
Brian D Mason
14800 Cohagen Rd
Logan OH 43138

Call Sign: KB8PWE
Orville M Lewis
692 E 2nd St
Logan OH 43138

Call Sign: KC8NMH
Jackie G Smith Jr
498 E Hunter St
Logan OH 43138

Call Sign: N8BUS
Jackie G Smith Jr
498 E Hunter St
Logan OH 43138

Call Sign: KB8OTU
David G Brimner

522 E Main St
Logan OH 43138

Call Sign: KC8DPE
Nancy A Brimner
522 E Main St
Logan OH 43138

Call Sign: KC8DLY
Donna J Berry
516 East St
Logan OH 43138

Call Sign: KC8MAB
Albert G Coulson
581 Edgehill Cir
Logan OH 43138

Call Sign: KD8RYK
Lawrence B Peters
778 Edgehill Dr
Logan OH 43138

Call Sign: N8RQM
John W Smart
258 Elm St
Logan OH 43138

Call Sign: KC8DPA
Dennis G Keels
248 Eulalia Ave
Logan OH 43138

Call Sign: KD8PRY
Charles S Barron
29658 Fairhaven Dr
Logan OH 43138

Call Sign: WD8CIW
Milton C Mason
101 Florence Ave
Logan OH 43138

Call Sign: KB8VJW
Geoffrey F Perry

138 Fountain St
Logan OH 43138

Call Sign: KD8LPW
Mark W Edgar
30800 Freeman Rd
Logan OH 43138

Call Sign: KB8CXM
Tona Carter
22980 Griffith Rd
Logan OH 43138

Call Sign: KB8NZB
Philip M Stanley
18510 Hartshell Rd
Logan OH 43138

Call Sign: KC8DPF
Patricia J Stanley
18510 Hartshell Rd
Logan OH 43138

Call Sign: KC8TEM
Douglas D Wolfe
219 Hocking Ave
Logan OH 43138

Call Sign: WA8DUG
Douglas D Wolfe
219 Hocking Avc
Logan OH 43138

Call Sign: KC8FOM
John R Reeves
1147 Homer St
Logan OH 43138

Call Sign: KC8TUZ
Roman A Wilshanetsky
33510 Inboden Rd
Logan OH 43138

Call Sign: KD8NFZ
Joanne T Wilshanetsky

33510 Inboden Rd
Logan OH 43138

Call Sign: W8TUZ
Roman A Wilshanetsky
33510 Inboden Rd
Logan OH 43138

Call Sign: KC8ZIP
James B Conner
14105 Julie Rd
Logan OH 43138

Call Sign: KD8QDM
Thomas F Davis
29890 Lake Logan Rd
Logan OH 43138

Call Sign: KC8TUX
Joni L Tornwall
251 Mae St
Logan OH 43138

Call Sign: KC8TUY
Katherine E Tornwall
251 Mae St
Logan OH 43138

Call Sign: KC8UVD
Jeffrey A Tornwall
251 Mae St
Logan OH 43138

Call Sign: KC8UVC
Michael S Tornwall
251 Mae St
Logan OH 43138

Call Sign: KC8THJ
Thomas J Odell
993 Marla Ave
Logan OH 43138

Call Sign: AB8SJ
Thomas J Odell

993 Marla Ave
Logan OH 43138

Call Sign: KB8USO
Gregg A Russell
37376 Maysville
Greendale Rd
Logan OH 431389116

Call Sign: KC8WMF
Donald G Jeffries
37855 Maysville
Greendale Rd
Logan OH 43138

Call Sign: KC8YAH
Jeffrey T Doty
273 Midland Pl
Logan OH 43138

Call Sign: N8WLQ
Merle E Dietz
298 Midland Pl
Logan OH 43138

Call Sign: KB8WQJ
Donald D Rose Jr
15100 Mohler Rd
Logan OH 43138

Call Sign: KC8JIV
Deborah W Snyder
1255 New York Ave
Logan OH 43138

Call Sign: KC8KAC
Richard C Martin
1255 New York Ave
Logan OH 43138

Call Sign: N8RHJ
Richard C Martin
1255 New York Ave
Logan OH 43138

Call Sign: KD8ORN
Scot A Freeman
15045 Nickel Plate Rd
Logan OH 43138

Call Sign: K8TUK
Karen E Tucker
152 S Walnut
Logan OH 43138

Call Sign: KC8CMJ
Harold B Sanders
14493 St Rt 328
Logan OH 43138

Call Sign: AH2JD
James E Ditty Jr
1015 Ohio Ave
Logan OH 43138

Call Sign: KC8WRX
Raymond G Tucker
152 S Walnut St
Logan OH 43138

Call Sign: KC8SYT
Walter F Fisher
13574 St Rt 595
Logan OH 43138

Call Sign: K8JED
James E Ditty Jr
1015 Ohio Ave
Logan OH 43138

Call Sign: W8TUK
Raymond G Tucker
152 S Walnut St
Logan OH 43138

Call Sign: W3JAY
Walter F Fisher
13574 St Rt 595
Logan OH 43138

Call Sign: W8LGX
William R Hopstetter
19503 Rauber Rd
Logan OH 431388895

Call Sign: N8TRJ
Raymond L Turner Sr
32247 Shaw Rd
Logan OH 43138

Call Sign: WB8WEK
John L Wilkinson
600 St Rt 664
Logan OH 43138

Call Sign: KC8PNQ
Robert H Mc Manaway
195 Ruth Ave
Logan OH 43138

Call Sign: KD8NGB
Anthony W Moscato
35251 Smith Chapel Rd
Logan OH 431389454

Call Sign: KC8PHA
Max L Ringwald
6933 St Rt 664 N
Logan OH 43138

Call Sign: K8VVG
Robert H Mc Manaway
195 Ruth Ave
Logan OH 43138

Call Sign: KD8NGA
Sharon E Moscato
35251 Smith Chapel Rd
Logan OH 431389454

Call Sign: KC8PHC
Michael L Dillard
6933 St Rt 664 N
Logan OH 43138

Call Sign: KC8CML
Florence E Reeves
50 S High St 306
Logan OH 43138

Call Sign: KC8YBZ
Phillip L Wolfe
2319 SR 935
Logan OH 43138

Call Sign: KC8ZQP
Donald L Dupler
8565 St Rt 664 N
Logan OH 43138

Call Sign: KC8LPV
William S Meyer
50 S High St Apt 407
Logan OH 43138

Call Sign: KD8ANO
Billy J Helber
13710 St Rt 278
Logan OH 43138

Call Sign: KB8WUG
Patricia A Baum
9560 St Rt 664 N Lot 12
Logan OH 43138

Call Sign: KD8EZE
Karen E Tucker
152 S Walnut
Logan OH 43138

Call Sign: KD8POO
Michael L Castor Jr
7285 St Rt 312
Logan OH 43138

Call Sign: KB8VFC
Ray E Baum
9560 St Rt 664 N Lot 12
Logan OH 43138

Call Sign: KF8MW
Anthony E Mills
13664 St Rt 664 S
Logan OH 43138

Call Sign: N0WAW
Mark R Smith
13907 St Rt 664S
Logan OH 431389503

Call Sign: KF8OZ
Mack D Bailey
14475 St Rt 93 S
Logan OH 43138

Call Sign: KB8OIM
Deborah S Stevens
17351 St Rt 93 S
Logan OH 43138

Call Sign: KC8MEG
Karen S Lipp
28070 Starr Rd
Logan OH 43138

Call Sign: KF8OU
James W Lipp Sr
28070 Starr Rt Rd
Logan OH 43138

Call Sign: N8TXL
Melissa J Finney Shaffer
28433 Starr Rt Rd
Logan OH 43138

Call Sign: KB8NPS
Terry L Stevens
17651 State Rd 93 S
Logan OH 43138

Call Sign: KC8EJZ
Hocking Valley ARC
5550 Twp Rd 250
Logan OH 431389218

Call Sign: W8LXC
Harry C Vollmer
5550 Twp Rd 250 SW
Logan OH 431389218

Call Sign: KD8DPG
Kenneth A Berry
1286 Vermont Ave
Logan OH 43138

Call Sign: KC8NPQ
William K Webb
330 Vine St
Logan OH 43138

Call Sign: KD8GUN
William K Webb
330 Vine St
Logan OH 43138

Call Sign: KB8OKE
Mark A Wetzel
199 W Betty Ave
Logan OH 43138

Call Sign: KC8KNO
Richard W Sams
231 W Main St
Logan OH 431381607

Call Sign: W8LNX
Richard W Sams
231 W Main St
Logan OH 431381607

Call Sign: KC8TFX
Danielle N Lehman
292 W Main St
Logan OH 43138

Call Sign: KD8PSB
David R Kunkler
9722 Walnut Dowler Rd
Logan OH 43138

Call Sign: KD8GD
Gary P Kanode
9786 Walnut Dowler Rd
Logan OH 43138

Call Sign: N8TCA
Deborah F Kanode
9786 Walnut Dowler Rd
Logan OH 43138

Call Sign: N8PHI
Donald E Shaffer
11680 Walnut Dowler
Rd
Logan OH 43138

Call Sign: KC8VOI
Jon E Lehman
799 Walnut Dr
Logan OH 43138

Call Sign: KD8NFY
Mark J Potter
719 Warner Ave
Logan OH 43138

Call Sign: KD8LPY
Carolyn D Swank
31403 Zeigler Rd
Logan OH 43138

Call Sign: KD8LPZ
Jerry L Swank
31403 Zeigler Rd
Logan OH 43138

Call Sign: KC8YAI
Gary T Snider
7320 Zwickle Rd
Logan OH 43138

Call Sign: W8GTS
Gary T Snider
7320 Zwickle Rd
Logan OH 43138

Call Sign: KD8FTX
Sandra K Snider
7320 Zwickle Rd
Logan OH 431389493

Call Sign: KB8NPQ
Willa J Walters
Logan OH 43138

Call Sign: KC8HIU
Gary L Messer
Logan OH 43138

Call Sign: N8ZUK
Dennis J Mc Nally
Logan OH 43138

Call Sign: KD8FJL
Patricia A Frye
Logan OH 43138

Call Sign: KD8OKT
Sarah E Swayne
Logan OH 43138

Call Sign: KD8OKU
Steven W Swayne
Logan OH 431380903

**FCC Amateur Radio
Licenses in London**

Call Sign: KA8YYG
Joseph G Reeves Jr
320 Andrew Ct
London OH 43140

Call Sign: KD8NLA
Mark R Case
2741 Arbuckle Rd NW
London OH 43140

Call Sign: KC8ZVP
Anna M Bingman

107 Berkshire Rd
London OH 43140

Call Sign: KC8ZVQ
Christopher N Bingman
107 Berkshire Rd
London OH 43140

Call Sign: KD8NTA
Joseph A Harris
113 Berkshire Rd
London OH 43140

Call Sign: KB8PDB
Brian J Carlson
9241 Big Plain
Circleville Rd
London OH 43140

Call Sign: N8ME
Mark E Erbaugh
3105 Big Plain
Circleville Rd
London OH 43140

Call Sign: AA8LX
Clyde D Nimal
80 Cedar Wood Ln
London OH 43140

Call Sign: W8BQ
Gregg M Alexander
93 Chandler Ave
London OH 43140

Call Sign: K8EIJ
James S Hartzler
2515 Chickasaw Dr
London OH 43140

Call Sign: N8JAF
Stephen D Coates
1860 Choctaw Cir
London OH 43140

Call Sign: KD7PQD
Michael G Durller
51 Deger Dr
London OH 431401056

Call Sign: KC8ZVN
Stephen E Buckley
7758 Drury Rd
London OH 43140

Call Sign: KB8USC
Kenneth S Brooks
190 E 1st St
London OH 43140

Call Sign: N6AKL
Michael R Donaldson
1374 E Choctaw Dr
London OH 431408727

Call Sign: KD8PQB
Michael R Byars
140 E High St
London OH 431401260

Call Sign: KD8DSJ
Kassie K France
95 E Lincoln Ave
London OH 43140

Call Sign: N8LPX
Ronald L France
95 E Lincoln Ave
London OH 43140

Call Sign: KB8ODY
David R Swartz
55 Elm St
London OH 43140

Call Sign: KD8RMY
Paul Yackey
1076 Hartford Ln
London OH 43140

Call Sign: N8MNI
Mark Crosbie
231 Jacqueline Dr
London OH 43140

Call Sign: N8CZO
Michael L Flaharty
1025 Josiah Morris Rd
London OH 43140

Call Sign: KD8JLF
Jeffery L Higgins
2567 Karok Dr
London OH 43140

Call Sign: AC8IZ
Jeffery L Higgins
2567 Karok Dr
London OH 43140

Call Sign: KB8VGH
Bart W Landes
1093 Kelsey Ct
London OH 43140

Call Sign: N8KHO
Monte H Weisheimer
5675 Lafayette Plain
City Rd
London OH 431409579

Call Sign: KB0NAY
Jody N Cromer
387 Landis Ln
London OH 43140

Call Sign: KD8NLW
Nathan M Martin
7440 Lilly Chapel
Georgesville Rd
London OH 43140

Call Sign: WE8R
Donald P Kovalchik

4665 Lilly Chapel
Opossum Rd
London OH 43140

Call Sign: W8DPK
Donald P Kovalchik
4665 Lilly Chapel
Opossum Rd
London OH 43140

Call Sign: KD8DPH
Terri L Iden
4665 Lilly Chapel
Opossum Rd
London OH 43140

Call Sign: N8TLK
Terri L Kovalchik
4665 Lilly Chapel
Opossum Rd
London OH 43140

Call Sign: KE8RV
Madison County ARC
4665 Lilly Chapel
Opossum Rd
London OH 431408875

Call Sign: KD8PGE
Thomas L Robinson
3972 Little Darby Rd
London OH 43140

Call Sign: WD8QMX
Ronald M Schiering
3800 Little Darby Rd
NE
London OH 43140

Call Sign: KD8NHW
John K Hill
261 Locust Dr
London OH 43140

Call Sign: KB8FNK

Kellie D Medors
128 Logan Ave
London OH 43140

Call Sign: KD8DFA
Ric Arbogast
3531 Lundy Ln
London OH 43140

Call Sign: KD8MBW
Raymond S Salyer
5095 Main St NE
London OH 43140

Call Sign: WA5QCV
Dennis L Vannerson
167 Maplewood Ln
London OH 431409584

Call Sign: WA8TRH
Charles R Morrison
581 Markley Rd
London OH 43140

Call Sign: N8BUE
David B Ridenour
300 McLene Ave
London OH 43140

Call Sign: N8IBS
Orville E Russell
165 N Main St
London OH 43140

Call Sign: KC8ZZE
John C Gaynard
243 N Main St
London OH 431401146

Call Sign: K8WDN
John C Gaynard
243 N Main St
London OH 431401146

Call Sign: KF8HH

C Michael Southard
313 Northview Dr
London OH 43140

Call Sign: KD8MVO
Griffin S Bluestone
440 Old US 42 SE
London OH 43140

Call Sign: KD8NLT
Daniel R Imboden
2515 Old US Hwy 40
NW
London OH 43140

Call Sign: KD8KYF
Joshua A Coffey
1135 Roberts Mill Rd
London OH 43140

Call Sign: AC8KA
Jeffrey L Conley
27.5 S Main St
London OH 43140

Call Sign: WB8NBC
Jeffrey L Conley
27.5 S Main St
London OH 43140

Call Sign: WB8WHQ
Ernest H Young Sr
212 S Oak St
London OH 43140

Call Sign: N8BUG
John M Watkins
1048 Seacove Cir B
London OH 431409158

Call Sign: N8CGV
Robert V Mason
1830 Shoshone Dr
London OH 43140

Call Sign: N8RGP
Ruben M Pierce
11840 SR 38 SW
London OH 43140

Call Sign: WA8CGP
Lamar L Gossard
2110 SR 56 SW
London OH 43140

Call Sign: KD8NLS
Orestes J Waddle
9865 St Rt 38
London OH 43140

Call Sign: KA8WEX
Philip E Hardman
Stump Ln
London OH 43140

Call Sign: WB8DML
James L Dieguez
6155 Taylor Blair Rd
London OH 43140

Call Sign: WA8TTZ
Bert W Buganski
4105 Taylor Blair Rd
London OH 43140

Call Sign: NX8P
Gregory R Stark
340 Thomas Ln
London OH 43140

Call Sign: AB8DU
Gene W Pierce
3141 Tradersville
Brighton Rd
London OH 43140

Call Sign: KC8UOI
James L Shuff
61 W 5th St
London OH 43140

Call Sign: KB8EPL
Sharon L Coates
2220 W Choctaw Dr
London OH 43140

Call Sign: KF9IV
Richard B Hartnett
2609 W Choctaw Dr
London OH 43140

Call Sign: KC8MYP
Thomas A Breckenridge
3725 W Jefferson
Kiousville Rd
London OH 43140

Call Sign: KA8MYN
John B Balderson Sr
146 Washington Ave
London OH 43140

Call Sign: KE8RV
Wanda F Cutlip
30 Westmoor Dr
London OH 43140

Call Sign: KB8TCG
Randall C Hazelton
2180 Yuma Dr
London OH 43140

Call Sign: KA8TTR
Jill M Littleton
2345 Yuma Dr
London OH 43140

Call Sign: KA8TTT
William G Littleton
2345 Yuma Dr
London OH 43140

Call Sign: KA8UCE
Gene M Pass
London OH 43140

Call Sign: N8OIC
Forrest E Penwell
London OH 43140

FCC Amateur Radio Licenses in Londonberry

Call Sign: KD8HHG
Donald E Barnhart
31 Anna Marie Dr
Londonderry OH 45647

Call Sign: KD8IIN
Ronald E Cochenour
23 Jason Ln
Londonderry OH 45647

Call Sign: N8RGS
Allen E Karshner
33518 Nichols Rd
Londonderry OH 45647

Call Sign: AB8MW
Franklin E Sturgill Jr
493 Smith Ln
Londonderry OH 45647

Call Sign: KD8EAD
Justin A Drummond
1375 Smith Ln
Londonderry OH 45647

FCC Amateur Radio Licenses in Long Bottom

Call Sign: KB8DEM
Delmar G Pullins
50280 Bigley Ridge Rd
Long Bottom OH 45743

Call Sign: N8UBF
Don A Harris

47620 SR 248
Long Bottom OH 45743

FCC Amateur Radio Licenses in Lore City

Call Sign: KD8OEN
Dwayne A Lashley
62437 County Home Rd
Lore City OH 43755

Call Sign: W8EQO
David E Scholik
140 East St
Lore City OH 43755

Call Sign: KD8BTL
Dean A Gilpin
69800 Glen View Rd
Lore City OH 43755

Call Sign: KB8OLG
Doris M Brown
69800 Glenview Rd
Lore City OH
437559726

Call Sign: N3DZP
Walter R Brown
69800 Glenview Rd
Lore City OH
437559726

Call Sign: KD8HGZ
Deward E Stalnaker
61791 Institute Rd
Lore City OH 43755

Call Sign: N8IIY
David L Galloway
Lore City OH 43755

FCC Amateur Radio Licenses in Lowell

Call Sign: KB8ZMK
John R Reed
Box 12B
Lowell OH 45744

Call Sign: K8RST
Robert F Farson
Box 173
Lowell OH 45744

Call Sign: WD8IVB
Robert E Moynihan
Box 57
Lowell OH 45744

Call Sign: KB8GZV
Wendy A Cook
742 Highland Ridge Rd
Lowell OH 45744

Call Sign: KB8GYG
Dennis O Cook
742 Highland Ridge Rd
Lowell OH 45744

Call Sign: KB8KBH
Daryl R Ullman
Lowell OH 45744

FCC Amateur Radio Licenses in Lower Salem

Call Sign: KB8UEP
Daniel J Betts
Box 158
Lower Salem OH 45745

Call Sign: W8NFL
Daniel J Betts
Box 158
Lower Salem OH 45745

Call Sign: N8OG
Daniel J Betts

7375 Dalzell Rd
Lower Salem OH
457458983

Call Sign: WC8Z
Daniel J Betts
7375 Dalzell Rd
Lower Salem OH
457458983

Call Sign: N8HOC
Joseph E Nagel
40503 Harriettsville Rd
Lower Salem OH
457459401

Call Sign: KC9AED
Ann C Mchale
Lower Salem OH 45745

Call Sign: KC8YAD
John M Mchale
Lower Salem OH 45745

FCC Amateur Radio Licenses in Lucasville

Call Sign: KD8BTB
Terry L Duncan
867 Back Run Rd
Lucasville OH 45648

Call Sign: WB8VRN
Ronald L Caudill
1974 Blue Run Rd
Lucasville OH 45648

Call Sign: WD8CFH
Larry C Gullett
4384 Blue Run Rd
Lucasville OH
456488382

Call Sign: KC8OFP
Steven Z Thompson

746 Bowen Rd
Lucasville OH 45648

Call Sign: WB8HLF
David K Jackson
Box 11683
Lucasville OH 45648

Call Sign: KB8SCZ
Elisabeth A Bell
Box 256
Lucasville OH 45648

Call Sign: N8ZFN
Jennifer R Murphy
Box 326A
Lucasville OH 45648

Call Sign: KB8SDC
Phillip J Short
2299 Camp Crk Rd
Lucasville OH 45648

Call Sign: K4YJ
Dwight D Kelly
9345 Camp Crk Rd
Lucasville OH 45648

Call Sign: K3YJ
Eileen Kelly
9345 Camp Crk Rd
Lucasville OH 45648

Call Sign: WB8WBR
Charles F Ramsey
1098 Cook Rd
Lucasville OH
456488544

Call Sign: KC8ADF
Cynthia K Castle
2378 Duck Run Rd
Lucasville OH
456488803

Call Sign: KG8SG
John D Castle
2378 Duck Run Rd
Lucasville OH
456488803

Call Sign: KB8WHH
Clifford Wolfe III
3485 Duck Run Rd
Lucasville OH 45648

Call Sign: KA8ZOE
Clarence Tackett
523 Germany Rd
Lucasville OH 45648

Call Sign: KD8EZD
Brian D Buckle
266 Greenbriar Rd
Lucasville OH 45648

Call Sign: KC8MFY
Alice A Kuhner
57 Hartford Dr
Lucasville OH 45648

Call Sign: WA8WAG
Roger D Jackson
1979 Hunting Run Rd
Lucasville OH 45648

Call Sign: KA8LHS
Homer E Duncan
3380 Huston Long Run
Rd
Lucasville OH 45648

Call Sign: KB8QEL
Jeffrey E Bell
15 Lakewood
Lucasville OH 45648

Call Sign: KC8FIZ
Grover F Jones
55 Linda Ave

Lucasville OH 45648

Call Sign: KA8ZAF
Charles G Compton
Mack Rd
Lucasville OH 45648

Call Sign: KB8QEI
Sandra L Compton
Mack Rd
Lucasville OH 45648

Call Sign: KB8SCY
Brian A Lewis
77 Morgan Dr Apt 10
Lucasville OH 45648

Call Sign: AA4ZI
Orville A Jones
5900 N St Rt 139
Lucasville OH 45648

Call Sign: KA8RWG
David H Carver
192 Nesbitt Rd
Lucasville OH 45648

Call Sign: KC8OFN
Maynard D Thompson
322 Rapp Montgomery
Rd
Lucasville OH 45648

Call Sign: N8NHQ
Mark E Mc Daniel
1289 Salt Crk Rd
Lucasville OH 45648

Call Sign: WD8OKG
John G Ridout
656 Schuler Hollow Rd
Lucasville OH 45648

Call Sign: N8WBT
Bruce W Culp

2161 Sedan Crabtree Rd
Lucasville OH 45648

Call Sign: N8CUG
Michael J Rafferty Sr
45 Shawnee Ln
Lucasville OH 45648

Call Sign: KD8FZP
Danny W Edwards
87 Skyline Dr
Lucasville OH 45648

Call Sign: KB8WGW
Alfred J Malo
SR 104 9400
Lucasville OH 45648

Call Sign: KB8WHD
Larry D Mullins
12717 SR 348
Lucasville OH 45648

Call Sign: KC8AMQ
Timothy G Atkins
10321 St Rt 104
Lucasville OH 45648

Call Sign: N8DYU
Bonnie J Jackson
11683 St Rt 104
Lucasville OH 45648

Call Sign: WB8YZO
Ralph H Jackson
11683 St Rt 104
Lucasville OH 45648

Call Sign: KB8VDY
Anthony R Selbee
13179 St Rt 335
Lucasville OH 45648

Call Sign: KC8HZA
Amanda S Mitchell

12834 St Rt 348
Lucasville OH 45648

Call Sign: KB8IIH
Christopher B Kemper
16830 St Rt 348
Lucasville OH 45648

Call Sign: KC8FAN
Etheldreth Caldwell
17056 St Rt 348
Lucasville OH 45648

Call Sign: KC8INQ
Ralph G Stephens
10824 St Rt 348
Lucasville OH 45648

Call Sign: KC8FAM
Toni K Kritzwiser
17056 St Rt 348
Lucasville OH 45648

Call Sign: N8IDW
Charles O Collins
542 Thomas Hollow
Lucasville OH 45648

Call Sign: KA8RZP
Paul D Phillips
Lucasville OH 45648

Call Sign: KB8TKP
Rodney E Gossett
Lucasville OH 45648

Call Sign: W8EPV
Charles R Taylor
Lucasville OH 45648

Call Sign: KC8USE
Paul R Taylor
Lucasville OH 45648

FCC Amateur Radio Licenses in Macksburg

Call Sign: KD8CNE
Shawn M Devol
640 Downard Rd
Macksburg OH 43701

Call Sign: N8GP
Eugene P Gildow
401 Franks Ln
Macksburg OH
457468015

FCC Amateur Radio Licenses in Malta

Call Sign: N8KSS
Chester L Sanders
3470 Conk Palmer Rd
NW Rfd 3
Malta OH 43758

Call Sign: WB8WLW
Frederick S Ruland
822 Echo St
Malta OH 43758

Call Sign: KD8JVW
Matthew R Junn
911 Echo St
Malta OH 43758

Call Sign: WB8QXF
Charles E Lewis
2262 N Newlon Rd
Malta OH 43758

Call Sign: WD8OGD
Eleanor B Manning
2909 N Riverview Rd
Malta OH 43758

Call Sign: KC8OBJ
Harold D French

4037 Poplar Ridge Rd
Malta OH 43758

Call Sign: KD8RIL
Austen B Erwin
16255 Timberman Rd
Malta OH 43758

Call Sign: KD8BYY
Randall E Poore
2647 Vanhornhill Rd
Malta OH 43758

Call Sign: KD8XJ
Brooks L Wilson
7605 W Morganville Rd
Malta OH 43758

Call Sign: KB8ERT
Benjamin L Heppner
Malta OH 43758

Call Sign: KD8PED
Bradley B Mcgrath
Malta OH 43758

FCC Amateur Radio Licenses in Marietta

Call Sign: KB8EXQ
Christopher W Murphy
616 10th St
Marietta OH 45750

Call Sign: N8UPK
Anne Caseman
817 2nd St
Marietta OH 45750

Call Sign: WB8BSC
Larry D Caseman
817 2nd St
Marietta OH 45750

Call Sign: KB8UGD

David M Paskawych
421 3rd St
Marietta OH 45750

Call Sign: KC8ICF
Kevin M Paskawych
421 3rd St
Marietta OH 45750

Call Sign: KB8DP
David M Paskawych
421 3rd St
Marietta OH 45750

Call Sign: KC2LJU
Peter F Prigge
519 3rd St
Marietta OH 45750

Call Sign: KC8MAC
Christopher B Pfeiffer
431 4th St
Marietta OH 45750

Call Sign: KA8RJC
Stanley H Lang
529 4th St
Marietta OH 45750

Call Sign: KC8ZZS
Gary B Bosworth Jr
215 5th St Box P39
Marietta OH 45750

Call Sign: KD8CRJ
Caroline A Perruci
432 6th St
Marietta OH 45750

Call Sign: WD8QNA
Christina I Kaplan
626 7th St
Marietta OH 45750

Call Sign: KB0CPL

Colleen M Kesselring
722.5 7th St
Marietta OH 45750

Call Sign: K4ICQ
Zane B Kesselring
7th St
Marietta OH 45750

Call Sign: N8DYF
Thelda J Hall
141.5 Acme St Apt A
Marietta OH 457503467

Call Sign: KD8FMJ
John E Triplett Jr
107 Alden Ave
Marietta OH 45750

Call Sign: KD8IWN
Karen P Shaner
106 Alta St Apt 1 I
Marietta OH 45750

Call Sign: K8JAY
Jay B Stowe
625 Ash Rd
Marietta OH 45750

Call Sign: KD6LGY
Peter W Whittock
211 Barber St
Marietta OH 45750

Call Sign: KA8GVG
Robert S Gerken
102 Becker Ln
Marietta OH 45750

Call Sign: KD8LXJ
Christopher C English
106 Bel Aire Dr
Marietta OH 45750

Call Sign: WN8AMA

Duane A Grubb
375 Belavista Dr
Marietta OH 457508223

Call Sign: N8OJ
 Southeastern OH
Repeater Association
300 Belle Meadow Dr
Marietta OH 45750

Call Sign: W8JL
John C Lee
300 Belle Meadow Dr
Marietta OH 45750

Call Sign: K8SKI
Cathy J Lee
300 Belle Meadow Dr
Marietta OH 45750

Call Sign: WB8UHP
Louis E Urschel Jr
420 Bellevue St
Marietta OH 45750

Call Sign: W8JTW
Joseph T Wigal
1952 Bender Rd
Marietta OH 45750

Call Sign: KC8PZK
Jessica K Wigal
1952 Bender Rd
Marietta OH 45750

Call Sign: KD8DLY
Jonna R Wigal
1952 Bender Rd
Marietta OH 45750

Call Sign: W8AMO
James A Stanley
200 Bohl Dr
Marietta OH 45750

Call Sign: KC8MGU
 Jtw RC
Box 157
Marietta OH 45750

Call Sign: KC8KAE
Ellsworth R Lane
Box 196
Marietta OH 45750

Call Sign: N8YXV
Michael A Hupp
Box 205C
Marietta OH 45750

Call Sign: N8LNK
Richard E Brown
Box 247
Marietta OH 45750

Call Sign: KC8KGO
Charles G Marshall
Box 260
Marietta OH 45750

Call Sign: N8YXU
Daniel L Campbell
Box 271
Marietta OH 45750

Call Sign: KB8YOY
Matthew M Hansell
Box 302
Marietta OH 45750

Call Sign: K8LTS
Donald R Patterson
Box 307
Marietta OH 45750

Call Sign: KJ8L
Stephen M Hobensack
Box 311A
Marietta OH 45750

Call Sign: KB8MWV
Brion E Thomas
Box 328
Marietta OH 45750

Call Sign: N8KMM
Rowdy J Freeland
Box 362A
Marietta OH 45750

Call Sign: KA8VEI
D Wade Angle
Box 73
Marietta OH 45750

Call Sign: KB8ZTR
Grant D Brown
Box 76
Marietta OH 45750

Call Sign: KB8PWF
Kevin G Betzing
102 Brandy Dr
Marietta OH 45750

Call Sign: WD4LOS
Phillip J Kimble
104 Brandy Dr
Marietta OH 45750

Call Sign: N8JPS
Darwin Mayle
117 Brandy Dr
Marietta OH 45750

Call Sign: K8KYE
Richard L Miller
206 Brittigan Cir
Marietta OH 45750

Call Sign: KC8EEO
Leslie S Mc Intyre
223 Broughton Ave
Marietta OH 45750

Call Sign: KC8RSK
Earl L Mc Intyre
223 Broughton Ave
Marietta OH 45750

Call Sign: KA8QNW
James D Fernihough
1665 Brown Rd
Marietta OH 45750

Call Sign: N8XBE
Paul R Hickman
Bx 192A
Marietta OH 45750

Call Sign: KB8HRG
Earl E Hulce
104 Circle Dr
Marietta OH 45750

Call Sign: N8PYE
Diane E Hulce
104 Circle Dr
Marietta OH 45750

Call Sign: WD8JYB
Ronald E Wright
700 Cisler Dr
Marietta OH 45750

Call Sign: N8MPR
William E Hathaway
1308 Cisler Dr
Marietta OH 45750

Call Sign: KB8ZTU
Edward L Fox
1560 Coal Run Rd
Marietta OH 45750

Call Sign: KC8YZQ
Alisha M Smithberger
350 Cole Coffman Rd
Marietta OH 45750

Call Sign: AA8SD
Vicki L Anderson
365 Cole Coffman Rd
Marietta OH 45750

Call Sign: KB8BRN
Wendell W Grimm
1175 Cole Coffman Rd
Marietta OH 457506774

Call Sign: KA8QNV
Leah W Grimm
1175 Cole Coffman Rd
Marietta OH 475506774

Call Sign: KA0ZAV
Dean C Hirschi Jr
703 Colegate Dr
Marietta OH 457509299

Call Sign: KC8IRZ
Washington State
Community College RC
710 Colegate Dr
Marietta OH 45750

Call Sign: N8KM
William L Hurte
806 Colegate Dr
Marietta OH 45750

Call Sign: K8OBL
Jack A Kemp
1009 Colegate Dr
Marietta OH 45750

Call Sign: W8IIM
Earl E Ritchie
1689 Colegate Dr Apt
122
Marietta OH 45750

Call Sign: KI8CS
William L Hurte
806 Colgate Dr

Marietta OH 45750

Marietta OH 45750

Marietta OH 45750

Call Sign: KB8VLQ
William E Campbell
58 Cornerville Rd
Marietta OH 45750

Call Sign: NO8F
Carl D Apple
306 Franklin St
Marietta OH 45750

Call Sign: WD8LTB
Richard E Saltzwedel
919 Hadley Hollow Rd
Marietta OH 45750

Call Sign: KD8ODS
Sean W Brady
845 County House Ln
Marietta OH 45750

Call Sign: K8RYU
Ralph E Matheny Jr
207 Gibbons Pl
Marietta OH 45750

Call Sign: AD7BR
Bradley J Thomas
112 Hanson Dr
Marietta OH 45750

Call Sign: K8AXK
Jon F Bergen
121 Devol Dr
Marietta OH 45750

Call Sign: W8HH
Marietta ARC
207 Gibbons Pl
Marietta OH 45750

Call Sign: KB8ZTS
Nancy D Owens
141 Harvest Run Rd
Marietta OH 45750

Call Sign: WB8BRZ
Lyle G Farmer
107 Dun Wrentin Rd
Marietta OH 45750

Call Sign: W8PBA
Edgar M Walters
774 Glendale Rd
Marietta OH 45750

Call Sign: KB8ZTT
Daniel E Owens
141 Harvest Run Rd
Marietta OH 45750

Call Sign: N8HPH
Richard F Glenn
220 E Spring St
Marietta OH 45750

Call Sign: KD8ITF
Joshua K Page
1483 Green Hill Rd
Marietta OH 45750

Call Sign: KA8CWJ
Glennis E Daugherty
210 Holly St
Marietta OH 45750

Call Sign: KC8UQC
James E Desouza
217 Fairview Ln
Marietta OH 45750

Call Sign: KC8YUX
Jessica M Page
1483 Green Hill Rd
Marietta OH 45750

Call Sign: W8LSE
Michael L Daugherty
210 Holly St
Marietta OH 457502420

Call Sign: W8JED
James E Desouza
217 Fairview Ln
Marietta OH 45750

Call Sign: W8CFL
Milton K Page
1483 Greenhill Rd
Marietta OH 457508403

Call Sign: N8IP
Ellsworth R Lane
310 Jennings Hill Rd
Marietta OH 45750

Call Sign: KB8HDD
Loretta J Phelps
776 Ferncliff Dr
Marietta OH 45750

Call Sign: WO8G
Milton K Page
1483 Greenhill Rd
Marietta OH 457508403

Call Sign: KC8LND
Charles W Sayre Jr
114 Kingman Rd
Marietta OH 45750

Call Sign: WD8BRZ
Allen F Phelps
776 Ferncliff Dr

Call Sign: N8LCY
Terry L Burner
1925 Greenhill Rd

Call Sign: WD8COW
Eugene M Cooke
811 Lancaster St

Marietta OH 45750   Marietta OH 45750   Marietta OH 45750

Call Sign: K8YLW   Call Sign: N8PJ   Call Sign: N8KKX
Louis E Urschel Sr   Paul D Jett   Lesa A Wigal
939 Lancaster St   123 Mound Dr   180 Pleasant Ridge Rd
Marietta OH 457509497   Marietta OH 45750   Marietta OH 45750

Call Sign: KD8AUF   Call Sign: KB8RUM   Call Sign: N8KKY
Matthew A Pooler   Harold D Copple   Peter A Wigal
1005 Lancaster St   515 Mt Tom Rd   180 Pleasant Ridge Rd
Marietta OH 45750   Marietta OH 45750   Marietta OH 45750

Call Sign: N8FGD   Call Sign: KR5N   Call Sign: W8LYL
Glenn T Miller   Marcus C Leatham   Roger W Beck
400 Lawton Rd   1710 Mt Tom Rd   250 Pleasant Ridge Rd
Marietta OH 45750   Marietta OH 457506894   Marietta OH 45750

Call Sign: KB8TDJ   Call Sign: KD8EZG   Call Sign: WB8WKM
Jonathan G Orr   Russell H Nutter   Emory L Parker
301 Masonic Park Rd   404.5 Mulberry St   12 Putnam Pl
Marietta OH 45750   Marietta OH 45750   Marietta OH 45750

Call Sign: N8NUR   Call Sign: W6XG   Call Sign: KD8GWN
Raymond L Williams   Russell H Nutter   Tyler C Arnold
135 Melody Ln   404.5 Mulberry St   145 Rauch Dr
Marietta OH 45750   Marietta OH 45750   Marietta OH 45750

Call Sign: WB8IHT   Call Sign: N8JKC   Call Sign: KC8LNN
George O Grady Sr   Lynn M Barnhart   Peggy J Blasko
105 Michigan Ave   124 Muskingum Dr   Ridgewood Dr
Marietta OH 45750   Marietta OH 45750   Marietta OH 45750

Call Sign: WD5EXD   Call Sign: KA8MFZ   Call Sign: KA8HQU
Robert E Patterson Jr   Vance R Cogar   Herman J Wunderlich
65 Millers Ln   716 Orchard St   286 Riggenbach Hill Rd
Marietta OH 45750   Marietta OH 45750   Marietta OH 457508446

Call Sign: AA8GN   Call Sign: N8HHN   Call Sign: W8OTH
Paul D Jett   Allan K Cumberledge   Robert Stewart
123 Mound Dr   1110 Phillips St Apt 2   133 Riverview Dr
Marietta OH 45750   Marietta OH 45750   Marietta OH 45750

Call Sign: N8RMZ   Call Sign: KD8PYF   Call Sign: W8BNH
Barbara A Jett   Robert E Mercer   Richard V Rogers
123 Mound Dr   1024 Pike St   135 Riverview Dr

Marietta OH 45750   Marietta OH 45750   Marietta OH 45750

Call Sign: KD8ELC
Michael J Marks
2474 Robinson Hill Rd
Marietta OH 45750

Call Sign: KG8WV
Ted Walter
110 Shade St
Marietta OH 45750

Call Sign: KC8TEO
Lloyd C Wilson
85 Smoke Rise Dr
Marietta OH 45750

Call Sign: KE8WL
Milton K Page
Rt 4
Marietta OH 45750

Call Sign: KC8OGT
Cathy J Morgnstern
106 Shawnee Dr 7
Marietta OH 45750

Call Sign: KC8TKY
Kimberly D Wilson
85 Smoke Rise Dr
Marietta OH 45750

Call Sign: KA7LIG
Charles R Raines
255 Rummer Rd
Marietta OH 45750

Call Sign: N8HEO
Gerald R Hamilton
105 Sheridan St
Marietta OH 457503450

Call Sign: WD8MME
C Daniel Schramm
27370 SR 7
Marietta OH 45750

Call Sign: NQ0D
Ronald B Kuhn
370 Rummer Rd
Marietta OH 45750

Call Sign: WD8MIO
Constance L Hamilton
105 Sheridan St
Marietta OH 457503450

Call Sign: KA8AKB
James E White
9110 St Rt 26
Marietta OH 45750

Call Sign: KD8AGK
Lloyd L Marcum
535 Rummer Rd
Marietta OH 45750

Call Sign: N8GRH
Gerald R Hamilton
105 Sheridan St
Marietta OH 457503450

Call Sign: WD8JFT
Bernd Berendts
2875 St Rt 821
Marietta OH 45750

Call Sign: KB8TRR
David G Boley
270 Rummer Rd
Marictta OH 45750

Call Sign: N8IO
Constance L Hamilton
105 Sheridan St
Marietta OH 457503450

Call Sign: KD8NXD
Nicholas A Hugh
404 Strecker Ln
Marietta OH 45750

Call Sign: N8YE
Stephen M Hobensack
2440 Sandhill Rd
Marietta OH 45750

Call Sign: KA8VVE
Howard E Guenther
101 Skyvue Cir
Marietta OH 45750

Call Sign: WD8MZC
Philip D Schramm
106 Summerset Dr
Marietta OH 45750

Call Sign: KD8HWA
Steven J Tomasko
5745 Sandhill Rd
Marietta OH 45750

Call Sign: W8RTS
Richard T Seebaugh
880 Smith Hill Rd
Marietta OH 45750

Call Sign: KC8SIP
Michael F Davis
206 Summit Rd
Marietta OH 45750

Call Sign: KC8TGP
Gary R Goodwin
107 Schilling St

Call Sign: KG4ZDW
Sheilah Seebaugh
880 Smith Hill Rd

Call Sign: KC8VPN
Pamela S Davis
206 Summit Rd

Marietta OH 45750

Call Sign: WA8AKV
Dale S Eddy
110 Sunset Ln
Marietta OH 45750

Call Sign: KD8FMN
James S Huggins
132 Sylvan Way
Marietta OH 45750

Call Sign: K8HUG
James S Huggins
132 Sylvan Way
Marietta OH 45750

Call Sign: N8UPM
Charles F Powell
130 Terrace Ave
Marietta OH 45750

Call Sign: KB8CCQ
Stephen D Ritchie
2186 Vickers Rd
Marietta OH 45750

Call Sign: KC8ZLK
Daniel S Ritchie
2186 Vickers Rd
Marietta OH 45750

Call Sign: WD8IFQ
Walter W Worthington
Jr
118 Victory Pl
Marietta OH 45750

Call Sign: WE8H
Samuel G Stewart
214 Walnut Dr
Marietta OH 45750

Call Sign: KD8PXY
Melissa K Duff

107 Washington St
Marietta OH 457502141

Call Sign: N8JCY
John R Ellison
707 Washington St
Marietta OH 45750

Call Sign: N7MLT
Jaime V Ondrusek
713.5 Washintgon St
Marietta OH 45750

Call Sign: KG8JR
Edwin G Reno
3421 Waterford Rd
Marietta OH 45750

Call Sign: WB5CVA
George E Thomas
2215 Wynnecrest Dr
Marietta OH 45750

Call Sign: KC8TCG
Diane Duskey
Marietta OH 45750

FCC Amateur Radio Licenses in Martins Ferry

Call Sign: KC8NZS
Kristi J Burge
69921 Brady Rd
Martins Ferry OH 43935

Call Sign: KC8NSR
Kenneth S Burge
69921 Brady Rosd
Martins Ferry OH 43935

Call Sign: WB8U
Karl W Kindberg Jr
815 Broadway

Martins Ferry OH
439352004

Call Sign: KC8YCR
Rebecca G Horne
56341 Buckeye Run Rd
Martins Ferry OH 43935

Call Sign: WD8KCS
William A Lyden
924 Carlisle St
Martins Ferry OH 43935

Call Sign: N8TAL
Michael J Ackermann Jr
434 Cemetery Rd
Martins Ferry OH 43935

Call Sign: N8WLW
John M Smith
517 Concord St
Martins Ferry OH 43935

Call Sign: KC8GDX
Diana S Holcombe
58544 Deep Run Rd
Martins Ferry OH 43935

Call Sign: KD8LNT
Suzanne Escott
509 Elm St
Martins Ferry OH 43935

Call Sign: KG8NB
Robert A George Jr
628 Hanover St
Martins Ferry OH 43935

Call Sign: WB8WHF
Morris W Rees
1201 Hughes Ave
Martins Ferry OH 43935

Call Sign: KB8AAL
Nina W Brown

411 Jefferson St
Martins Ferry OH 43935

Call Sign: KB8AAM
Wendy S Brown
411 Jefferson St
Martins Ferry OH 43935

Call Sign: KB8DNK
Elizabeth J Hutchinson
809 Jefferson St 3
Martins Ferry OH 43935

Call Sign: WB8ZUB
Alexander Da Re
71561 Lake End Rd
Smith Addtn
Martins Ferry OH 43935

Call Sign: KB8TRE
David R Grenier
722 Monroe St
Martins Ferry OH 43935

Call Sign: KC8VLD
Terrance R Lewis
1403 N 6th St
Martins Ferry OH 43975

Call Sign: KC8NRC
Jeffrey Davis
N 7th St
Martins Ferry OH 43935

Call Sign: KC8NUE
Daniel N Phillips Jr
N 7th St
Martins Ferry OH 43935

Call Sign: KC8VOF
Jamie N Richards
414 N 7th St
Martins Ferry OH 43935

Call Sign: KC8AVF

Jamie N Richards
417 N 7th St Apt A
Martins Ferry OH 43935

Call Sign: KC8CMZ
Victor W Davis Jr
240 N 8th St
Martins Ferry OH 43935

Call Sign: W8VAP
Victor W Davis Jr
240 N 8th St
Martins Ferry OH 43935

Call Sign: KD8MTF
Clifton D Reintzel Sr
1801 N 9th St Apt F
Martins Ferry OH 43935

Call Sign: KB8MRN
William H Ellis Jr
58540 Nixon Run Rd
Martins Ferry OH 43935

Call Sign: KD8AU
Russell E Brown
723 Pearl Rd
Martins Ferry OH 43935

Call Sign: K8QYA
Frank Fregiato
1109 Pearl St
Martins Ferry OH 43935

Call Sign: N8BH
Charles T Deaton
1 S 11th
Martins Ferry OH 43935

Call Sign: KC8BJM
Thomas Q Cresap Sr
100 S 3rd St Apt 608
Martins Ferry OH 43935

Call Sign: KC8NQB

Richard L Laughman Sr
611 S Zane Hwy
Martins Ferry OH 43935

Call Sign: KC8NZN
Richard L Laughman Jr
611 S Zane Hwy
Martins Ferry OH 43935

Call Sign: NQ8B
Jerry B Arnold
1026 S Zane Hwy
Martins Ferry OH 43935

Call Sign: KA8VAH
Vivian L Arnold
1026 S Zane Hwy
Martins Ferry OH
439352067

Call Sign: N8DQH
Floyd T Smith
832 Seabrights Ln
Martins Ferry OH 43935

Call Sign: WB8TQA
William E De Bolt
640 Tulip Ln
Martins Ferry OH 43935

Call Sign: KG4IJM
David Heath
501 Virginia St
Martins Ferry OH 43935

Call Sign: KC8URN
Richard N Postlethwaite
1102 Virginia St
Martins Ferry OH 43935

Call Sign: W8ZER
Howard L Daubenmeyer
1105 Virginia St
Martins Ferry OH 43935

Call Sign: KB8AUL
Louis A Yurkovitch
1112 Virginia St
Martins Ferry OH
439351947

Call Sign: KA8CDM
Louis A Yurkovitch
1112 Virginia St
Martins Ferry OH
439351974

Call Sign: KB8FEC
Clara B Glaspell
1119 W Jefferson St
Martins Ferry OH 43935

Call Sign: KD8KRN
Amber N Lutz
818 W Vine St
Martins Ferry OH 43935

Call Sign: KQ8X
Paul A Zavislak
70910 Zavislak Dr
Martins Ferry OH 43935

Call Sign: KC8NTI
Bert Duff Jr
Martins Ferry OH 43935

**FCC Amateur Radio
Licenses in McArthur**

Call Sign: KD8OXZ
Frank A Alder
36381 Alder Rd
McArthur OH 45651

Call Sign: KB8NF
Kenneth E Neal
Box 467
McArthur OH 45651

Call Sign: N8YHX

Charles M Williams
Box 992
McArthur OH 45651

Call Sign: KD8BWU
Timothy M Allison
72733 Brooks Martin
Rd
McArthur OH 45651

Call Sign: AB8CF
Thomas J Ferguson
31722 Circle Dr
McArthur OH 45651

Call Sign: KD8HAA
Diane K Coelho
62130 Locker Plant Rd
McArthur OH 45651

Call Sign: KD8DDG
Thomas J Coelho
62130 Locker Plant Rd
McArthur OH
456518627

Call Sign: N8TJC
Thomas J Coelho
62130 Locker Plant Rd
McArthur OH
456518627

Call Sign: AA8QE
George L Knox
100 Lynwood Dr
McArthur OH 45651

Call Sign: KB6CQ
Henry E Burr
35018 Martindill Rd
McArthur OH 45651

Call Sign: KC8DFO
Nancy Jane Brame
59460 McKee Rd

McArthur OH 45651

Call Sign: KC8FOK
Sarah R Brame
59460 McKee Rd
McArthur OH 45651

Call Sign: W8RY
Michael A Brame
59460 McKee Rd
McArthur OH 45651

Call Sign: KI8EK
William D Welker
201 N Locust St
McArthur OH 45651

Call Sign: KC8GPG
James E Shiveley
30237 Powder Plant Rd
McArthur OH 45651

Call Sign: KA8VUE
William A Armstrong
186 S Walnut St
McArthur OH 45651

Call Sign: WA6VGB
Patricia L Speck
64575 Siverly Crk Rd
McArthur OH 45651

Call Sign: KC8UVE
John L Collins
32776 St Forest Rd
McArthur OH 45651

Call Sign: KC8WIV
Paul C Cecil Jr
59723 US Hwy 50
McArthur OH 45651

Call Sign: KC8GCM
Valerie R Burns
66566 US Hwy 50

McArthur OH 45651

Call Sign: KI8FV
Steven L Burns
66566 US Hwy 50
McArthur OH 45651

Call Sign: KC8YKI
Jason A Holstine
418 W High St
McArthur OH 45651

Call Sign: KC8DFN
Clyde W Pinney
28021 Wheelabout Rd
McArthur OH 45651

Call Sign: KB8TNL
John T Goodman
McArthur OH 45651

Call Sign: KB8TNM
Jean L Goodman
McArthur OH 45651

Call Sign: KC8SRW
John R Bethel
McArthur OH 45651

Call Sign: AB8LZ
John R Bcthcl
McArthur OH 45651

Call Sign: K1YAK
John R Bethel
McArthur OH 45651

**FCC Amateur Radio
Licenses in
McConnelsville**

Call Sign: K8RYW
Edward L North
810 E Main St

McConnelsville OH
43756

Call Sign: WA8LZV
Ray B Kissick
212 E St Rt 60 NE
McConnelsville OH
43756

Call Sign: K8TFG
Dorothy M Baker
383 E Union Ave
McConnelsville OH
43756

Call Sign: KB8GNT
Loren W Baker
2771 Hooppole Ridge
McConnelsville OH
43756

Call Sign: KC8ENJ
Russell E Mendenhall
814 Marietta Rd
McConnelsville OH
437560453

Call Sign: WB8YIT
Timothy W Scholl
4725 Mercer Ln
McConnelsville OH
43756

Call Sign: W9NTX
Edward L Schweikert
8487 N Bush Rd NW
McConnelsville OH
437569591

Call Sign: WA8BMK
Roger H Calendine
661 N Reynolds Rd NE
McConnelsville OH
437569628

Call Sign: KD8MPH
Wendy J Donnelly
8850 N St Rt 60
McConnelsville OH
43756

Call Sign: KC8HAJ
James W Stewart
6660 N St Rt 60 NW
McConnelsville OH
43756

Call Sign: KD8PXN
Patrick J Roberts
4551 N St Rt 669
McConnelsville OH
43756

Call Sign: KD8DFT
Patrick M Roberts
4551 N St Rt 669 NW
McConnelsville OH
43756

Call Sign: KD8MQR
Carter J Reed
3425 N Terrace Cir Dr
McConnelsville OH
43756

Call Sign: WB8NTA
Jon R Barkhurst
5710 Rodeback Ln
McConnelsville OH
43756

Call Sign: KD8JUW
Mike T Wood
720 S Riverside Dr
McConnelsville OH
43756

Call Sign: N8VWO
William M Strate
4594 Srt 669 NW

McConnelsville OH
43756

Call Sign: KC8BVW
Jason H Perry
St Rt 60 N
McConnelsville OH
43756

Call Sign: KB8OGY
Dixie L Strate
4594 St Rt 669 NW
McConnelsville OH
43756

Call Sign: WB8VQV
David R Davis
4333 Taylor Dr
McConnelsville OH
43756

Call Sign: KD8MPV
Travis C Eddleblute
1042 W Bone Rd
McConnelsville OH
43756

Call Sign: KC8PVX
Shawn R Smith
129 W Jefferson Ave
McConnelsville OH
43756

Call Sign: N8YVG
Fredrick R Morris
3530 Wise Ln
McConnelsville OH
43756

**FCC Amateur Radio
Licenses in McDermott**

Call Sign: KC8HYZ
Darlene Call
596 Arion Rd

McDermott OH 45652

Call Sign: KC8HZD
James E Call
596 Arion Rd
McDermott OH 45652

Call Sign: KB8NKQ
Samuel T Crabtree
1895 Arion Rd
McDermott OH 45652

Call Sign: KB8VFN
Sherri L Howell
1909 Arion Rd
McDermott OH 45652

Call Sign: KB8WGU
Brian R Howell
1909 Arion Rd
McDermott OH 45652

Call Sign: KB8WHG
Eric N Thompson
39 Barbara Ave
McDermott OH 45652

Call Sign: KB8WHE
Evelyn J Murphy
100 Blanford Rd
McDermott OH 45652

Call Sign: KD8OCQ
David F Rose
42 Hanley Comstock Rd
McDermott OH 45652

Call Sign: KC8PWP
Eddie A Sowards
84 John St
McDermott OH 45652

Call Sign: N8ERP
Omalee F Mathews

2672 McDermott Pond
Crk Rd
McDermott OH 45652

Call Sign: N8WAS
Jason L Johnson
2153 Pollock Rd
McDermott OH 45652

Call Sign: N8YMJ
Virginia H Johnson
2153 Pollock Rd
McDermott OH 45652

Call Sign: N8YMK
Benjamin S Johnson
2153 Pollock Rd
McDermott OH 45652

Call Sign: KC8HYX
Jack E James
1189 Rushtown
Mcdermott Rd
McDermott OH 45652

Call Sign: KB8RBT
Mark S Spradlin
12745 St Rt 73
McDermott OH 45652

Call Sign: KB8VFK
Melissa F Spradlin
12745 St Rt 73
McDermott OH 45652

Call Sign: KC8DKP
Terry L Lacy
119 Wrights Run Rd
McDermott OH 45652

**FCC Amateur Radio
Licenses in Middleport**

Call Sign: W8TRI
Joseph J Davis

939 Ash St
Middleport OH 45760

Call Sign: KB8NKR
Robert K Hedrick
410 Broadway
Middleport OH 45760

Call Sign: KA8AQR
Charles L Neutzling
36774 Leading Crk Rd
Middleport OH 45760

Call Sign: KT4TY
Brian S Borthwick
5 Main St
Middleport OH 45760

Call Sign: N8ZYU
Madeline Neece
30915 Neece Rd
Middleport OH 45760

Call Sign: WD8IFR
Perry O Rupe
227 Rutherford Rd
Middleport OH 45760

Call Sign: N8GZF
David M Horton
285 S 3rd Ave
Middleport OH 45760

Call Sign: KB8PGO
David L Cole
158 S 3rd St
Middleport OH 45760

Call Sign: KB8BZR
Gary C Harper
35790 Titus Rd
Middleport OH 45760

Call Sign: KA8NIA
Brian G Jones

1037 Vine St
Middleport OH
457601218

FCC Amateur Radio Licenses in Millfield

Call Sign: KB8GBJ
Robert Wachenschwarz
16287 6th St Box 104
Millfield OH 45761

Call Sign: KC8RRI
Michael S Moore
16933 Bell Rd
Millfield OH 45761

Call Sign: KC8RHH
Molly K Cottrill
18047 Jacksonville Rd
Millfield OH 45761

Call Sign: N8TDY
Mark E Rollins
12606 Liars Corner Rd
Millfield OH 45761

Call Sign: N8TRY
Jo Ann K Rollins
12606 Liars Corner Rd
Millfield OH 45761

Call Sign: KB8OIZ
Rachel S Fox
16067 Main St
Millfield OH 45761

Call Sign: KA8NHX
Don R Anderson
13210 St Rt 13
Millfield OH 45761

Call Sign: KC8MZB
Edward J Chilcote
16366 Utah Ridge Rd

Millfield OH 45761

Call Sign: N8UVM
Robert L Peoples Jr
8300 W Bailey Rd
Millfield OH 45761

FCC Amateur Radio Licenses in Minford

Call Sign: KC8KY
Donald W Jones
Box 227
Minford OH 45653

Call Sign: AB8FZ
Donald W Jones
725 Dewey Rd
Minford OH 45653

Call Sign: KC8JRE
John W Pick
443 Diana St
Minford OH 456538615

Call Sign: KC8HCR
Jeffrey L Gilliland
1591 Furnace Crk Rd
Minford OH 45653

Call Sign: KB8SRN
Gary L Miller
938 Rases Mountain Dr
Minford OH 45653

Call Sign: KA8IGI
John A Coburn
12738 SR 139
Minford OH 45653

Call Sign: N8RGW
Ronald A Pasquinelli
10243 St Rt 139
Minford OH 45653

Call Sign: KC8MVJ
Dan L Caudill
10260 St Rt 139
Minford OH 45653

Call Sign: KC8ZQU
Robert J Borders
8795 St Rt 335
Minford OH 45653

Call Sign: KC8EF
James C Crabtree
7184 White Gravel Rd
Minford OH 45653

Call Sign: N8WBX
James M Rogers Jr
Minford OH 45653

FCC Amateur Radio Licenses in Morristown

Call Sign: WB8TPX
Warren D Groves
Church St
Morristown OH 43759

Call Sign: N8EES
Mark A Calvert
Morristown OH 43759

FCC Amateur Radio Licenses in Mount Perry

Call Sign: KB4SGF
Donald L Minor
6345 Cimarron Rd
Mount Perry OH 43760

Call Sign: KD8MHU
James E Miller
2050 Harden Dr
Mount Perry OH 43760

Call Sign: KD8KRO
Jody L Stevens
6460 Kroft Rd
Mount Perry OH 43760

Call Sign: KD8KRP
Matthew W Stevens
6460 Kroft Rd
Mount Perry OH 43760

Call Sign: KA8HQL
Jeffrey P Van Meter
10535 Madison Twp Rd 56
Mount Perry OH 43760

Call Sign: KC8ESP
Dawn M Van Meter
10535 Madison Twp Rd 56
Mount Perry OH 43760

Call Sign: KD8PVJ
Grant T Wilcox
9268 Mulberry Rd
Mount Perry OH 43760

Call Sign: KD8ETH
Kyle T Pickrell
3095 Opera Rd
Mount Perry OH 43760

Call Sign: WE8G
Richard L Mellon
11600 Palmer Rd
Mount Perry OH
437609626

Call Sign: KC8UVB
Michael D Erdy
Mount Perry OH 43760

FCC Amateur Radio Licenses in Moxahala

Call Sign: KC8KKQ
Ronald E Osborn
Moxahala OH 43761

FCC Amateur Radio Licenses in Murray City

Call Sign: W8WBR
Eugene F Six
Orchard Aly
Murray City OH 43144

FCC Amateur Radio Licenses in Nashport

Call Sign: KD8JVB
Kimberly A Ross
5645 Bishop Ct
Nashport OH 43830

Call Sign: KC8VNH
Roger E Bowen
8860 Black Run Rd
Nashport OH 43830

Call Sign: WB8STN
Bernard E Brailer
6355 Brailer Ln
Nashport OH 43830

Call Sign: KD8JVG
Ryan E Mayberry
6365 Brentcrest Dr
Nashport OH 43830

Call Sign: KD8PIR
Ryan M Harris
5085 Brentwood Park
Nashport OH 43830

Call Sign: N8FXB
Terence R Cost
3470 Briarcliff Rd NE

Nashport OH 43830

Call Sign: K8QG
Terence R Cost
3470 Briarcliff Rd NE
Nashport OH 43830

Call Sign: KB8AFY
William J Scott
1388 CR 273A NE
Nashport OH 43830

Call Sign: KD8PEK
Cody M Steele
3430 Creamery Rd
Nashport OH 43701

Call Sign: KA8UWV
Patrick S Tanner
7340 Frazeysburg Rd
Nashport OH 43830

Call Sign: KD8CNF
Jason A Dillon
5965 Frazeysburg Rd
Lot 15
Nashport OH 43830

Call Sign: KD8HKZ
Nicholas B Mcconaha
7830 Gause Rd
Nashport OH 43830

Call Sign: KD8CNR
Kenneth A Fulks
2820 Idle Cr
Nashport OH 43830

Call Sign: W6MOX
Larry L Leifried
3055 Jacks Fairway
Nashport OH
438309114

Call Sign: KE6SGC

Phyllis J Leifried
3055 Jacks Fairway
Nashport OH
438399114

Call Sign: N8BAV
Shaun R Strahm
5512 Licking Vly Rd
Nashport OH 43830

Call Sign: KD8PGR
Tom C Greiner
2830 Lisa Kim Ln
Nashport OH 43830

Call Sign: K8TCG
Tom C Greiner
2830 Lisa Kim Ln
Nashport OH 43830

Call Sign: WT8X
Tom C Greiner
2830 Lisa Kim Ln
Nashport OH 43830

Call Sign: WD8BXU
Harry S Lett
6615 Lookout Dr
Nashport OH 43830

Call Sign: KD8PDS
John M Dillon
16970 Mary Ann
Furnace Rd
Nashport OH 43830

Call Sign: KC8VPJ
Lynn D Morrison
17019 Mary Ann
Furnace Rd
Nashport OH 43830

Call Sign: KC8UQR
Thomas E Morrison Jr

17019 Mary Ann
Furnace Rd
Nashport OH 43830

Call Sign: K9TEC
Thomas E Morrison Jr
17019 Mary Ann
Furnace Rd
Nashport OH 43830

Call Sign: KC8RU
Donald W Moore
5805 Melody Ln
Nashport OH 43830

Call Sign: KC8AAN
Charles A Hunt
6970 Minnick Dr
Nashport OH 43836

Call Sign: KC8BEV
James J Dickson
6980 Minnick Dr
Nashport OH 43830

Call Sign: K8JJD
James J Dickson
6980 Minnick Dr
Nashport OH 43830

Call Sign: KD8CMZ
Jason M Smeltzer
6650 Prior Rd
Nashport OH 43830

Call Sign: KD8MQH
Jeremy N Anders
6009 Shala Cir
Nashport OH 43830

Call Sign: KD8PEB
Jacob D Hindel
6635 Swing A Long Ln
Nashport OH 43830

Call Sign: KB8UVV
Mark A Spiker
6650 Swing A Long Ln
Nashport OH 43830

Call Sign: KD8BUF
Willard L Bailey
6270 Tanglewood Dr
Nashport OH 43830

Call Sign: KD8AAY
Todd E Wilson
6295 Tanglewood Dr
Nashport OH 43830

Call Sign: KD8MQF
Steven A Welch
2545 Tarkman Dr
Nashport OH 43830

Call Sign: KD8MPP
Chase R Tippie
2640 Vista View Dr
Nashport OH 43830

Call Sign: KD8MQC
Brady N Stephens
605 Welsh Rd
Nashport OH 43830

Call Sign: KD8MQA
Jordan B Miller
6287 Welsh Rd
Nashport OH 43830

Call Sign: N8HNE
Susan E Small
5520 Woodside Dr
Nashport OH 43830

Call Sign: N8TS
Terry W Small
5520 Woodside Dr
Nashport OH 43830

Call Sign: KC8HAQ
Gregory A Starcher
Nashport OH 43830

FCC Amateur Radio Licenses in Neffs

Call Sign: N8TAC
Janet L Olexa
54060 Belmont St
Neffs OH 43940

Call Sign: N8TAD
Cara A Olexa
54060 Belmont St
Neffs OH 43940

Call Sign: N8TFM
Abby T Olexa
54060 Belmont St
Neffs OH 43940

Call Sign: WK8T
Allan Olexa
54060 Belmont St
Neffs OH 43940

Call Sign: KC8IEG
Bradley J Jenkins
64690 Campbell
Johnson Rd
Neffs OH 43940

Call Sign: KC8QNJ
Earnest W Kennedy Jr
65360 McCurdy Rd
Neffs OH 43940

Call Sign: WM8N
Duane Olexa
64672 Sand Hill Rd
Neffs OH 439400342

Call Sign: WB8TQG
Floyd E Dailey

Neffs OH 43940

Call Sign: WD8JYG
Jo Ann H Olexa
Neffs OH 43940

FCC Amateur Radio Licenses in Nelsonville

Call Sign: KD8HEL
James R Whitney
156 Adams St
Nelsonville OH 45764

Call Sign: KD8HVV
Jeffrey A Stull II
298 Adams St
Nelsonville OH 45764

Call Sign: WB8JFU
Wallace W Pickett
42257 Carb Hill Buchtel
Rd
Nelsonville OH 45764

Call Sign: KC8WBY
Greg E Stufflebeam
42743 Carbon Hill
Buchtel Rd
Nelsonville OH 45764

Call Sign: N8QHR
Ralph C Hinerman
354 Chestnut St
Nelsonville OH 45764

Call Sign: KC8PND
Mike J Blake
13892 Dawley Rd
Nelsonville OH 45764

Call Sign: W8ACO
Orvil C Midkiff
182 E Canal St
Nelsonville OH 45764

Call Sign: N8VYA
Matthew R Phillips
147 Fort St
Nelsonville OH 45764

Call Sign: WD8LKU
Richard L Adams
738 High St
Nelsonville OH 45764

Call Sign: KC8PNE
Leonard D Bentley
28 Jefferson St
Nelsonville OH 45764

Call Sign: KD8QNI
Eric D Juniper
13808 Kimberley Rd
Nelsonville OH
457649537

Call Sign: N8TRB
Joel Christian
255 Kontner St
Nelsonville OH 45764

Call Sign: N8TRK
Leslie H Westfall
265 Kontner St
Nelsonville OH 45764

Call Sign: KB8NOG
Robert A Mohney
96 Mill St
Nelsonville OH 45764

Call Sign: KB8VXQ
Charles G Mohney
96 Mill St
Nelsonville OH 45764

Call Sign: KD8FNM
Amy R Hook

5316 New Floodwood
Rd
Nelsonville OH 45764

Call Sign: KD8FNL
Robert J Clark
5316 New Floodwood
Rd
Nelsonville OH 45764

Call Sign: KC8STA
Larry Owens
842 Poplar St
Nelsonville OH 45764

Call Sign: KD8PON
Brenda L Ferguson
577 Railroad St
Nelsonville OH 45764

Call Sign: KD8PJB
Daniel R Ferguson
577 Railroad St
Nelsonville OH 45764

Call Sign: KB8DTU
Gary M Carter
95 Robbins Rd
Nelsonville OH 45764

Call Sign: KB8DYH
Barbara L Carter
95 Robbins Rd
Nelsonville OH 45764

Call Sign: KD8MSR
Gary M Carter
95 Robbins Rd
Nelsonville OH 45764

Call Sign: N8ION
Ron W Pittman Sr
1040 SR 56
Nelsonville OH 45764

Call Sign: KA8URX
Thomas H Brooks
11658 SR 691
Nelsonville OH 45764

Call Sign: KB8GXS
Jeffrey J Hiles
16975 St Rt 278 NE
Nelsonville OH 45764

Call Sign: KD8PKV
Roy E Plant III
14794 St Rt 691
Nelsonville OH 45764

Call Sign: KC8EAC
David M Mc Bride
15577 St Rt 691 Apt
221
Nelsonville OH 45764

Call Sign: KD8PSA
Kay R Gabriel
17670 Sylvania Ave
Nelsonville OH 45764

Call Sign: KD8PRZ
Patrick L Gabriel
17670 Sylvania Ave
Nelsonville OH 45764

Call Sign: WB8BSQ
William M Mc Connell
17671 Sylvania Ave
Nelsonville OH 45764

Call Sign: WB8RGW
John W Hartley
231 W Washington St
Nelsonville OH 45764

Call Sign: WB8BSR
Richard W Hopstetter
4244 Woodlane Dr
Nelsonville OH 45764

Call Sign: KA8LGK
Gus M Morris
Nelsonville OH 45764

FCC Amateur Radio Licenses in New Boston

Call Sign: AB8DR
Larry M Stephenson
4241 Gallia
New Boston OH 45662

Call Sign: KC8IYX
Gary D Blackburn
3446 Gallia St
New Boston OH 45662

Call Sign: KF8NL
Gary G Stephenson
3763 Grace St
New Boston OH 45662

Call Sign: KA8YFU
Wanda L Stephenson
3763 Grace St
New Boston OH
456624926

Call Sign: KC8SYJ
Wanda L Stephenson
3763 Grace St
New Boston OH
456624926

Call Sign: WW8O
Gary G Stephenson
3763 Grace St
New Boston OH
456624926

Call Sign: WM8O
Wanda L Stephenson
3763 Grace St

New Boston OH
456624926

Call Sign: N8VKH
Robert R Cooley
930 Maple Ct
New Boston OH 45662

Call Sign: KF8ER
Larry M Stephenson
4203 Oak St
New Boston OH 45662

Call Sign: KB8PPS
Timothy J Poole
4228 Oak St
New Boston OH 45662

Call Sign: KD8JQR
Willard E Estep II
3309 Rhodes Ave
New Boston OH 45662

Call Sign: KB8VFM
Theodore F Elkins Jr
4230 Spruce St
New Boston OH 45662

Call Sign: AB8EV
Larry M Stephenson
3902 Stanton Ave Apt B
New Boston OH 45662

FCC Amateur Radio Licenses in New Concord

Call Sign: KC8YFP
Chad A Hulboy
60073 Bliss Rd
New Concord OH
43762

Call Sign: WK8L
Chad A Hulboy

60073 Bliss Rd
New Concord OH
43762

Call Sign: KD8ESU
Sean A Taft
5825 Cambridge Rd
New Concord OH
43762

Call Sign: KB3OAD
James M Weigele
16 Depot St Apt 101
New Concord OH
437621272

Call Sign: KB8GTH
Deborah M Marshall
13 E High St
New Concord OH
43762

Call Sign: KC8IEB
Sean P Mc Donough
152 E Main St
New Concord OH
43762

Call Sign: WB8DQE
Charles E Montague
800 Friendship Dr
New Concord OH
43762

Call Sign: WB8TRK
Billie L Dickson
1900 Friendship Dr
New Concord OH
43762

Call Sign: KD8KGH
Carol A Emerson
2215 Friendship Dr
New Concord OH
43762

Call Sign: KD8CNM
Shannon L Simmerman
3400 Friendship Dr
New Concord OH
43762

Call Sign: KA8RCJ
Kevin C Jones
5470 Friendship Dr
New Concord OH
43762

Call Sign: KD8HKT
Jonathan M Winsley
57284 Fritter Rd
New Concord OH
43762

Call Sign: KD8ESY
Shane A Dale
59285 Fritter Rd
New Concord OH
43762

Call Sign: KA8UQE
Francis J Hall
7 Garfield Ave
New Concord OH
43762

Call Sign: KD8MQJ
Zachary M Bishop
270 Homestead Dr
New Concord OH
43762

Call Sign: WB8WLL
Cloyd W Eddy
58687 Keiser Ln
New Concord OH
43762

Call Sign: N4KNS
Edith F Best

201 Lakeside Dr Apt 36
New Concord OH
43762

Call Sign: KA8YYI
Jill K Stewart
53 Maple Ave
New Concord OH
43762

Call Sign: N8HFD
Edward C Stewart
53 Maple Ave
New Concord OH
43762

Call Sign: KA8JIM
James V Houser
157 N Liberty St
New Concord OH
43762

Call Sign: WA8JIM
James V Houser
157 N Liberty St
New Concord OH
43762

Call Sign: KC8OBK
James S Houser
157 N Liberty St
New Concord OH
43762

Call Sign: KC8OBL
Phyllis A Houser
157 N Liberty St
New Concord OH
43762

Call Sign: KD8JVM
Blake M Patton
12240 Patton Ln
New Concord OH
43762

Call Sign: W8KUA
George S Quillia
1950 Peters Crk Rd
New Concord OH
43762

Call Sign: WA8ZMN
Steven R La Monica
2045 Rix Mills Rd
New Concord OH
43762

Call Sign: KC8OVH
Darren L Sears
2795 Rix Mills Rd
New Concord OH
43762

Call Sign: WD8NXD
Donald A Snedden
3900 Rough & Ready
Rd
New Concord OH
43762

Call Sign: N8FXL
John W Taylor
4335 Taylor Rd
New Concord OH
43762

Call Sign: KC8HNX
Paul D Davis
58 W High St
New Concord OH
43762

Call Sign: KC8WXB
Mark R Hoffer
59550 West Rd
New Concord OH
43762

Call Sign: KB4GPR

Martha L Sims
New Concord OH
43762

FCC Amateur Radio Licenses in New Lexington

Call Sign: WD8BBN
Larry E Williams
695 Cemetery Rd Rt 1
New Lexington OH
437649728

Call Sign: N8PHL
Paul H Linkous III
121 E Broadway St
New Lexington OH
43764

Call Sign: KC8JCI
Helen F Hankinson
556 Fowler St
New Lexington OH
437641542

Call Sign: KA8EUA
Charles A Hankinson Jr
556 Fowler St
New Lexington OH
437641542

Call Sign: KC8DTS
Nicky A Holter
259 Highland Dr
New Lexington OH
43764

Call Sign: KC8JBH
Max A Van Fossen
708 Johnson Ave
New Lexington OH
43764

Call Sign: KC8GWU

Robert A Gray
197 Knoll St
New Lexington OH
43764

Call Sign: KC8ZA
Gene C Dawson
4795 Marietta Rd SE
New Lexington OH
43764

Call Sign: N8EAQ
Margaret E Dawson
4795 Marietta Rd SE
New Lexington OH
43764

Call Sign: WB8ECK
Paul W Beckett
511 N Main St
New Lexington OH
43764

Call Sign: KC8JBG
Michael P Ferguson
2823 Old Somerset Rd
New Lexington OH
43764

Call Sign: KB8MQT
Stephanie F Allen
5179 Pke Twp Rd 225
SE
New Lexington OH
43764

Call Sign: W8FZI
Richard L Grimes Sr
8860 Portie Flamingo
SE
New Lexington OH
43764

Call Sign: W8FQZ
James E Mc Carty

720 Ridge Ave
New Lexington OH
43764

Call Sign: W8GDA
Fred J King
769 Ridge Ave
New Lexington OH
43764

Call Sign: KD8RED
Cynthia L Lampley Ms
208 S Maple Heights
New Lexington OH
43764

Call Sign: N8OFM
Douglas E Skillman
515 Shawnee St
New Lexington OH
43764

Call Sign: N8RGU
Bonnie C Skillman
515 Shawnee St
New Lexington OH
43764

Call Sign: W8BGS
Orville S Bingman
5550 St Rt 37
New Lexington OH
43764

Call Sign: KB8GHL
Jared P Hiles
292 Union St
New Lexington OH
43764

Call Sign: KC8OSC
Connie L Cote
616 W Brown St
New Lexington OH
43764

Call Sign: KC8DTR
Robyn L Seenes
204 W Lincoln St
New Lexington OH
43764

Call Sign: KC8EHO
Robert L Seenes
204 W Lincoln St
New Lexington OH
43764

Call Sign: KC8FAE
Edith J Seenes
204 W Lincoln St
New Lexington OH
43764

Call Sign: KC8KKT
Robert L Seenes Jr
204 W Lincoln St
New Lexington OH
43764

FCC Amateur Radio Licenses in New Marshfield

Call Sign: KC8KBW
Ernest Michael Brown
7721 Hawk Rd
New Marshfield OH
45766

Call Sign: AB8NA
Ernest Michael Brown
7721 Hawk Rd
New Marshfield OH
45766

Call Sign: N8VOV
Warren G Ferguson
10100 Lightfritz Ridge
Rd

New Marshfield OH
457669739

Call Sign: KA8TKM
Melvin L Brooks
8450 Rt 356
New Marshfield OH
45766

Call Sign: KC8SPQ
Gary B Lemley
9155 St Rt 691
New Marshfield OH
45766

Call Sign: KC8MAL
Alice R Van Doren
New Marshfield OH
457660085

Call Sign: KC8MAM
Margaret A Van Doren
New Marshfield OH
457660085

Call Sign: KC8MAN
Helen M Van Doren
New Marshfield OH
457660085

Call Sign: KC8MAO
Mary E Van Doren
New Marshfield OH
457660085

Call Sign: KC8MAP
Mark R Van Doren
New Marshfield OH
457660085

FCC Amateur Radio Licenses in New Matamoras

Call Sign: K8ULE

John G Knowlton
611 2nd St
New Matamoras OH
45767

Call Sign: KC8JWO
Boger L Bunner
Box 324A
New Matamoras OH
45767

Call Sign: N8PYP
Norma G Yoho
4421 Brownsville Rd
New Matamoras OH
45767

Call Sign: W8FL
Gerald W Yoho
4421 Brownsville Rd
New Matamoras OH
457676053

Call Sign: KB8GRZ
Phillip R Voight
C Hill Rd
New Matamoras OH
45767

Call Sign: KD8MCD
Earnest P Hulsey
35205 Rock Camp Rd
New Matamoras OH
45767

Call Sign: WD8PVL
Chester M Slonaker
Williamson Ave
New Matamoras OH
45767

Call Sign: K8LEM
Stafford D Merckle
New Matamoras OH
45767

Call Sign: KA8TBX
Chester M Slonaker II
New Matamoras OH
45767

Call Sign: KC8IEF
Jennifer L Grimes
New Matamoras OH
45767

Call Sign: KI8AK
Gary P Grimes
New Matamoras OH
45767

FCC Amateur Radio Licenses in New Plymouth

Call Sign: KB8TKZ
Jack D Mc Clain
20193 St Rt 328
New Plymouth OH
45654

FCC Amateur Radio Licenses in New Straitsville

Call Sign: KA8GNM
Gary W Edgell
103 E Main St
New Straitsville OH
43766

Call Sign: KD8KFJ
Gary W Edgell
103 E Main St
New Straitsville OH
43766

Call Sign: K8RVV
David J Blosser
221 N Cunningham St

New Straitsville OH
43766

Call Sign: KC8TFW
Roy P Vickers
5898 Twp Rd 133 SE
New Straitsville OH
43766

Call Sign: KC8URA
Rebecca E Vickers
5898 Twp Rd 133 SE
New Straitsville OH
43766

FCC Amateur Radio Licenses in North Waterford

Call Sign: N8JIU
Gail L Loveland
6501 Raley Rd
North Waterford OH
44445

FCC Amateur Radio Licenses in Norwich

Call Sign: KD8KGI
Traci R Graham
9990 E Pike
Norwich OH 43767

Call Sign: KA8OKF
Terry L Simmons
71 Lincoln Ln
Norwich OH 43767

Call Sign: KD8EZZ
Jeremy M Barnhart
10025 Matchett Rd
Norwich OH 43767

Call Sign: KD8EZX
Grace A Barnhart

Matchett Rd
Norwich OH 43767

Call Sign: KD8EZY
Mark A Barnhart
10005 Mattchett Rd
Norwich OH 43767

Call Sign: N8IMW
Linda D Alfman
1975 N Moose Eye Rd
Norwich OH 43767

Call Sign: W8FHF
George A Alfman
1975 N Moose Eye Rd
Norwich OH 43767

Call Sign: KD8PEC
Justin K Lowry
10255 North St
Norwich OH 43767

Call Sign: W8LBB
Wayne H Ely
140 Riley Rd
Norwich OH 43767

Call Sign: KD8MPX
Micah M Jordan
1660 S Cove Ln
Norwich OH 43767

Call Sign: KD8MQM
Megan L Geyer
580 Southern Rd
Norwich OH 43767

Call Sign: KD8HWK
Jeffrey A Hayes
181 Sundale Rd
Norwich OH 43767

Call Sign: KB3RDR
Kathleen M Frederico

905 W Union Rd
Norwich OH 43767

Call Sign: KB3SWO
Valerie L Smith
905 W Union Rd
Norwich OH 43767

Call Sign: KZ8VAL
Valerie L Smith
905 W Union Rd
Norwich OH 43767

**FCC Amateur Radio
Licenses in Oak Hill**

Call Sign: KA8PJU
John A Black
1277 Clay Banner Rd
Oak Hill OH 45656

Call Sign: AB8KT
Patty Vaughn
1898 Clay Banner Rd
Oak Hill OH 45656

Call Sign: AB8KU
John T Vaughn
1898 Clay Banner Rd
Oak Hill OH 45656

Call Sign: KC8AOM
Warren C Crabtree
218 Cozy Glen Rd
Oak Hill OH 45656

Call Sign: WD8LTO
Donald J Morgan
2693 Flat Woods Rd
Oak Hill OH 456569708

Call Sign: N8KWM
Perry P Horton
173 Gallia Sardis Rd
Oak Hill OH 45656

Call Sign: KD8ICX
Robert E Czechlewski
888 Maybee Karn Rd
Oak Hill OH 45656

Call Sign: WB8JLV
Paul M Crabtree
723 Monroe Hickory Rd
Oak Hill OH 45656

Call Sign: WD8LYF
James ARCadipane Jr
438 Oak St
Oak Hill OH 45656

Call Sign: KC8ASG
Todd B Stambaugh
119 Palmyra St
Oak Hill OH 45656

Call Sign: KD8HCK
Todd B Stambaugh
119 Palmyra St
Oak Hill OH 45656

Call Sign: KB8PKT
Malcolm D Case
4519 Riegel Ridge
Oak Hill OH 45656

Call Sign: KB8GTT
William C Burke
682 Shady Point Rd
Oak Hill OH 45656

Call Sign: KB8HNT
Kevin T Clark
120 Smith St
Oak Hill OH 45656

Call Sign: KB8ZRQ
Jerry P Foster
342 Sonne Kolb Rd
Oak Hill OH 45656

Call Sign: KC8FIX
Dennis E Wallace
St Rt 140
Oak Hill OH 45656

Call Sign: KD8NMX
Gaylen J Smith
210 W Main
Oak Hill OH 45656

Call Sign: AA8TD
James R Sturgill Jr
503 Zane Oak Rd
Oak Hill OH 45656

**FCC Amateur Radio
Licenses in Otway**

Call Sign: N8WBU
Thomas E Webb
706 Big Run Rd
Otway OH 45657

Call Sign: KB8NBH
Jonathan D King
744 Big Run Rd
Otway OH 45657

Call Sign: KB8QNS
Ethel M King
1425 Big Run Rd
Otway OH 45657

Call Sign: KB8NBI
Jack E King
1425 Big Run Rd
Otway OH 456578983

Call Sign: KB8WGV
Martha W King
1475 Big Run Rd
Otway OH 45657

Call Sign: N8ZNO

William E Murphy
1081 Big Run Rd
Otway OH 45657

Call Sign: N8ZNP
Jacqueline M Murphy
1081 Big Run Rd
Otway OH 45657

Call Sign: WA8ZUS
Robert R Higgins
165 Dry Run Rd
Otway OH 45657

Call Sign: KC8CXH
Loyd E Gilley
1136 Hackworth Hill Rd
Otway OH 45657

Call Sign: WA8PAS
Ronald I Knisley
1834 Hackworth Hill Rd
Otway OH 45657

Call Sign: KD8EUL
Jeanne L Mountjoy
3397 Mt Hope Rd
Otway OH 45657

Call Sign: KB8SCX
Eric O Lewis
5205 Rocky Fork Rd
Otway OH 45657

Call Sign: N8DFI
Sandra L Lewis
5205 Rocky Fork Rd
Otway OH 456578993

Call Sign: KB8LOJ
Floyd E Shelton Sr
25830 St Rt 125
Otway OH 45657

Call Sign: KC8CXF

Becki Hoffer
7316 St Rt 16
Otway OH 45657

Call Sign: KB8PPQ
Melissa R Hurst
9906 St Rt 348
Otway OH 45657

Call Sign: KC8CXG
Anthony Hoffer
7316 St Rt 73
Otway OH 45657

FCC Amateur Radio Licenses in Patriot

Call Sign: W8UV
Philip M Roberts
96 Dundee Ave
Patriot OH 45658

Call Sign: KC8VJK
Craig E James
12762 St Rt 141
Patriot OH 45658

Call Sign: WD8LYG
James ARCadipane
3756 St Rt 233
Patriot OH 45658

Call Sign: KD8DJC
Robert S Oehler
6215 St Rt 775
Patriot OH 45658

FCC Amateur Radio Licenses in Pedro

Call Sign: KB8LWZ
David M Barber
113 CR 29
Pedro OH 456599602

Call Sign: WA8GTQ
Richard L Jones
1085 CR 51
Pedro OH 45659

Call Sign: KC8WDU
Otto R Schweickart Jr
3100 CR 51
Pedro OH 45659

Call Sign: N8URU
Eddie L Jenkins
3167 CR 51
Pedro OH 45659

Call Sign: KB8TGI
Annabelle L Jenkins
3167 CR 51
Pedro OH 45659

Call Sign: KD8QME
Timothy J Hosto
11708 CR S
Pedro OH 45659

Call Sign: KD8FPY
Larry A Chinn
176 Private Dr 8649
Pedro OH 45659

FCC Amateur Radio Licenses in Philo

Call Sign: KC8WFQ
David D Swingle
2015 Butterbean Ridge
Philo OH 43771

Call Sign: KC8WFP
Sue E Swingle
2015 Butterbean Ridge
Philo OH 43771

Call Sign: KD8WA
David L Higley

5625 Center Rd
Philo OH 43771

Call Sign: KC8LPI
Terry W Smedley
2720 Johnson Hill Rd
Philo OH 43771

Call Sign: KC8MAA
Sally L Smedley
2720 Johnson Hill Rd
Philo OH 437719718

Call Sign: KC8LPJ
Darrell W Jenkins
4125 Old River Rd
Philo OH 43771

Call Sign: WB8TNB
James E Kretschmar
6970 Sealover Hollow
Rd
Philo OH 43771

**FCC Amateur Radio
Licenses in Piketon**

Call Sign: KC8EWL
John W Tackett
1884 Chenoweth Fork
Rd
Piketon OH 45661

Call Sign: KC8LZZ
Lee H Music
1884 Chenoweth Fork
Rd
Piketon OH 45661

Call Sign: KC8OFM
Robert L Smith Jr
160 Church Rd
Piketon OH 45661

Call Sign: KB8KCX

David E Darst
220 Donns Way
Piketon OH 45661

Call Sign: W8YPH
Walden H Rheinfrank
E Main
Piketon OH 45661

Call Sign: KD8CDJ
Beverly K Metheney
2094 Happy Hollow Rd
Piketon OH 45661

Call Sign: KC8UDN
Delbert A Metheney Jr
2094 Happy Hollow Rd
Piketon OH 45661

Call Sign: KC8ADJ
James H Rebman
5747 Long Fork Rd
Piketon OH 45661

Call Sign: KC8QLI
John J Foster
2779 Shyville Rd
Piketon OH 45661

Call Sign: KD8KOL
Jeremy K Satterfield
841 Smokey Hollow Rd
Piketon OH 45661

Call Sign: KB8DHP
Edward E O Bryant
4976 St Rt 772
Piketon OH 45661

Call Sign: KC8JMD
Jeannette O Bryant
4976 St Rt 772
Piketon OH 45661

Call Sign: KC8YZR

William C New
436 Wakefield Mnd Rd
Piketon OH 45661

Call Sign: KC8WDZ
Delores J Oyer
2514 Waldren Hill Rd
Piketon OH 45661

Call Sign: N8WJS
Thomas D Oyer Sr
2514 Waldren Hill Rd
Piketon OH 45661

Call Sign: KC8VOJ
Thomas D Oyer II
2514 Waldron Hill Rd
Piketon OH 45661

Call Sign: K8KPE
Russell M Mc Dowell
Piketon OH 45661

Call Sign: WB8WDX
James D Litteral
Piketon OH 45661

**FCC Amateur Radio
Licenses in Pleasant
City**

Call Sign: N8VFM
Todd R Lucas
10598 Clay Pike Rd
Pleasant City OH 43772

Call Sign: KD8MPG
Tony A Delong
509 High St
Pleasant City OH 43772

Call Sign: KD8PYO
Levi E Wade
9942 Pleasant Rd
Pleasant City OH 43772

Call Sign: KD8JVL
Melanie L Wood
19313 West Rd
Pleasant City OH 43772

Call Sign: KD8RIU
Richard J Mcvicker
Pleasant City OH 43772

FCC Amateur Radio Licenses in Pomeroy

Call Sign: KB8LZG
Terry D Pack
39571 Carpenter Hill Rd
Pomeroy OH 45769

Call Sign: KD8DKO
Daemon R Zen-Eagle
43249 Cherry Ridge Rd
Pomeroy OH 45769

Call Sign: KD8DKP
Re Jn
43249 Cherry Ridge Rd
Pomeroy OH 45769

Call Sign: KB8OZF
Dean H Sexton
43881 Cherry Ridge Rd
Pomeroy OH 45769

Call Sign: WA8AKD
Jed J Webster
310 Condor St
Pomeroy OH 45769

Call Sign: KB8KUO
Roger D Trovi
114 E Main St
Pomeroy OH 45769

Call Sign: KB8NKS
John C Beaver

34471 Flatwoods Rd
Pomeroy OH
457699770

Call Sign: KC8LOE
 Meigs County Amateur
Radio
35190 Flatwoods Rd
Pomeroy OH 45769

Call Sign: KZ8U
Brian T Taylor
35190 Flatwoods Rd
Pomeroy OH 45769

Call Sign: N8SSU
Melvin S Henry
3 Hill St
Pomeroy OH 45769

Call Sign: KB8UAH
Charles M Lemley
15 Hill St
Pomeroy OH 45769

Call Sign: W8CML
Charles M Lemley
15 Hill St
Pomeroy OH 45769

Call Sign: KD8PYE
Liberty A King
106 Holly Ln
Pomeroy OH 45769

Call Sign: KC8NUY
Michael B Test
34478 Hysell Run Rd
Pomeroy OH 45760

Call Sign: WM8D
James E Stacy Jr
176 Mulberry Ave
Pomeroy OH 45769

Call Sign: KD8PYP
Scott L Walton
113 Peacock Ave
Pomeroy OH 45769

Call Sign: N8WON
Debra K Phelps
197 Pleasant Ridge
Pomeroy OH 45769

Call Sign: NQ8Y
Wiley L Phelps
197 Pleasant Ridge
Pomeroy OH 45769

Call Sign: KC8MPA
Robert E Brewer
41720 Pomeroy Pike
Pomeroy OH 45769

Call Sign: KD8DCR
Nick J Goodwin
38430 Rocksprings Rd
Pomeroy OH 45764

Call Sign: KB8MSE
Linda L Powell
40778 SR 681
Pomeroy OH 45769

Call Sign: N8UBG
Allan L Harris
34796 SR 7
Pomeroy OH 45769

Call Sign: KC8LNC
Jason B Ridenour
34815 SR 7
Pomeroy OH 45764

Call Sign: N8GQN
David A Lipscomb
St Rt 124
Pomeroy OH 45769

Call Sign: KB8OZG
Claude K Nease
43012 St Rt 124 Lot 12
Pomeroy OH 45769

Call Sign: KD8DKM
John L Hursey
42994 St Rt 124 Lot 21
Pomeroy OH 45769

Call Sign: N8UXV
Jimmy B Mc Clure
Union Ter
Pomeroy OH 45769

Call Sign: KC8UYO
Harley E Johnson
35491 Wolf Pen Rd
Pomeroy OH 45769

Call Sign: KD8KND
Scott A Warner
35795 Wolf Pen Rd
Pomeroy OH 45769

FCC Amateur Radio Licenses in Portland

Call Sign: KG6DI
Robin J Kinney
51795 Eaton Rd
Portland OH 45770

Call Sign: KC8JRO
Sarah B Bayer
481 Forest Ave
Portland OH 44514

Call Sign: KB8GRS
Randy D Taylor
54420 New Portland Rd
Portland OH 45770

Call Sign: KD8OOF
William R Snyder

57881 SR 124
Portland OH 45770

FCC Amateur Radio Licenses in Portsmouth

Call Sign: KA8COE
Margie Mutter
2024 27th St
Portsmouth OH 45662

Call Sign: KA8COF
Eugene Mutter
2024 27th St
Portsmouth OH 45662

Call Sign: K8NCE
Richard W Smith
1610 28th St Apt 3210
Portsmouth OH 45662

Call Sign: WB8BRO
George N Spears
1610 28th St Apt 3G29
Portsmouth OH
456622641

Call Sign: K8LPI
Betty R Richey
1015 29th St
Portsmouth OH 45662

Call Sign: W8LP
James D Richey
1015 29th St
Portsmouth OH 45662

Call Sign: KA8ATK
Herbert F Schuette
1063 29th St
Portsmouth OH 45662

Call Sign: KC8QCL
Florence A Meade
500 2nd St Apt 213

Portsmouth OH 45662

Call Sign: W8NK
Richard D Gibson
1631 3rd St
Portsmouth OH 45662

Call Sign: KC8GPH
Donald H Harrison
2047 5th St
Portsmouth OH 45662

Call Sign: KA8MBO
Diana R Gullett
1422 6th St Apt 1
Portsmouth OH 45662

Call Sign: KC8EXS
Debra D Lewis
1726 7th St
Portsmouth OH 45662

Call Sign: WD8IFH
Garey L Bashford Sr
2105 Argonne Rd
Portsmouth OH 45662

Call Sign: W8BTB
William C Gammon
5526 Auburn Ave
Portsmouth OH 45662

Call Sign: N4GHS
David A Erwin
2131 Baird Ave
Portsmouth OH 45662

Call Sign: W8VVT
Robert L Gilmer
2743 Blue Rock Dr
Portsmouth OH 45662

Call Sign: KA8CHF
Bernard F Wessel
Box 354

Portsmouth OH 45662   Portsmouth OH 45662   Portsmouth OH 45662

Call Sign: KB8QEJ   Call Sign: K8RFW   Call Sign: N8NWI
John B Collins Jr   Velton P Graham   Daniel L Burk
74 Brouse St   811 Findlay St Apt 601   24 High St
Portsmouth OH 45663   Portsmouth OH 45662   Portsmouth OH 45662

Call Sign: KD8OCR   Call Sign: KB8YKN   Call Sign: KB8PEH
David G Vetter   Gregory L Pate   Timothy A Hileman
2902 Cedar St   1226 Franklin   1808 High St
Portsmouth OH 45662   Portsmouth OH 45662   Portsmouth OH 45662

Call Sign: K0IDV   Call Sign: N8UYI   Call Sign: KD8GCY
David G Vetter   Larry A Shepherd   Ashley N Morris
2902 Cedar St   1225 Franklin Ave   1824 High St
Portsmouth OH 45662   Portsmouth OH 45662   Portsmouth OH 45662

Call Sign: KC8DZX   Call Sign: WA8FBZ   Call Sign: N8HAW
George L Davis III   Russell W Harcha   Garry L Hale
3202 Chateau Dr   2004 Franklin Blvd   1612 Highland Ave
Portsmouth OH 45662   Portsmouth OH 45662   Portsmouth OH 45662

Call Sign: KC8AMM   Call Sign: W8RWH   Call Sign: KC8QLA
George H Link   Russell W Harcha   Garry L Hale
1213 Cole Blvd   2004 Franklin Blvd   1612 Highland Ave
Portsmouth OH 45662   Portsmouth OH 45662   Portsmouth OH 45662

Call Sign: N8GXD   Call Sign: KB8RYE   Call Sign: N8HAW
Sue E Bissell   Joseph R Ferguson   Garry L Hale
1715 Coles Blvd   309 Front St   1612 Highland Ave
Portsmouth OH 45662   Portsmouth OH 45662   Portsmouth OH 45662

Call Sign: N8VCA   Call Sign: KC8LGW   Call Sign: KG8FQ
David M Huddleston   William D Smith   Wayne C Cooley
1909 Dorman Dr   445 Front St   4117 Hill Rd
Portsmouth OH 45662   Portsmouth OH 45662   Portsmouth OH 45662

Call Sign: WD8CDY   Call Sign: N8NWL   Call Sign: N8VKG
Paul R Ison   Scott W Thomas   Brenda K Cooley
2326 Elmwood Dr   3164 Gallia St 5   4117 Hill Rd
Portsmouth OH 45662   Portsmouth OH 45662   Portsmouth OH 45662

Call Sign: WD8CVU   Call Sign: N8YVA   Call Sign: W8UPI
Orville E Mower Sr   Robert A Storey   Dale W Gillette
5554 Endicott   2108 Grandview Ave   2749 Hillview Ct 4

Portsmouth OH
456622664

Call Sign: K8GAB
William R Brown
1329 Holmes Ave
Portsmouth OH 45662

Call Sign: AA8WI
Bernard L Cooper Jr
1611 Jackson Ave
Portsmouth OH 45662

Call Sign: KC8FWH
Nicholas J Kongos
40 Kongos Rd
Portsmouth OH 45662

Call Sign: N8NUB
Elaine K Le Master
1301 Linden Ave
Portsmouth OH 45662

Call Sign: KC8HPN
Gino P Milani
1623 Linden Ave
Portsmouth OH 45662

Call Sign: WA8VWW
Richard D Manley
1605 Mabert Rd
Portsmouth OH 45662

Call Sign: KB8QED
Tamatha A Williams
55 Maple St
Portsmouth OH 45662

Call Sign: N8PBB
Scott A Williams
55 Maple St
Portsmouth OH 45662

Call Sign: K8QLU
Leslie O Stir Jr

315 Market St Apt 1F
Portsmouth OH 45662

Call Sign: KB8QEF
Ryan E Robirds
158 Mathiott St
Portsmouth OH 45662

Call Sign: KG8EX
Donald A Daniels
1218 Mayo St
Portsmouth OH 45662

Call Sign: KC8NKM
Timothy W Taylor
2137 Micklethwaite Rd
Portsmouth OH 45662

Call Sign: W8TWT
Timothy W Taylor
2137 Micklethwaite Rd
Portsmouth OH 45662

Call Sign: KC8DZW
Richard A Chapman
2924 N Hill Rd
Portsmouth OH 45662

Call Sign: KE8BU
Robert L Warnock
65 N Mathiott St
Portsmouth OH 45662

Call Sign: N8WBV
Jerry L Swords
231 Nauvoo Pond Crk
Rd
Portsmouth OH 45663

Call Sign: WB8AUI
Harold D Leininger
4638 New Garden Rd
Portsmouth OH 45662

Call Sign: AA8KY

William N Massie
3019 Noddin Way
Portsmouth OH 45662

Call Sign: N8WQW
Caroline M Massie
3019 Noddin Way
Portsmouth OH 45662

Call Sign: KB8PPR
Mark D Mershon
1367 Normandy Dr
Portsmouth OH 45662

Call Sign: WA8BRZ
James R Schneider
1135 Orm Ave
Portsmouth OH 45662

Call Sign: KC8UYG
Richard M Calver
1822 Outlook Dr
Portsmouth OH 45662

Call Sign: KC8HZB
Thomas O James
1329 Park Ave
Portsmouth OH 45662

Call Sign: N8LEX
Michael D Musser
97 Pershing St
Portsmouth OH 45662

Call Sign: N8MBD
Donald E James Sr
2531 Ritchie St
Portsmouth OH 45662

Call Sign: KB8AAK
Russell L Jett
426 Roosevelt Ct
Portsmouth OH 45662

Call Sign: WB8RCF

Raymond B
Cunningham
1342 Rosemont Rd
Portsmouth OH
456626650

Call Sign: KC8RCC
Ceda S Minturn
1513 Rosemount Rd
Portsmouth OH 45662

Call Sign: KB8WGT
Jeff S Holmes
4020 Rosemount Rd
Portsmouth OH 45662

Call Sign: KC8HYY
Kevin D Call
1117 Ruhlman Ave
Portsmouth OH 45662

Call Sign: WA8NRC
David G Weber
1248 Sarasue Ave
Portsmouth OH 45662

Call Sign: WB8VRG
Brent A James
2517 Scioto Trl
Portsmouth OH 45662

Call Sign: WD8ICT
Ralph W Miller
6812 Shela Blvd
Portsmouth OH 45662

Call Sign: KG8MF
Ronald E Vastine
94 Shenandoah Ct
Portsmouth OH 45662

Call Sign: KD8IIR
Tien-Chien Chang
3671 Sheridan Rd
Portsmouth OH 45662

Call Sign: KO8H
Lynn R Wessel
St Rt 335
Portsmouth OH 45662

Call Sign: KC8FAP
Jodi A Call
4304 Sterling Ave
Portsmouth OH 45662

Call Sign: KD8AAP
Edwin L Hemminger Jr
297 Stout Hollow Rd
Portsmouth OH 45662

Call Sign: W8BLI
Richard J Frederick
2111 Sunrise Ave
Portsmouth OH 45662

Call Sign: WB8YIC
Donald L Goodwin
2613 Sunrise Ave
Portsmouth OH
456622544

Call Sign: KB8JO
Donald E Henry
46 Swickert St
Portsmouth OH 45662

Call Sign: KA8OBU
Paul F Elrod
104 Ter Ave
Portsmouth OH 45662

Call Sign: KC8HPM
Curtis D Conrad
583 Unita St Rt 140
Portsmouth OH 45662

Call Sign: WA8FMQ
Chester A Kilgore Jr
1925 Valley St

Portsmouth OH 45662

Call Sign: N8DPJ
Richard D Renison
508 Waller St
Portsmouth OH 45662

Call Sign: KJ8WW
Kim R Lozier
2400 Woods Ridge
Portsmouth OH 45662

Call Sign: N8ZW
Kim R Lozier
2400 Woods Ridge
Portsmouth OH 45662

Call Sign: K8RU
Ishmael F Groves
3398 Woods Ridge
Portsmouth OH 45662

Call Sign: N8QA
Portsmouth RC
Portsmouth OH 45662

Call Sign: KB8WHI
Billy R Woodall
Portsmouth OH 45662

Call Sign: KC8FKP
Portsmouth RC
Portsmouth OH 45662

Call Sign: KD8MBN
Elijah S Allen
Portsmouth OH 45662

**FCC Amateur Radio
Licenses in Powhatan
Point**

Call Sign: KB8KFL
Jerry E Knight
114 1st St

Powhatan Point OH
43942

Call Sign: KD8LNV
Charles L Haught Jr
247 Belt St Apt 32
Powhatan Point OH
43942

Call Sign: N8CGC
Darryl A Walters
110 Carrie St
Powhatan Point OH
43942

Call Sign: KA8TAJ
John Galavich Jr
52821 Geaman Hill Rd
Powhatan Point OH
43942

Call Sign: KF4SOR
Everett D Ours
51247 German Ridge
Rd
Powhatan Point OH
423945268

Call Sign: KD8JXP
Frank W Wojewodka
51737 German Ridge
Rd
Powhatan Point OH
43942

Call Sign: N8HYV
Arlie F Henry
107 Morgan St
Powhatan Point OH
43942

**FCC Amateur Radio
Licenses in Proctorville**

Call Sign: KB8KSS

Donald E Layman
Box 158
Proctorville OH 45669

Call Sign: N8SUJ
Deron T Lundy
Box 28B
Proctorville OH 45669

Call Sign: KC8AJA
Kevin S Mc Clanahan
Box 525
Proctorville OH 45669

Call Sign: N8SKK
Vicki D Dillon
Box 549A
Proctorville OH 45669

Call Sign: N8GOF
Mackey S Carpenter
Box 588
Proctorville OH 45669

Call Sign: KC8BBK
Cynthia L Henderson
Box 645
Proctorville OH 45669

Call Sign: KB8YLS
Thomas E Henderson
Box 645
Proctorville OH 45669

Call Sign: KC8ABL
Jonathan K Henderson
Box 645
Proctorville OH 45669

Call Sign: WD4KIC
Donald F Crace
107 Broad Aly
Proctorville OH 45669

Call Sign: KD8CRX

David L Spears
1344 CR 12
Proctorville OH 45669

Call Sign: KB8UWM
Paul M Bias
536 CR 66
Proctorville OH 45669

Call Sign: KD8NQJ
Denise R Sparks
1850 CR 71
Proctorville OH 45669

Call Sign: KD8NQK
Johnnie M Sparks Jr
1850 CR 71
Proctorville OH 45669

Call Sign: K8UHC
Larry E Brammer
260 Private Dr 10463
Proctorville OH 45669

Call Sign: KD8CSN
Nicholas M Kuhn
84 Private Dr 267
Proctorville OH 45669

Call Sign: N8IXX
Arnold D Kidd
63 Private Dr 514
Proctorville OH 45669

Call Sign: KD8QII
Ashton A Killen
96 Private Dr 601
Proctorville OH 45669

Call Sign: KD8QIG
Mark L Killen
96 Private Dr 601
Proctorville OH 45669

Call Sign: KD8QIH

Teresa L Killen
96 Private Dr 601
Proctorville OH 45669

Call Sign: KC8FHO
Larry T Murray Jr
74 Private Dr 8029 St Rt
7
Proctorville OH 45669

Call Sign: KC8IXQ
John F Williamson
177 Private Dr 8323
Proctorville OH 45669

Call Sign: KE4ZRI
James K Martin
203 Private Rd 574
Proctorville OH 45669

Call Sign: KE8RM
Robert E Fletcher
221 Pvt Rd 6 Twp Rd
1306
Proctorville OH 45669

Call Sign: KC8MBR
Barbara E Mannon
9617 SR 7
Proctorville OH 45669

Call Sign: K8WZM
Durward L Callicoat
22436 St Rt 243
Proctorville OH 45669

Call Sign: KB8FMU
Larry C Kimler
22921 St Rt 243
Proctorville OH
456698652

Call Sign: WA8JDT
Harry G Miller
14326 St Rt 7

Proctorville OH 45669

Call Sign: KC8SJS
Donald G Mccomas
105 Stanley St
Proctorville OH 45669

Call Sign: N8TVN
Elizabeth A Lundy
108 Stanley St
Proctorville OH 45669

Call Sign: KC0OQS
Eric C Wallace
159 TR 1052
Proctorville OH 45669

Call Sign: W8AFX
Stephen H Sheers
212 TR 1134
Proctorville OH 45669

Call Sign: KC8TDO
Georgia C Sheers
212 TR 1134
Proctorville OH 45669

Call Sign: KD8FMD
Georgia C Sheers
212 TR 1134
Proctorville OH 45669

Call Sign: W8GMS
Georgia C Sheers
212 TR 1134
Proctorville OH 45669

Call Sign: KB8PIB
Robert L Lawhon
49 TR 1152
Proctorville OH 45669

Call Sign: KC8JXH
Brian S Mannon
230 TR 1161

Proctorville OH 45669

Call Sign: KC8KLX
John A Harris
332 TR 1175
Proctorville OH 45669

Call Sign: KC8ZPK
Eric A Kuhn
202 TR 1196
Proctorville OH 45669

Call Sign: K8UHN
Eric A Kuhn
202 TR 1196
Proctorville OH 45669

Call Sign: KD4JQG
Bridget M Waters
265 TR 1196
Proctorville OH 45669

Call Sign: N4GQ
Gordon M Waters III
265 TR 1196
Proctorville OH 45669

Call Sign: W8LQD
Larry T Murray Sr
259 TR 1204
Proctorville OH 45669

Call Sign: KC8WJL
Ian S Mc Comas
364 TR 1229
Proctorville OH 45669

Call Sign: KC4DSK
Clifford G Wilson III
437 TR 1233
Proctorville OH
456698417

Call Sign: KE4JNM
Suzanne S Wilson

437 TR 1233
Proctorville OH
456698417

Call Sign: N8KKZ
John P Ratcliff
486 TR 1233
Proctorville OH
456698417

Call Sign: AL7AH
Cyril W Reich
76 TR 1244
Proctorville OH 45669

Call Sign: N8SEA
Christine D Cartee
99 TR 1248 Burd Dr
Proctorville OH 45669

Call Sign: KB8TGK
John O Davis
130 TR 1252
Proctorville OH 45669

Call Sign: KC8YGW
Windell D Ely
42 TR 1307
Proctorville OH 45669

Call Sign: WD8CLR
James B Massie
180 TR 1387
Proctorville OH 45669

Call Sign: KC8CDT
Matthew J Maxson
1005 TR 149
Proctorville OH 45669

Call Sign: WA8HSY
James A Wheeler
46 TR 1539
Proctorville OH 45669

Call Sign: KC8LTY
Adam K Weed
168 Twp Rd 1053
Proctorville OH 45669

Call Sign: KC8WDS
Catherine Rice
280 Twp Rd 1163
Proctorville OH 45667

Call Sign: KD8HTB
James M Williams
132 Twp Rd 1244
Proctorville OH 45669

Call Sign: KC8YMC
Wayne A Elkins
72 Twp Rd 1305
Proctorville OH 45669

Call Sign: N8UNQ
Michael W Walker Jr
583 Twp Rd 221
Proctorville OH 45669

Call Sign: KF8WH
James W Smallridge
96 Twp Rd 87 W
Proctorville OH 45669

Call Sign: N8KDE
Ricky F Thacker
Proctorville OH 45669

Call Sign: K8WOI
Robert R Jeter Jr
Proctorville OH 45669

Call Sign: KC8ZAL
Roger D Dillon II
Proctorville OH 45669

Call Sign: K8CAP
James A Pierce

Proctorville OH
456690995

Call Sign: KA8CVU
Mary D Galloway
69509 Batesville Rd
Quaker City OH 43773

Call Sign: WD8KNY
Charles L Galloway
69509 Batesville Rd
Quaker City OH 43773

Call Sign: KD8HWB
Gerald W Shaffer
300 E Main St
Quaker City OH 43773

Call Sign: KD8ETP
Shane A Roe
59564 Eldon Rd
Quaker City OH 43773

Call Sign: K8BTD
Myron W Gilcher
23672 Penrose Rd
Quaker City OH
437739521

Call Sign: N8RAF
Larry R Mason
56569 St Johns Rd
Quaker City OH 43773

Call Sign: KD8MFB
Anne L Mason
56569 St Johns Rd
Quaker City OH 43773

Call Sign: N8ANA
Anne L Mason

56569 St Johns Rd
Quaker City OH 43773

Call Sign: WB8UXX
Robert E Dunn
56472 Sycamore Rd
Quaker City OH 43773

Call Sign: N8RFD
Carl R Hulse
56834 Whiskey Run
Quaker City OH 43773

Call Sign: KB8YDL
Gail L Garrett
56860 Whiskey Run
Quaker City OH 43773

Call Sign: KB8WBG
Larry M Garrett
56860 Whiskey Run
Quaker City OH 43773

Call Sign: KA8JAS
Greg Bergman
56717 Wilson Rd
Quaker City OH 43773

Call Sign: WB8KUA
Gary R Dollison
56288 Yoker Rd
Quaker City OH 43773

Call Sign: N8DQB
April Y Carpenter
Quaker City OH 43773

FCC Amateur Radio Licenses in Racine

Call Sign: KC8QDO
Jeffery M Rose
30679 Bashan Rd
Racine OH 45771

Call Sign: KB8MSD
Ivan P Powell
33101 Johnson Rd
Racine OH 45771

Call Sign: KC8MKW
Ronald W Wilson
49680 Manuel Rd
Racine OH 45771

Call Sign: WD8PHV
Jay E Pedigo
47741 TR 100
Racine OH 45771

Call Sign: KC8MPB
Gene D Lyons
Racine OH 457710101

FCC Amateur Radio Licenses in Radcliff

Call Sign: KB8UKV
Mary M Nairn
35819 Knox Rd
Radcliff OH 45695

Call Sign: KC8SVI
Jacqulyn J Jardine
36459 Malone Rd
Radcliff OH 45695

FCC Amateur Radio Licenses in Rarden

Call Sign: KC8BBU
Kennie L Cooper
1409 Back St
Rarden OH 45671

Call Sign: KF8YO
Randy N Groves
6069 Rarden Crk Rd
Rarden OH 45671

Call Sign: KB8VFL
Carl D Barber
Rarden OH 45671

FCC Amateur Radio Licenses in Ray

Call Sign: N8PNX
Steven C Benson
54399 Benson Rd
Ray OH 45672

Call Sign: N8ZOY
Louis C Hyman
1960 Bronx Cor Rd
Ray OH 45672

Call Sign: KC8LPY
David E Massie
56325 Doles Rd
Ray OH 45672

Call Sign: WA8WZT
Chester W Meadows
9092 Raysville Rd
Ray OH 45672

Call Sign: KD8GSO
Crystal D Spires
2617 Woodrow Hale Rd
Ray OH 45672

Call Sign: KD8FZM
Guy Spires
2617 Woodrow Hale Rd
Ray OH 45672

Call Sign: KD8GSQ
Kayla R Spires
2617 Woodrow Hale Rd
Ray OH 45672

FCC Amateur Radio Licenses in Reedsville

Call Sign: KC8UYS
William D Durst
55498 4th Ave
Reedsville OH 45772

Call Sign: KD8ALH
Angela K Powell
54920 Hudson Rd
Reedsville OH 45772

Call Sign: K8ZUY
Virgil C Shook
50655 Lickskillet Rd
Reedsville OH 45772

Call Sign: KC8OQB
Dirk J Kreiss
66010 St Rt 124
Reedsville OH 45772

Call Sign: KD8IEO
Benjammin T Sampson
49495 St Rt 681
Reedsville OH 45772

Call Sign: K8BTS
Benjammin T Sampson
49495 St Rt 681
Reedsville OH 45772

Call Sign: KD8HQI
Jenah M Sampson
49495 St Rt 681
Reedsville OH 45772

Call Sign: KC8LFH
Anthony M Sampson
49495 St Rt 681
Reedsville OH
457729738

Call Sign: KI8JK
Anthony M Sampson
49495 St Rt 681

Reedsville OH
457729738

Call Sign: KI4ZWC
Matthew L Ware
50101 St Rt 681
Reedsville OH 45772

Call Sign: KB8OFY
Ronald E Dodderer
50726 St Rt 681
Reedsville OH 45772

Call Sign: N8JQW
Karen A Criss
53166 St Rt 681
Reedsville OH 45772

Call Sign: KC8SHD
Travis L Fridenstine
53166 St Rt 681
Reedsville OH 45772

Call Sign: KD8KTR
Marcus T Carroll
39381 St Rt 7
Reedsville OH 45772

Call Sign: KI4OLA
Curtis E Pooler
41893 St Rt 7
Reedsville OH 45772

Call Sign: WA8NEC
Clyde J Gillilan
39137 Success Rd
Reedsville OH 45772

FCC Amateur Radio Licenses in Reno

Call Sign: KD8KFO
Jason M Riggs
2021 County Nine Rd
Reno OH 45773

FCC Amateur Radio Licenses in Rio Grande

Call Sign: KE8EC
Robert N Adkins
396 Buckeye Hills Rd
Rio Grande OH 45674

Call Sign: N8PRY
Ronald E Johnson
410.5 E College St
Rio Grande OH 45674

Call Sign: KC8NWY
Sarah M Miller
Rio Grande OH 45674

FCC Amateur Radio Licenses in Rock Camp

Call Sign: KC8MFW
John M Anson
Rock Camp OH 45675

FCC Amateur Radio Licenses in Rockbridge

Call Sign: KB8VJX
Robert L Majors
23744 Bigham Rd
Rockbridge OH 43149

Call Sign: KB8VPS
Mary L Majors
23744 Bigham Rd
Rockbridge OH 43149

Call Sign: KD8FSK
Patsy L Cartwright
10325 Buena Villa Rd
Rockbridge OH 43149

Call Sign: WD8KTO

Gary R Lamb
19541 Buena Vista Rd
Rockbridge OH
431499725

Call Sign: KD8HHX
Jasmine A Nicholson
23840 Dunlap Rd
Rockbridge OH 43149

Call Sign: W8FRY
Patricia A Frye
23840 Dunlap Rd
Rockbridge OH 43149

Call Sign: KA8EWM
Linn E Altman
25203 Extine Rd
Rockbridge OH 43149

Call Sign: KD8HPT
Paul H Linkous III
10532 Jackson St
Rockbridge OH 43149

Call Sign: KD8NEL
Harvey M Raynard Jr
15659 Kreashbaum Rd
Rockbridge OH 43149

Call Sign: KB8SIS
Gene A Pearsall
26664 Main St
Rockbridge OH 43149

Call Sign: KD8GST
Lacy P Barnes
22464 St Rt 180
Rockbridge OH 43149

Call Sign: KD8PRX
John Hill
26039 St Rt 180
Rockbridge OH 43149

Call Sign: KC8MEF
Timothy F Lehman
10681 St Rt 374
Rockbridge OH 43149

Call Sign: KC8NCH
Debra S Lehman
10681 St Rt 374
Rockbridge OH 43149

Call Sign: KD8PRW
Theodore A Cox
15938 Toad Run Rd
Rockbridge OH 43149

**FCC Amateur Radio
Licenses in Roseville**

Call Sign: N8GKL
Patrick J Robarge
5515 Cannelville Rd
Roseville OH 43777

Call Sign: N8ROA
Darrin L Strate
164 E Athens Rd
Roseville OH 43777

Call Sign: KA8GOO
Harold R Ansel
10475 Elks Run Rd
Roseville OH 43777

Call Sign: WD8CDV
Dwight R Barnhart
7330 Fultonrose Rd
Roseville OH 43777

Call Sign: KD8MSK
Michael B Sowers
7990 Fultonrose Rd
Roseville OH 43777

Call Sign: N8LJF
Donald J Parmiter

8125 Goose Crk Rd
Roseville OH 43777

Call Sign: KC8IHT
Dean R Parmiter
8125 Goosecreek Rd
Roseville OH 43777

Call Sign: KC8MBZ
Lynne H Parmiter
8125 Goosecreek Rd
Roseville OH
437779778

Call Sign: KD8ETD
Aaron B Miller
9055 Goosecreek Rd
Roseville OH 43777

Call Sign: KC8AN
Charles L Bishop
220 High St
Roseville OH 43777

Call Sign: KD8PDT
Austin M Dunn
8645 Maysville Pike
Roseville OH 43777

Call Sign: KC8AT
Ronald R Wesney
87 Old Rainer Rd
Roseville OH 43777

Call Sign: KD8HKQ
Joe E Grimm Jr
11964 Old Rainer Rd
Roseville OH 43777

Call Sign: KD8PEI
Thomas B Sefton
78 Peggy St
Roseville OH 43777

Call Sign: KC8PVU

George D Gillogly
140 Peggy St
Roseville OH 43777

Call Sign: KD8MPL
Isaiah J Hiles
6610 Sheila Cir
Roseville OH 43777

Call Sign: KC8QCB
Ronald M Rollison
112 Summit St
Roseville OH 43777

Call Sign: N8BOZ
David E Desguin
266 Tad Dr
Roseville OH 43777

Call Sign: KC8AVP
David L Williamson
242 W Athens Rd
Roseville OH 43777

Call Sign: N8XBC
David C Williamson
242 W Athens Rd
Roseville OH 43777

Call Sign: KD8MQW
Christopher J Walker
155.5 W Lake St
Roseville OH 43777

Call Sign: KC8AVO
Royston A Cleary
505 Zanesville Rd
Roseville OH 43777

FCC Amateur Radio Licenses in Rutland

Call Sign: KD8EZF
Eric S Sayre
39012 Carpenter Hill Rd

Rutland OH 45775

FCC Amateur Radio Licenses in Saint Clairsville

Call Sign: KC8DKR
Matthew E Mowrer
67610 Airport Rd
Saint Clairsville OH
43950

Call Sign: WB8EBT
Edward M Mowrer
67610 Airport Rd
Saint Clairsville OH
43950

Call Sign: WB8WHE
Russell T Rouse
104 Allen St
Saint Clairsville OH
43950

Call Sign: N8MTW
William J Woods
47054 Almar Cir
Saint Clairsville OH
43950

Call Sign: WO0DS
William J Woods
47054 Almar Cir
Saint Clairsville OH
43950

Call Sign: N8PPN
George T Cowen
67755 Almar W
Saint Clairsville OH
43950

Call Sign: KD8EFZ
Daniel J Eaton
108 Belmont Dr

Saint Clairsville OH
43950

Call Sign: KD8HAP
Richard W Eaton
108 Belmont Dr
Saint Clairsville OH
43950

Call Sign: KC8YAB
Gregory S Seese
203 Bethel Ln
Saint Clairsville OH
439501108

Call Sign: W6CPT
Gregory S Seese
203 Bethel Ln
Saint Clairsville OH
439501108

Call Sign: WB8JGY
Terence T Wadsworth
105 Bett Mar Ln
Saint Clairsville OH
43950

Call Sign: N8EJW
Robert R Sowinski
64635 Bull Run Rd
Saint Clairsville OH
43950

Call Sign: AB8DH
Donald J Houck Jr
50595 Cindy Dr Apt 22
Saint Clairsville OH
43950

Call Sign: N8HQO
Theodore C Shaffer
67081 Clark Rd
Saint Clairsville OH
43950

Call Sign: KC8FZI
Joel A Habursky
67379 Clark Rd
Saint Clairsville OH
43950

Call Sign: KC8WLB
Jeffrey D Ault
49822 Clyde St
Saint Clairsville OH
43950

Call Sign: KB3IVB
John H Wright
104 Coroline Dr
Saint Clairsville OH
43950

Call Sign: KC8GDW
William A Milan Jr
70900 CR 4
Saint Clairsville OH
43950

Call Sign: KB8TFQ
William L Stidd
69240 Crescent Rd
Saint Clairsville OH
43950

Call Sign: KB8UEN
Donald D Semancik
71178 Crescent Rd
Saint Clairsville OH
43950

Call Sign: KB8DNF
Cloyd R Michael Jr
38 E Almar Ln
Saint Clairsville OH
43950

Call Sign: WB8ZTR
Stephen A Mularcik
253 E Main St

Saint Clairsville OH
43950

Call Sign: KD8SAL
Nora J Holtsclaw
259 E Main St
Saint Clairsville OH
43950

Call Sign: KD8KOD
Bruce A Smith
282 E Main St
Saint Clairsville OH
43950

Call Sign: KD8NNV
Sheila S Smith
282 E Main St
Saint Clairsville OH
43950

Call Sign: KB8BUZ
Eleanor E Harris
71475 Fairpoint
Sheperdstown Rd
Saint Clairsville OH
43950

Call Sign: KD8NNW
Shayna L Smith
133 Franklin St
Saint Clairsville OH
43950

Call Sign: N8MTS
Robert L Thomason
66769 Glencoe Rd
Saint Clairsville OH
43950

Call Sign: KB8BIZ
Duncan C Kinder
68761 Hammond Rd
Saint Clairsville OH
43950

Call Sign: KB8EXB
Robert J Holubeck
244 Harbel Dr
Saint Clairsville OH
43950

Call Sign: KB8HVH
Jeffrey S Gazdik
51931 Hells Kitchen Rd
Saint Clairsville OH
43950

Call Sign: N8GMU
Cara L Gazdik
51931 Hells Kitchen Rd
Saint Clairsville OH
43950

Call Sign: WB8TQD
Charles R Meske
111 Hutchinson Dr
Saint Clairsville OH
439501116

Call Sign: K8IP
Isaac R Price
138 Hutchinson Dr
Saint Clairsville OH
43950

Call Sign: KC8RUH
William E Fairbanks
67066 Joella Dr
Saint Clairsville OH
43950

Call Sign: KA8VAY
Betty W Sharp
67156 Joella Dr
Saint Clairsville OH
43950

Call Sign: W9WE

Disciples Amateur
Radio Fellowship
67156 Joella Dr
Saint Clairsville OH
43950

Call Sign: K8AAS
Abram A Sharp
67156 Joella Dr
Saint Clairsville OH
439509447

Call Sign: WB8FKQ
Charles D Adkins
316 Johnet Dr
Saint Clairsville OH
43950

Call Sign: KC8EUQ
Beulah R Stelmach
49384 Johnson Dr
Saint Clairsville OH
43950

Call Sign: KC8EUS
Edmund L Stelmach Sr
49384 Johnson Dr
Saint Clairsville OH
43950

Call Sign: KB8DNM
Gary B Davenport II
71330 Kagg Hill Rd
Saint Clairsville OH
43950

Call Sign: KD8IWK
Karen S Tanley
72524 Kinsman Rd
Saint Clairsville OH
439509669

Call Sign: N8TAH
Kevin S Stephens
72526 Kinsman Rd

Saint Clairsville OH
43950

Call Sign: WB8JHW
Joshua S Witsberger
50023 Lin Chris Dr Lot
7
Saint Clairsville OH
43950

Call Sign: KD8IHV
Joshua S Witsberger
50023 Lin Chris Dr Lot
7
Saint Clairsville OH
43950

Call Sign: N8NLY
Elaine C Norris
46779 Lynn Dr
Saint Clairsville OH
43950

Call Sign: N8HQP
Clyde E Carpenter
46515 Magee Rd
Saint Clairsville OH
43950

Call Sign: KD8RMK
Robert A Mansfield
71465 Main St Lot 10
Saint Clairsville OH
43950

Call Sign: KD8SAK
Robert A Mansfield Jr
71465 Main St Lot 10
Saint Clairsville OH
43950

Call Sign: N8WXI
Joyce A Dorsch
72889 Mercer Rd

Saint Clairsville OH
43950

Call Sign: KA8DJI
Marion T Ruminski
51070 Methodist Ridge
Rd
Saint Clairsville OH
439509217

Call Sign: W8GBH
Eastern OH Amateur
Wireless Assn
67689 Mills Rd
Saint Clairsville OH
43950

Call Sign: W8TPY
Eastern OH Amateur
Wireless Assn
67689 Mills Rd
Saint Clairsville OH
43950

Call Sign: N8UTS
Robert W Hunt
67810 Mills Rd
Saint Clairsville OH
43950

Call Sign: W8ROB
Robby L Fish
67689 Mills Rd
Saint Clairsville OH
43950

Call Sign: KD8DWB
Denise H Fish
67689 Mills Rd
Saint Clairsville OH
43950

Call Sign: WF1SHY
Denise H Fish
67689 Mills Rd

Saint Clairsville OH
43950

Call Sign: WD8CEP
Andrew R Wildman
197 Milrose Dr
Saint Clairsville OH
43950

Call Sign: KD8HWH
Susan L Stevens-Crosby
123 N Market St
Saint Clairsville OH
43950

Call Sign: KC8FQS
Emil J Slavik
124 N Sugar St
Saint Clairsville OH
43950

Call Sign: KB8DNN
Tony J Cavicchia
149 N Sugar St
Saint Clairsville OH
43950

Call Sign: KB5QJA
Matthew R Koch
45045 National Rd
Saint Clairsville OH
43950

Call Sign: N2NOF
Robert N Leonard
107 Newell Ave Apt
215
Saint Clairsville OH
439501253

Call Sign: WB8TQH
Martin S Bertus
107 Norris
Saint Clairsville OH
43950

Call Sign: KD8JXO
Jasmine A Anderson
104 Norris St
Saint Clairsville OH
43950

Call Sign: KA3GKG
James D Patrizi Jr
49495 Oldefield Dr
Saint Clairsville OH
43950

Call Sign: WB8WHD
William D Ryan
120 Orchard Dr
Saint Clairsville OH
43950

Call Sign: KD8LNU
Homer D Harden
119 Park Dr
Saint Clairsville OH
439501307

Call Sign: NM8D
Richard E Barr
114 Parshall Ave
Saint Clairsville OH
43950

Call Sign: WM8R
Ben Scales
67948 Pickering Rd
Saint Clairsville OH
43950

Call Sign: KC8GTC
Lois J Millhouse
71999 Prokes Rd
Saint Clairsville OH
43950

Call Sign: KC8HFS
Kenneth E Millhouse

71999 Prokes Rd
Saint Clairsville OH
43950

Call Sign: KD8DAB
Khorren M Lally
72441 Prokes Rd
Saint Clairsville OH
43950

Call Sign: KA8VAR
Richard A Howell
69641 Provident Rd
Saint Clairsville OH
43950

Call Sign: N8TOF
Ralph J Hadley Jr
49080 Randal Dr
Richland Acres
Saint Clairsville OH
43950

Call Sign: KD8OUI
Daniel E Tarleton
48271 Reservior Rd
Saint Clairsville OH
43950

Call Sign: WB8ZTN
Ted L Ruminski
48397 Reservoir Rd
Saint Clairsville OH
43950

Call Sign: WB8ZTO
Stanley J Ruminski
48397 Reservoir Rd
Saint Clairsville OH
43950

Call Sign: WA3OJH
David C Ruminski
48393 Reservoir Rd

Saint Clairsville OH
43950

Call Sign: W8DCR
David C Ruminski
48393 Reservoir Rd
Saint Clairsville OH
43950

Call Sign: WB8HKK
John E Sowinski
66397 Richwood Rd
Saint Clairsville OH
43950

Call Sign: KC8UJK
Sheila Lokosky
45761 Roscoe Rd
Saint Clairsville OH
43950

Call Sign: KC3EP
Richard F Ray
108 Sunset Dr
Saint Clairsville OH
439501128

Call Sign: KB8IPA
Brian R Sandridge
67821 Tulane Rd
Saint Clairsville OH
43950

Call Sign: KB8TFS
Richard P Steele
46637 W Almar Ln
Saint Clairsville OH
43950

Call Sign: K8RPS
Richard P Steele
46637 W Almar Ln
Saint Clairsville OH
43950

Call Sign: WA8RIW
Arthur J Hartman Jr
67300 Warnock Rd Rd 3
Saint Clairsville OH
43950

Call Sign: KC8URM
Robert M Ball Jr
103 Westminster Dr
Saint Clairsville OH
43950

Call Sign: WB8IIL
Arthur W Heiniger
108 Willinda Dr
Saint Clairsville OH
43950

Call Sign: WB8ZUE
Michael J Chaplin Jr
67398 Willow Grove
Pike
Saint Clairsville OH
43950

Call Sign: KB8VPL
Gladys L Landers
67474 Willow Grove Rd
Saint Clairsville OH
43950

Call Sign: WB4ZKO
Russell W Landers
67474 Willow Grove Rd
Saint Clairsville OH
43950

Call Sign: KB8OIV
Donald L Mc Cloud
Saint Clairsville OH
43950

Call Sign: KG9QP
Donald L Mc Cloud

Saint Clairsville OH
43950

FCC Amateur Radio
Licenses in Salesville

Call Sign: KA8TEH
Garrett R Jones
129 Main
Salesville OH 43778

Call Sign: KC8WOU
Theodore A Fidelholtz
126 Main St
Salesville OH 43778

Call Sign: N8XEV
Debra K Jones
129 Main St Box 29
Salesville OH 43778

Call Sign: N8BUR
Gary W Jones
Salesville OH 43778

FCC Amateur Radio
Licenses in Sarahsville

Call Sign: KD8HKW
Michael G Ramage
23120 Bates Rd
Sarahsville OH 43779

Call Sign: KD8JVZ
Joshua D Cowgill
50511 Cowgill Rd
Sarahsville OH 43779

Call Sign: KD8CNN
Michael J Branch II
51711 Mt Ephraim Pike
Sarahsville OH 43779

Call Sign: KD8ESO
Chris D Steed

48833 Seneca Lk Rd
Sarahsville OH 43779

Call Sign: KD8JWB
Corey G Bates
50715 Seneca Lk Rd
Sarahsville OH 43779

Call Sign: KD8JVC
William C Rich
51105 Seneca Lk Rd
Sarahsville OH 43779

Call Sign: KC8OXU
William H Smith
20820 TR 449
Sarahsville OH 43779

Call Sign: KC8WOV
Susan M Glunt
50550 Twp Rd 134
Sarahsville OH 43779

Call Sign: KD8MPR
Stephen B Watson
49301 Zep Rd W
Sarahsville OH 43779

FCC Amateur Radio Licenses in Sardis

Call Sign: KC8BTZ
Bernard K Knight
51421 Baptist Ridge Rd
Sardis OH 43946

Call Sign: KC8WNN
Bert K Knight
51421 Baptist Ridge Rd
Sardis OH 43946

Call Sign: WA8FMD
Leo R Cattabiani Sr
48375 Benwood Rd
Sardis OH 43946

Call Sign: KC8ECW
Loretta L Knight
37295 Marietta St
Sardis OH 43946

Call Sign: KN8BK
Bernard K Knight
37295 Marietta St
Sardis OH 43946

Call Sign: KB8LLY
Barry B Butler
48244 SR 255
Sardis OH 43946

Call Sign: N8NEB
William E Butler Jr
48244 SR 255
Sardis OH 43946

Call Sign: KB8ZZD
Stanley B Maienknecht
38648 SR 800
Sardis OH 43946

Call Sign: KC8AZO
Theresa A Maienknecht
38648 SR 800
Sardis OH 43946

Call Sign: WD8PVM
Robert N Mease
34375 St Rt 7
Sardis OH 43946

Call Sign: N8MTP
Gene R Morris
38475 St Rt 800
Sardis OH 43946

Call Sign: N8QFM
Doris J Morris
38475 St Rt 800
Sardis OH 439469724

Call Sign: KC8AZQ
Charles O Blue
Sardis OH 43946

Call Sign: WD8DZO
Gerald E Kocher
Sardis OH 439460125

FCC Amateur Radio Licenses in Sciotoville

Call Sign: W8MEM
Charles N Quillen
1201 Allard St
Sciotoville OH 45662

Call Sign: KC8JDZ
Beverly D Williams
5571 Auburn Ave
Sciotoville OH 45662

Call Sign: KA8NWV
Carl E Crabtree Sr
2211 Bonser Run Rd
Sciotoville OH 45662

Call Sign: N8NUC
Paul E Adams
Box 178A
Sciotoville OH 45662

Call Sign: N8NXK
Patricia A Adams
Box 178A
Sciotoville OH 45662

Call Sign: KA8CGY
Raymond E Atkins
Box 400
Sciotoville OH 45662

Call Sign: KC8RCB
Gib L Carver
416 Eastern Ave

Sciotoville OH 45662

Call Sign: K8GLC
Gib L Carver
416 Eastern Ave
Sciotoville OH 45662

Call Sign: KC8VSQ
Kimberly K Carver
416 Eastern Ave
Sciotoville OH 45662

Call Sign: W8KKC
Kimberly K Carver
416 Eastern Ave
Sciotoville OH 45662

Call Sign: K1TBL
Richard N Duffany
5916 Kentland Ave
Sciotoville OH 45662

Call Sign: KC8NTL
James R Minturn
49 Lower Camp Rd
Sciotoville OH 45662

Call Sign: N8ZO
James R Minturn
49 Lower Camp Rd
Sciotoville OH 45662

Call Sign: KB8QEG
Rita F Robirds
851 Mathiott St
Sciotoville OH 45662

Call Sign: KB8SSL
Vondon V Newman
7433 Ohio River Rd
Sciotoville OH 45662

Call Sign: WB8SLL
Allen W Keffer
Rt 2

Sciotoville OH 45662

**FCC Amateur Radio
Licenses in Scottown**

Call Sign: KD8MWI
Paul A Pierce
3124 CR 37
Scottown OH 45678

Call Sign: N8PAP
Paul A Pierce
3124 CR 37
Scottown OH 45678

Call Sign: KC8CWN
Chloe I Callicoat
1157 CR 67
Scottown OH 45678

Call Sign: WA8WOY
Cleo G Watson
9662 St Rt 217
Scottown OH 45678

Call Sign: KA8ANC
Danny J Watson
9748 St Rt 217
Scottown OH 45678

Call Sign: N8XZR
Tyrone J Jenkins
10 Twp Rd 212 S
Scottown OH 45678

**FCC Amateur Radio
Licenses in Senecaville**

Call Sign: KB8NHF
Dan E Timura
406 Bridge St
Senecaville OH 43780

Call Sign: KD8PKZ
Dan E Timura

406 Bridge St
Senecaville OH 43780

Call Sign: KD8PEJ
Adam M Smithberger
56880 Cherry Hill Rd
Senecaville OH 43780

Call Sign: N8GDH
Nickolas L Miller
54590 Lakeland Rd
Senecaville OH 43780

Call Sign: KC8MFK
Donald E Shoemaker Sr
14344 Leatherwood Cir
Senecaville OH
437809561

Call Sign: KC8MFL
Betty M Shoemaker
14344 Leatherwood Cir
Senecaville OH
437809561

Call Sign: WA8RPK
Thomas L Moore Sr
58071 Richport Dr
Senecaville OH
437809455

Call Sign: N8NJB
Alban L Hunter
58579 Soggy Run Rd
Senecaville OH 43780

Call Sign: N8RFC
Elvin L Wickham
14740 Walhonding Rd
Senecaville OH 43780

**FCC Amateur Radio
Licenses in Shade**

Call Sign: KC8KSM

Robert F Moore
40193 Burlingham Rd
Shade OH 45776

Call Sign: NJ8V
Dewey F King
1035 King Rd
Shade OH 45776

Call Sign: KC8UYP
Charles C Arnott
13855 Rainbow Lk Rd
Shade OH 45776

Call Sign: KB8WQM
Charles E Williams
41100 S 33
Shade OH 45776

Call Sign: N8FAA
William F Kane
15151 Slab Rd
Shade OH 45776

Call Sign: WR8C
Stephen D Kane
15500 Slab Rd
Shade OH 45776

Call Sign: KC8THG
David H Smith
39271 St Rt 681
Shade OH 45776

Call Sign: KA8WPU
Richard A Lawless
2310 US Hwy 33
Shade OH 45776

**FCC Amateur Radio
Licenses in Shadyside**

Call Sign: KB8MPH
Ronald R Brown
59321 Broadview Rd

Shadyside OH 43947

Call Sign: N8SIK
Rebecca J Brown
59321 Broadview Rd
Shadyside OH 43947

Call Sign: KB8WIM
Josef J Meholovitch
59550 Cash Hill Rd
Shadyside OH 43947

Call Sign: N8ZAI
Richard W Mason
59805 Cash Hill Rd
Shadyside OH 43947

Call Sign: N8ZEX
Chad R Mason
59805 Cash Hill Rd
Shadyside OH 43947

Call Sign: KB8WIL
Kandy L Oyler
55760 Cash Ridge Rd
Shadyside OH 43947

Call Sign: KC8TEC
Paul B Strope
3520 Central Ave
Shadyside OH 43947

Call Sign: KC8VFC
Allen R Rogers
4008 Central Ave
Shadyside OH
439470713

Call Sign: WD8DDE
Solomon E Crow
25 E 37th St
Shadyside OH 43947

Call Sign: KA8CDC
Robert T Crow

25 E 37th St
Shadyside OH 43947

Call Sign: N8KFA
William M Le Masters
Jr
126 Kennedy Ln
Shadyside OH 43947

Call Sign: WC8V
Carl W Williams
3750 Leona Ave
Shadyside OH 43947

Call Sign: KB8FEA
Glen L Crippen
3497 Prospect Ave
Shadyside OH 43947

Call Sign: N8HQM
David W Crippen
3497 Prospect Ave
Shadyside OH 43947

Call Sign: N8HQN
Gary L Crippen
3497 Prospect Ave
Shadyside OH 43947

Call Sign: N8XEU
Rose M Yourkovich
62003 Rolling Hills Ln
Shadyside OH 43947

Call Sign: WB8ZTK
Louis W Yourkovich Jr
62003 Rolling Hills Ln
Shadyside OH
439479749

Call Sign: KC8VMC
Bradley D Johnston
102 W 40th St
Shadyside OH 43947

Call Sign: K8QXS
James E Thomas Jr
319 W 40th St
Shadyside OH 43947

Call Sign: KA8CDF
Richard P Mc Gee
554 W 40th St
Shadyside OH
439471165

Call Sign: WA4BHA
Louis F Gross
170 W 45th St
Shadyside OH
439471035

Call Sign: W8AHU
Arthur E Fernandez Sr
444 W 45th St
Shadyside OH
439471037

Call Sign: KB8QOP
Connie D Thuring
61285 Webb Heights Rd
Shadyside OH 43947

Call Sign: KB8QVQ
Richard D Thuring
61285 Webb Heights Rd
Shadyside OH 43947

Call Sign: KB8TFR
Susan L Morgan
61360 Webb Heights Rd
Shadyside OH 43947

Call Sign: WD8CBC
John S Morgan
61360 Webb Heights Rd
Shadyside OH
439479744

Call Sign: KB8KKI

Bruce D Williams
55471 Wegee Rd
Shadyside OH 43947

FCC Amateur Radio Licenses in Shawnee

Call Sign: KD8HLB
Brandon A Spencer
7720 Twp Rd 498
Shawnee OH 43782

FCC Amateur Radio Licenses in Somerset

Call Sign: K6LHF
Wayne C Henderson
208 Fancy St
Somerset OH
437839509

Call Sign: KC8BUP
Kenneth E Eyerman
5870 SR 669 NE
Somerset OH 43783

Call Sign: K8SRJ
Charles R Dossett
9435 SR 757
Somerset OH 43783

Call Sign: KB8MRL
Jala L Ward
6530 St Rt 13 NE
Somerset OH 43783

Call Sign: KD8ETB
Jason M Saffell
6675 St Rt 13 NE
Somerset OH 43783

Call Sign: N8FFH
John R Dossett
9435 St Rt 757

Somerset OH
437839696

Call Sign: N8NKG
Sean K Benson
6650 Tollgate Rd NW
Somerset OH 43783

Call Sign: WB8DDA
Ronald O Smucker
3615 Twp Rd 123 NE
Somerset OH 43783

Call Sign: KB8YZG
Clarence O Duncan
3495 Twp Rd 418
Somerset OH 43783

Call Sign: KD8QCA
Timothy N Lentz
5284 US Hwy 22 NW
Somerset OH
437839661

Call Sign: KB8SIT
Richard F Hale Jr
2260 US Rt 22
Somerset OH 43783

Call Sign: KI8BZ
James D Ferguson Jr
113 W Sheridan Ave
Somerset OH
437830522

Call Sign: KA4IQD
Steven R Carter
Somerset OH 43783

FCC Amateur Radio Licenses in South Bloomingville

Call Sign: K8UID
Ronald A Diehl

19900 Lindsay Rd
South Bloomingville
OH 43152

Call Sign: KB8TKR
Kay G Gossett
22790 SR 56
South Bloomingville
OH 43152

**FCC Amateur Radio
Licenses in South Point**

Call Sign: WA8KPG
Merlin R Stanley
908 4th St E
South Point OH 45680

Call Sign: KB8CAU
Vinson L Kincaid
1202 4th St E
South Point OH 45680

Call Sign: N8SDY
Jeffrey A Gaskin
202 6th St
South Point OH 45680

Call Sign: KB8LIV
David Crabtree
Box 270
South Point OH 45680

Call Sign: KD8FGF
Glendale Mcclurg
2422 CR 1
South Point OH 45680

Call Sign: KD8GYB
Glendale L Mcclurg
2422 CR 1
South Point OH 45680

Call Sign: KD8MHX
Glendale L Mcclurg

2422 CR 1
South Point OH 45680

Call Sign: KD8QMA
Glendale L Mcclurg
2422 CR 1
South Point OH 45680

Call Sign: KD8ATA
Shawn G Smith
1084 CR 120
South Point OH 45680

Call Sign: KB8WQE
Zandra L King
79 CR 15
South Point OH 45680

Call Sign: KC8DXQ
Bill E King
79 CR 15
South Point OH 45680

Call Sign: KF8ZB
Robert M Harrison
405 Dean St
South Point OH 45680

Call Sign: W8HJR
Wayne Herald Jr
113 Franklin St
South Point OH 45680

Call Sign: W8IA
Wayne Herald Jr
113 Franklin St
South Point OH 45680

Call Sign: AB8BX
David E Snyder
118 Freeman Ct Apt B
South Point OH 45680

Call Sign: KA8QIY
Arnold R Vaughan

103 High St
South Point OH 45680

Call Sign: AA8EN
Gary N Booth
102 Lawrence Ave
South Point OH 45680

Call Sign: N8SDZ
Kevin L Mc Fann
104 Lea St
South Point OH 45680

Call Sign: KD8MI
Carl M Brammer
106 Mills Ln
South Point OH 45680

Call Sign: KC8WDQ
David H Staten
106 N Kenova Rd
South Point OH 45680

Call Sign: KT8I
Larry D Tawney
107 N Kenova Rd
South Point OH 45680

Call Sign: N8SLA
Timothy Breeding
Private Dr 54
South Point OH 45680

Call Sign: N8SKZ
Lesa D Breeding
160 Private Dr 54 Unit
C
South Point OH 45680

Call Sign: AG8Q
John P Goodson
102 Roberts St
South Point OH 45680

Call Sign: KF4GCI

Paul B Hannah
604 Solida Rd
South Point OH 45680

Call Sign: KA8ZZI
James M Brown
306 TR 1026
South Point OH 45680

Call Sign: KA8MVG
Jerry Harmon Jr
149 TR 1030
South Point OH
456807880

Call Sign: W8REY
Frederick W Schilling
127 TR 1034
South Point OH 45680

Call Sign: KB8LOV
John W Norris Jr
1195 TR 276 N
South Point OH 45680

Call Sign: KB8QLM
Frances J Norris
1195 TR 276N
South Point OH 45680

Call Sign: KD8NCQ
James F Costello
Trl 1430 Apt 19
South Point OH 45680

Call Sign: KB8NWR
Kenneth K Hileman
65 Twp Rd 1428 W
South Point OH 45680

Call Sign: KB8ZRU
Barbara J Hileman
65 Twp Rd 1428 W
South Point OH 45680

Call Sign: KB8CJB
Charles E Callicoat
94 Twsp Rd 1187
South Point OH 45680

Call Sign: KD8JEA
Julie A Suiter
106 Washington Ave
South Point OH 45680

Call Sign: KA8VWR
Joseph F Brown Jr
201 Washington Ave
South Point OH
456809654

Call Sign: K8QZQ
Kenneth J Bell
South Point OH 45680

Call Sign: N8XXT
Paul W Niles
South Point OH 45680

Call Sign: WA8FOE
Rita A Bell
South Point OH 45680

Call Sign: N8TVS
Thomas L Dobbins
South Point OH 45680

Call Sign: WB8LUR
Donald E Pennisten
South Point OH 45680

Call Sign: KC8VYC
Robert L Slaughter
South Point OH 45680

Call Sign: KD8JDY
Sammy K Suiter Jr
South Point OH 45680

FCC Amateur Radio Licenses in South Salem

Call Sign: WD8AII
Jamima I Schiller
4526 Broadway St
South Salem OH 45681

Call Sign: KD8ONY
Rick L Boggs
701 Fordyce Rd
South Salem OH 45681

Call Sign: KA8EQT
Arthur J Corbin
2555 Pricer Ridge
South Salem OH 45681

Call Sign: KA8HDC
Betty D Corbin
2555 Pricer Ridge Rd
South Salem OH 45681

Call Sign: KB8BZL
Larry J Corbin
2555 Pricer Ridge Rd
South Salem OH 45681

Call Sign: KB8OTS
Rebecca A Corbin
2555 Pricer Ridge Rd
South Salem OH 45681

Call Sign: KB8OWJ
Robert P Jones
7321 Upper Twin Rd
South Salem OH 45681

Call Sign: KC8DYD
Sharon K Crusie
8110 Upper Twin Rd
South Salem OH 45681

FCC Amateur Radio Licenses in South Webster

Call Sign: KC8DZY
Mary L Slone
30 Bear Run Rd
South Webster OH
45682

Call Sign: N8EAS
Edward A Sims
15055 Lick Run Lyra
Rd
South Webster OH
45682

Call Sign: N8WUU
Kevin L Roark
South Webster OH
45682

FCC Amateur Radio Licenses in South Zanesville

Call Sign: KB8KV
Randall L Kirkbride
48 Beechrock Dr
South Zanesville OH
43701

Call Sign: KD8ONP
Amy J Lent
2755 Chandlersville Rd
South Zanesville OH
43701

Call Sign: KB8MGQ
Robert L Kirkbride
80 Charles St
South Zanesville OH
43701

Call Sign: KD8MSQ

William L Rowe
2656 Cinema Dr
South Zanesville OH
43701

Call Sign: KC8MN
Granvil Bolen
62 Codell Ln
South Zanesville OH
43701

Call Sign: N8DFM
Cleta M Bolen
62 Codell Ln
South Zanesville OH
43701

Call Sign: KC8PLO
Paul E Gibbons
3700 Colony Hill Dr
South Zanesville OH
43701

Call Sign: KC8SUM
Robert J Miller
30 Crown Cir
South Zanesville OH
43701

Call Sign: KD8MPS
Adam P Young
285 Deerfield Rd
South Zanesville OH
43701

Call Sign: KD8PDR
William Dalrymple
3475 Foxfire Dr
South Zanesville OH
43701

Call Sign: KD8RZW
Jerod S Untied
18 Gaslight Dr

South Zanesville OH
43701

Call Sign: KD8MPN
Jeffery W Lloyd
37 Hazel Ave
South Zanesville OH
43701

Call Sign: KD8PDU
Jacob M Durant
705 Jersey Ridge Rd
South Zanesville OH
43701

Call Sign: KD8PEO
Tanner P Wilson
3154 Lakewood Dr
South Zanesville OH
43701

Call Sign: KD8PEN
Seth A Williamson
323 Lucia Ct
South Zanesville OH
43701

Call Sign: KD8PDZ
Abraham J Hajjar
1115 Maple Ave
South Zanesville OH
437013030

Call Sign: KB8JVL
Chester F England
98 Montague Ave
South Zanesville OH
43701

Call Sign: KD8PPA
Brittney N Hartley
231 N Blackwood Dr
South Zanesville OH
43701

Call Sign: KD8MPI
Coleman E Forrestal
2427 Oakwood Ave
South Zanesville OH
43701

Call Sign: KC8US
Benjamin F Bender Sr
125 Rains Cir
South Zanesville OH
437016292

Call Sign: KD8MVG
David L Delaney
6800 Ridge Rd
South Zanesville OH
43701

Call Sign: KB8JVM
Leonard L Fluhart Jr
67 Shawnee Ave
South Zanesville OH
43701

Call Sign: KD8PDO
Jacob H Ball
100 Sletzer Dr
South Zanesville OH
43701

Call Sign: KD8KZO
James Cash
1657 Spruce St
South Zanesville OH
43701

Call Sign: KB8OHJ
John L Mc Elfresh
20 W Berkley St
South Zanesville OH
43701

Call Sign: KD8PJC
Edward R Gallis
3715 Wesley Chapel Rd

South Zanesville OH
43701

Call Sign: KD8PDV
Steven A Durant
1294 Wheeling Ave
South Zanesville OH
43701

FCC Amateur Radio Licenses in Stewart

Call Sign: KA8TKO
Jon D Tobin
10070 Featherstone Rd
Stewart OH 45778

Call Sign: KC8JWS
Adam K Brozak
9903 New England Rd
Stewart OH 45778

Call Sign: KA8PJQ
Donald E Carter
11499 St Rt 329
Stewart OH 45778

Call Sign: KD8MN
Patrick D Quinn
19790 Winner Ln
Stewart OH 45778

FCC Amateur Radio Licenses in Stockport

Call Sign: AA8JC
Rodney G Mc Grew
1725 Broadway St
Stockport OH 43787

Call Sign: KC8OIH
Ty R James
3223 Chase Hill Rd
Stockport OH 43787

Call Sign: KD8ESR
Samantha C Drobina
520 Groah Rd
Stockport OH 43787

Call Sign: WB8TVO
Ralph E Bosworth Jr
6375 Lightner Ridge Rd
Stockport OH 43787

Call Sign: KD8PEE
Rodney B Ponchak
1077 McCoy Ridge Rd
Stockport OH 43787

Call Sign: KC8LN
Donald W Rode
1015 Pugh Rd
Stockport OH 43787

Call Sign: KC8SZ
Betty Jo Rode
1015 Pugh Rd
Stockport OH 43787

Call Sign: KD8MSW
John W Hickerson
565 S Elliott Rd
Stockport OH 43787

Call Sign: N8FID
Richard R Tuten
480 S St Rt 266 SE
Stockport OH 43787

Call Sign: WA8GVX
Michael C Turner
3977 Turner Rd
Stockport OH 43787

Call Sign: KC8HFU
Jennifer L Mc Grew
Stockport OH 43787

FCC Amateur Radio Licenses in Summerfield

Call Sign: KD8MPW
Aaron C Grywalski
49455 Glady Rd
Summerfield OH 43788

Call Sign: K8NBZ
Francis E Yuncker
50910 TR 228
Summerfield OH 43788

Call Sign: KD8MPT
Aaron W Bridgman
27025 Woodsfield Rd
Summerfield OH 43788

FCC Amateur Radio Licenses in Syracuse

Call Sign: KC8MOW
Trisha I Gibson
2377 4th St
Syracuse OH 45779

Call Sign: KB8PUV
Patsy A Warner
2383 4th St
Syracuse OH 45779

Call Sign: KC8LFI
Robert E Byer
2227 7th St
Syracuse OH
457790117

Call Sign: KA8GUH
Daniel A Hayman
2176 Karr St
Syracuse OH
457790422

Call Sign: KC8JWT

Matthew F Morris
Marina Dr
Syracuse OH 45779

Call Sign: KD8FL
Jeffrey L Fields
Syracuse OH 45779

Call Sign: KG8IT
James D Warner
Syracuse OH 45779

Call Sign: KC8UYR
Travis L Gibson
Syracuse OH 45779

FCC Amateur Radio Licenses in The Plains

Call Sign: KC8SIN
Shane A Sloan
99 Bean Rd Lot51
The Plains OH 45780

Call Sign: KC2JGV
Aaron D Venezia
4 Blossom Ln
The Plains OH 45780

Call Sign: KD8FRN
Garry E Bruce
93 Clinton St
The Plains OH 45780

Call Sign: KC8ZBR
Jonathan A Jarvis
6 Cross St
The Plains OH 45780

Call Sign: KC8ZBS
Scott H Jarvis
6 Cross St
The Plains OH 45780

Call Sign: AB8SQ

Scott H Jarvis
6 Cross St
The Plains OH 45780

Call Sign: K8GWH
Lloyd M Graham Sr
14 E 1st St
The Plains OH 45780

Call Sign: KC8YXV
Olena S Wilshanetsky
E 1st St
The Plains OH 45780

Call Sign: KC8AAP
Daniel L Adams
7924 Floyd Dr
The Plains OH 45780

Call Sign: KB8TFL
David J Moorehead
7931 Floyd Dr
The Plains OH
457801403

Call Sign: WI8G
Jason D Licht
28 Grant St
The Plains OH 45780

Call Sign: AC8GA
Jason D Licht
28 Grant St
The Plains OH 45780

Call Sign: W8QO
Jason D Licht
28 Grant St
The Plains OH 45780

Call Sign: KG8JL
Jason D Licht
28 Grant St
The Plains OH 45780

Call Sign: K8AHS
Athens High School
ARC
1 High School Rd
The Plains OH 45780

Call Sign: KC8DXZ
Athens High School
ARC
1 High School Rd
The Plains OH 45780

Call Sign: N3GDC
James E Staebler
7 Main St
The Plains OH 45780

Call Sign: KC8ZUZ
Nathan A Chapman
65 N Plains Rd
The Plains OH 45780

Call Sign: KB8LPT
N Matthew Wright III
34 Poston Rd
The Plains OH 45780

Call Sign: KD8MZA
Peter A Wickman
36 Poston Rd Apt 4
The Plains OH 45780

Call Sign: N8MUQ
Alex C,Neimayer
36 Poston Rd Apt 5
The Plains OH 45780

Call Sign: WD8IUY
Robert E Williams
184 S Plains Rd
The Plains OH 45780

Call Sign: KD8NLI
Hans Hake
10450 St Rt 682

The Plains OH 45780

Call Sign: KA8YMH
William M Johnson Jr
26 Sunset Ln
The Plains OH 45780

Call Sign: W8VKJ
Carrol A Riley
35 W 1st St
The Plains OH 45780

Call Sign: N8CCM
Clyde D Baker
53 W 1st St
The Plains OH 45780

Call Sign: KC8UYQ
Curtis E Barnes
The Plains OH 45780

Call Sign: W8CEB
Curtis E Barnes
The Plains OH 45780

Call Sign: KC8WMZ
Darry V Michael
The Plains OH 45780

Call Sign: KC8MNA
Marcia A Welch
The Plains OH
457800159

**FCC Amateur Radio
Licenses in Thornville**

Call Sign: KC8PWC
Terry L Sykes
7440 Baltimore
Somerset Rd
Thornville OH 43076

Call Sign: K8DRM
Dennis R Blank

15078 Harbor Point Dr
W
Thornville OH 43076

Call Sign: N8RQG
Charles K Lawrence
328 Hickory Way
Thornville OH 43076

Call Sign: KC8ASA
Ray H Blair Jr
4956 Island Ave
Thornville OH 43076

Call Sign: KA8ZPF
John T Camm
13404 Ivy Rd
Thornville OH 43076

Call Sign: W8JTC
John T Camm
13404 Ivy Rd
Thornville OH 43076

Call Sign: KB8ESR
Thomas E Camm
13404 Ivy Rd
Thornville OH 43076

Call Sign: K8CSE
Roxie L Kern
13420 King Rd
Thornville OH 43076

Call Sign: K8CSF
Roland L Kern
13420 King Rd
Thornville OH 43076

Call Sign: KA8YBT
Phyllis I Murnane
12115 Laurel Hill Rd
Thornville OH 43076

Call Sign: W8WRP

James A Horvat
86 N Court
Thornville OH 43076

Call Sign: KC8LVQ
Kevin L Page
18 N Main St
Thornville OH 43076

Call Sign: AC8GI
Kevin L Page
18 N Main St
Thornville OH 43076

Call Sign: KA8AFE
Robert M Cunningham
10817 National Rd
Thornville OH 43076

Call Sign: KB8OEC
Deborah K Cunningham
10817 National Rd
Thornville OH 43076

Call Sign: KB8OEL
Robert M Cunningham
Jr
10817 National Rd
Thornville OH 43076

Call Sign: WA8STF
Henry C Robinson
13341 NE Pine Rd Rr 3
Thornville OH 43076

Call Sign: KB8POS
Jamie R Wilson
10587 Roley Hills SE
Thornville OH 43076

Call Sign: KB7QBB
Gregory A Ardrey
7400 Rushcreek Rd NW
Thornville OH 43076

Call Sign: N8NUG
Paul D Hester
10443 Shelley Rd
Thornville OH 43076

Call Sign: KC8NGP
Nicholas A Hester
10443 Shelly Rd
Thornville OH 43076

Call Sign: KB8SXJ
George W Franey
8477 Somerset Rd
Thornville OH
430769390

Call Sign: WE8V
Ronald N Jones
8221 Somerset Rd SE
Thornville OH
430768810

Call Sign: KB8NAN
Gwen M West
11479 St Rd 204
Thornville OH 43076

Call Sign: KB8ZUD
Barry Moore
11711 St Rt 13 NW
Thornville OH 43076

Call Sign: KB8LRR
Michael W Harris II
25 St Rt 204
Thornville OH 43076

Call Sign: AA8GH
George M West
11479 St Rt 204
Thornville OH 43076

Call Sign: KB8NAM
Becky E West
11479 St Rt 204

Thornville OH 43076

Call Sign: KB8PWD
Jarrod L Rhodes
7640 Star Rd
Thornville OH 43076

Call Sign: W8APD
Harry E Secrest
11800 TR 406
Thornville OH 43076

Call Sign: K7WE
Richard E Loeckel
5120 TR 98
Thornville OH 43076

Call Sign: K8FS
Donald J Murphy
11559 Twp Rd 390 NW
Thornville OH 43076

Call Sign: KB8GWB
Kelly J Snoke
7255 Woolard Rd
Thornville OH
430768707

Call Sign: WD8IXO
Scott A Snoke
7255 Woolard Rd NE
Thornville OH
430768707

Call Sign: KB5KCN
Roger H Lucas
Thornville OH 43076

Call Sign: KC8COO
James E Smith
Thornville OH 43076

Call Sign: KD8ORP
Kira D Harris
Thornville OH 43076

Call Sign: KD8LSV
Michael W Harris II
Thornville OH 43076

Call Sign: WA8P
Michael W Harris
Thornville OH 43076

FCC Amateur Radio Licenses in Thurman

Call Sign: K8HPO
Robert C Lewis
Rio Grande Est
Thurman OH 45685

Call Sign: N8PRW
Keith W Clark
650 Trails End
Thurman OH 45685

FCC Amateur Radio Licenses in Trimble

Call Sign: KC8VPO
Joshua Hogue
Trimble OH 45782

FCC Amateur Radio Licenses in Trinway

Call Sign: WD8OSU
Paul E Cater
12150 Main St
Trinway OH 43842

Call Sign: KD8PEH
Harrison J Ross
12390 Main St
Trinway OH 43821

Call Sign: W8MBX
Tom A Mathews
Trinway OH 43842

Call Sign: KD8LGV
Muskingam County
Ares
Trinway OH 43842

Call Sign: KC8BEW
Matthew R Murphy
Trinway OH 43842

FCC Amateur Radio Licenses in Tuppers Plains

Call Sign: KC8MOZ
Ronald E Dillon Sr
42240 Main St
Tuppers Plains OH
45783

Call Sign: AB8PB
Ronald E Dillon Sr
42240 Main St
Tuppers Plains OH
45783

Call Sign: N9LA
Nicolae A Leu
Tuppers Plains OH
45783

Call Sign: WA8NED
Norman O Weber
Tuppers Plains OH
45783

Call Sign: WD8OIK
Charles F Kim
Tuppers Plains OH
45783

Call Sign: KC8MOV
Chad E Griffith
Tuppers Plains OH
45783

FCC Amateur Radio Licenses in Union Furnace

Call Sign: KD8PAF
John A Rader
18193 Main St
Union Furnace OH
43158

Call Sign: KD8PRV
Roger L Stivison
35884 Moore Rd
Union Furnace OH
43158

FCC Amateur Radio Licenses in Vincent

Call Sign: N8IOM
Galen D Cox
85 Blue Gill Ln
Vincent OH 45784

Call Sign: K8DCZ
Elmo L Monroe
Box 314S
Vincent OH 45784

Call Sign: KC8ZOM
Michael A Rumer
1290 Brackenridge Rd
Vincent OH 45784

Call Sign: KG4JPN
Greg W Combs
490 Lewis Pointe Dr
Vincent OH 457849114

Call Sign: KB8JSV
Robert L Carlsen
115 Northlake Dr
Vincent OH 45784

Call Sign: KC8MRI
Kyle R Carlsen
115 Northlake Dr
Vincent OH 45784

Call Sign: KC8YAZ
Tara M Carlsen
115 Northlake Dr
Vincent OH 45784

Call Sign: KB8UWC
Ivy J Carlsen
115 Northlake Dr
Vincent OH 45784

Call Sign: KC8YMK
Linda K Morris
3010 Sealy Ridge Rd
Vincent OH 45784

Call Sign: KC8UYN
Robert E Morris
3010 Sealy Ridge Rd
Vincent OH 45784

Call Sign: KC8SSQ
Roger L Allberry
9673 St Rt 339
Vincent OH 45784

Call Sign: KD8GWM
Jason R Allberry
9673 St Rt 339
Vincent OH 45784

Call Sign: KD8LKK
Kathleen M Sulfridge
445 Timberline Dr
Vincent OH 45784

Call Sign: KD8LKJ
Luke J Sulfridge
445 Timberline Dr
Vincent OH 45784

FCC Amateur Radio Licenses in Vinton

Call Sign: KD8MNM
Thomas G Saunders
130 Amby Ln
Vinton OH 45686

Call Sign: KC8FOG
Jeffrey L Clark
1296 Cherry Pt Rd
Vinton OH 45686

Call Sign: KB8OZD
Charles W Greenlee
582 Greenlee Rd
Vinton OH 45686

Call Sign: KB8QMD
Hannah R Greenlee
582 Greenlee Rd
Vinton OH 45686

Call Sign: WB8MSN
Adrian F Gibson
558 Mt Carmel Rd
Vinton OH 45686

Call Sign: KB8WGQ
David J Maskew
84 S Main St
Vinton OH 456860065

Call Sign: K8AQO
Ralph J Fulks
199 Sailor Rd
Vinton OH 45686

Call Sign: KE6JAG
Thomas A Stephens II
13178 St Rt 160
Vinton OH 45686

Call Sign: KC8KDT
Emanuel Simpkins

72366 Stapelton Rd
Vinton OH 45686

Call Sign: KC8ZAB
Mid OH Valley ARC
Vinton OH 45686

FCC Amateur Radio Licenses in Wakefield

Call Sign: KQ4BW
David C Dilbeck
55 Salt Crk Rd
Wakefield OH 45687

FCC Amateur Radio Licenses in Waterford

Call Sign: WB8WPK
Bernard W Wright
Box 172
Waterford OH 45786

Call Sign: WD8IFP
Barbara L Coulter
Box 173
Waterford OH 45786

Call Sign: KC8KUK
Thomas C Watkins Jr
Box 215
Waterford OH 45786

Call Sign: K8SRW
David R Bidwell Sr
462 Echo Vly Rd
Waterford OH
457866280

Call Sign: W8WSM
Matthew M Hansell
1735 Hendershot Rd
Waterford OH 45786

Call Sign: KC8RYO

Timothy J Birkeland
2371 Righteous Ridge
Rd
Waterford OH
457866106

Call Sign: N8ZVD
Charles A Hathaway
2939 Righteous Ridge
Rd
Waterford OH 45786

Call Sign: W8ROX
Charles A Hathaway
2939 Righteous Ridge
Rd
Waterford OH 45786

Call Sign: W8FDU
Martin R Stapf Jr
545 Stapf Rd
Waterford OH
457866305

Call Sign: KD8LKO
Chris J Dehnart
80 Washington St
Waterford OH 45786

Call Sign: KD8LKR
James J Denart
80 Washington St
Waterford OH 45786

Call Sign: KD8LKQ
Timothy J Dehnart
80 Washington St
Waterford OH 45786

Call Sign: KB8KOZ
Steve L Rogers
Waterford OH 45786

Call Sign: W8HUB
William B Mason

Waterford OH 45786

Call Sign: W8RLA
Roger L Allberry
4975 Anderson Rd
Watertown OH 45787

Call Sign: WD8BGN
Richard D Newman
413 7th St
Waverly OH 45690

Call Sign: KA8PQC
Wayne E Cook
112 Alpine Dr
Waverly OH 456909636

Call Sign: KC8TYT
Scottie W Thomas
18 Barker Ln
Waverly OH 45690

Call Sign: KC8YTB
Scottie W Thomas
18 Barker Ln
Waverly OH 45690

Call Sign: AB8TI
Scottie W Thomas
18 Barker Ln
Waverly OH 45690

Call Sign: N8LGL
Paul D Besimer
108 Baywood Ln
Waverly OH 45690

Call Sign: KC8VOG
Loutishia M Snively

1831 Buchanan Rd
Waverly OH 45690

Call Sign: KC8VOH
Terry R Snively
1831 Buchanan Rd
Waverly OH 45690

Call Sign: KB8QXY
Richard W Dively
473 Carl Penn Rd
Waverly OH 45690

Call Sign: KD8HFD
Julie A Jonas
298 Copeland Rd
Waverly OH 45690

Call Sign: N8ULP
Sean R Jonas
298 Copeland Rd
Waverly OH 45690

Call Sign: KC8ZYV
Ryan B Saunders
306 E 3rd St
Waverly OH 45690

Call Sign: KB8BTD
Richard A Mc Cartney
523 E 3rd St
Waverly OH 45690

Call Sign: KC8TYS
James D Snodgrass
306 E 4th St
Waverly OH 45690

Call Sign: WD8ARB
Gareth D Baker
613 E 7th St
Waverly OH 456901564

Call Sign: KB8TVU
Frank E Dam

304 Elizabeth Ln
Waverly OH 45690

600 Markham Rd
Waverly OH 45690

746 Prosperity Rd
Waverly OH 45690

Call Sign: WB8SPV
Gary B Trustle
424 Franklin Ave
Waverly OH 45690

Call Sign: KD8NMT
Edward C Jordan
333 Morningside Dr
Waverly OH 45690

Call Sign: N8OUH
Gregory S Lang
2774 Prussia Rd
Waverly OH 45690

Call Sign: WB8AYU
James D Dameron
307 Hoffman Ln
Waverly OH 45690

Call Sign: KD8MZE
Gary C Damron
2996 Mt Tabor Rd
Waverly OH 45690

Call Sign: WB8GZL
Richard D Walsh
4235 Prussia Rd
Waverly OH 45690

Call Sign: N8BS
Robert B Schmitt
875 Howard Rd
Waverly OH 45690

Call Sign: KD8AAQ
Steven J Houk
160 Nye Rd
Waverly OH 45690

Call Sign: WB8GZM
Elizabeth M Walsh
4235 Prussia Rd
Waverly OH 45690

Call Sign: N8FIM
Judy L Schmitt
875 Howard Rd
Waverly OH 45690

Call Sign: AB8NL
Barratt R Banta
318 Oak Ave
Waverly OH 456901515

Call Sign: KD8FQV
Mark K Lewis
1447 Prussia Rd
Waverly OH 45690

Call Sign: KB8TKM
Cheryl A Dryden
56 Kennard Rd
Waverly OH 45690

Call Sign: KD8AQE
Walter M Tilley
1171 Pennington Rd
Waverly OH 45690

Call Sign: WO8A
Mark K Lewis
1447 Prussia Rd
Waverly OH 45690

Call Sign: KG8KC
Tony A Dryden Sr
56 Kennard Rd
Waverly OH 45690

Call Sign: KC8KYQ
James L Rinaldi II
1712 Pennington Rd
Waverly OH 45690

Call Sign: N8SBQ
Richard C Walsh
4237 Prussia Rd
Waverly OH 45690

Call Sign: KB8ZGR
Michael S Leach
609 Lock St
Waverly OH 45690

Call Sign: KB8ZYJ
Larry E Kempton
2629 Pennington Rd
Waverly OH 45690

Call Sign: KC8JRT
Dave L Easley
1483 Rainbow Trl Rd
Waverly OH 45690

Call Sign: WB8JOK
John L Harris
16 Maple St Omega
Waverly OH 45690

Call Sign: K8LEK
Larry E Kempton
2629 Pennington Rd
Waverly OH 45690

Call Sign: N4GX
Edwin H Lane
416 Ramble Rd
Waverly OH 45690

Call Sign: KB8UVJ
Albert T Whited

Call Sign: KD8DON
Jordan L Purpero

Call Sign: N3DDA
Thomas G Klinger

400 S Lock St
Waverly OH 45690

Call Sign: N8DAS
John D Call
405 S Lock St
Waverly OH 45690

Call Sign: KB9MVS
Jennifer E Kessler
131 Skyline Dr
Waverly OH 456909696

Call Sign: KB9MVT
David R Kessler
131 Skyline Dr
Waverly OH 456909696

Call Sign: KD8FZQ
Darryl J Hart
230 St Marys Ln
Waverly OH 45690

Call Sign: W8TSU
Goodsell L Mc Coy
378 St Rt 551
Waverly OH 45690

Call Sign: KD8EMT
Trent W Pekkala
650 St Rt 551
Waverly OH 45690

Call Sign: KB8TZA
Chris A Beatty
528 St Rt 552
Waverly OH 45690

Call Sign: WB8ZZY
John K Schmitt
620 St Rt 552
Waverly OH 45690

Call Sign: N8QWN
Ernest R Dickerson

21798 St Rt 772
Waverly OH 45690

Call Sign: KD8EMS
Van T Levier
5545 Straight Crk Rd
Waverly OH 45690

Call Sign: KA8WWI
Scioto Valley ARC
1878 US 23
Waverly OH 45690

Call Sign: W8BAP
Scioto Valley ARC
1878 US 23
Waverly OH 45690

Call Sign: K8KX
R Marvin Turner
1878 US 23
Waverly OH 45690

Call Sign: W8BAP
Scioto Valley ARC
1878 US 23
Waverly OH 45690

Call Sign: KD8CTB
Scioto Valley ARC
1878 US 83
Waverly OH 45690

Call Sign: KA8WWI
Scioto Valley ARC
1878 US 83
Waverly OH 45690

Call Sign: N8SBJ
James F Lico
875 USR 23
Waverly OH 45690

Call Sign: KB8QGO
Norman D Gillmore

321 Valerie Dr
Waverly OH 45690

Call Sign: KA6GGT
Walter T Price
212 Wells Jones Rd
Waverly OH 45690

Call Sign: KD8QZI
Walter T Price
212 Wells Jones Rd
Waverly OH 45690

Call Sign: K8VNL
Ray E Conrad
214 Wendy Ln
Waverly OH 45690

Call Sign: W8TRX
Donald Schwardt
Waverly OH 45690

Call Sign: K8BNF
Gerald E Davis
Waverly OH 45690

FCC Amateur Radio Licenses in Wellston

Call Sign: KB8TUX
James W Gregory
510 E Broadway
Wellston OH 45692

Call Sign: WA8YNF
Ernest F Meadows
223 Jackman Rd T203
Wellston OH 45692

Call Sign: WA8MIC
Dewey J Barr
21 N Illinois Ave
Wellston OH 45692

Call Sign: N8LOQ

Sidney W Grant
216 N Ohio Ave
Wellston OH 45692

Call Sign: KB8EJL
Velma M Meadows
253 S Illinois Ave
Wellston OH 45692

Call Sign: W9JLZ
Charles F Mc Claskey
1433 S Maine Ave
Wellston OH 45692

Call Sign: KC8ILV
Jackson County ARC
436 S Michigan Ave
Wellston OH 45692

Call Sign: W8SFC
Sidney W Grant
620 S Michigan Ave
Wellston OH 45692

Call Sign: KD8FZN
Willis E Martin
1240 S Michigan Ave
Wellston OH 45692

Call Sign: KC8TMY
Marilyn J Brady
23 S Wisconsin
Wellston OH 45692

Call Sign: K8MJB
Marilyn J Copas Brady
23 S Wisconsin
Wellston OH 45692

Call Sign: K8RLC
Richard L Copas
23 S Wisconsin Ave
Wellston OH 45692

Call Sign: KB8UNL

Hershel D Patton
205 Velma Dr
Wellston OH 45692

Call Sign: KC8HLG
Kenneth A Henson
219 W 2nd St
Wellston OH 45692

Call Sign: N8KXV
Richard R Drake
Wellston OH 45692

Call Sign: KC8BHM
Chris A Keller
Wellston OH 45692

Call Sign: W8CMI
Rick B Callebs
Wellston OH 45692

Call Sign: W8UU
Richard B Callebs
Wellston OH 45692

Call Sign: KD8ICY
Sidney W Grant
Wellston OH 45692

Call Sign: N8ORR
Gary L Green
Wellston OH
456920349

FCC Amateur Radio Licenses in West Portsmouth

Call Sign: WA8OHG
Robert E Penn
1545 3rd St
West Portsmouth OH
45663

Call Sign: KC8FM

Steven D Compton
3725 4th St
West Portsmouth OH
456636304

Call Sign: KG4HYY
Matthew S Maphis
1620 6th St
West Portsmouth OH
45663

Call Sign: KC8FWG
Charles D Kurtz
2922 Careys Run Pond
Crk Rd
West Portsmouth OH
456639075

Call Sign: WA8POE
Hubert S Steele Jr
Careys Run Rd
West Portsmouth OH
45663

Call Sign: KB8AAJ
Donna K Cowgill
1258 Careys Runpond
Crk Rd
West Portsmouth OH
45663

Call Sign: KA8JCU
James A Folsom
414 City View Ave
West Portsmouth OH
45663

Call Sign: KF8R
James E Folsom
414 City View Ave
West Portsmouth OH
45663

Call Sign: KA8YLB
Robert L Compton

263 Cole Ave
West Portsmouth OH
456636310

Call Sign: W8SV
Gary L Plummer
275 Crane Rd
West Portsmouth OH
45663

Call Sign: KB8ZTH
Kenneth N Silvey
1004 Main St
West Portsmouth OH
45663

Call Sign: KB8ZTI
Mary L Pennington
1004 Main St
West Portsmouth OH
45663

Call Sign: KC8UYH
Tobias B Nelson
1876 Moores Ln
West Portsmouth OH
45663

Call Sign: N8BLD
Paul J Weber
126 Raymond Ave
West Portsmouth OH
45663

Call Sign: KC8QCM
David E Timmer
321 Shump St
West Portsmouth OH
45662

Call Sign: KG8HF
Larry D Scott
1400 Washington Blvd
West Portsmouth OH
45662

Call Sign: N8GYQ
Brian D Lucas
202 Washington Blvd S
West Portsmouth OH
45663

FCC Amateur Radio Licenses in Wheelerburg

Call Sign: KB8WGS
Robert Z Henderson
1224 Allegheny Hill
Wheelersburg OH
45662

Call Sign: KC8AMO
Vicki J Henderson
1224 Allegheny Hill
Wheelersburg OH
45694

Call Sign: WD8BUO
Dan E Wells
17 Ashley Rd
Wheelersburg OH
45694

Call Sign: AC8BU
Dan E Wells
17 Ashley Rd
Wheelersburg OH
45694

Call Sign: WD8IFA
Bernard L Cooper
Box 131
Wheelersburg OH
45694

Call Sign: N8GJE
Jennie L Kegley
Box 2

Wheelersburg OH
45694

Call Sign: WD8ICU
Ralph L Kegley
Box 2
Wheelersburg OH
45694

Call Sign: N8CNB
Alan E Graff
84 Carty St
Wheelersburg OH
45694

Call Sign: KA8JLM
Carlton W Gallaher
854 Center St
Wheelersburg OH
45694

Call Sign: KD8HFE
Cassidy D Skaggs
1108 Charleviox Ave
Wheelersburg OH
45694

Call Sign: N8TH
Thomas T Hammond
93 Colony Dr Apt 405
Wheelersburg OH
45694

Call Sign: N8CNA
Bonnie L Fetters
1077 Crescent Dr
Wheelersburg OH
45694

Call Sign: WD8JWO
Bradley S Brandt
1241 Crescent Dr
Wheelersburg OH
45694

Call Sign: KB8EHN
Morris Fetters Jr
1077 Crescent Dr Rt 5
Wheelersburg OH
45694

Call Sign: WB8QNU
Alva A Warner
2332 Dogwood Ridge
Wheelersburg OH
456949492

Call Sign: KB8ZHV
April S Kegley
2554 Dogwood Ridge
Wheelersburg OH
45694

Call Sign: N8QZG
Randall G Tufts Sr
1811 Dogwood Ridge
Apt C
Wheelersburg OH
45694

Call Sign: KC8VJJ
Mary K Tufts
1811 Dogwood Ridge
Apt C
Wheelersburg OH
45694

Call Sign: KD8KUK
Gene E Smith
624 Dold Rd
Wheelersburg OH
45694

Call Sign: K8NJO
Norma J Ramsey
2719 Fairlane Dr
Wheelersburg OH
456949047

Call Sign: K8DN

Donald L Ramsey
2719 Fairlane Dr Rt 4
Wheelersburg OH
45694

Call Sign: N1XRF
David R Mc Dowell
9390 Galiia Pike Rd
Wheelersburg OH
45694

Call Sign: KD8PAU
Randall C Wickham
1165 Gleim Rd
Wheelersburg OH
45694

Call Sign: KB8QW
Harlan E Terry II
599 Goose Crk Rd
Wheelersburg OH
45694

Call Sign: N8QW
Harlan E Terry II
599 Goose Crk Rd
Wheelersburg OH
45694

Call Sign: KC8ENH
Robert K Risner
834 Hamilton Ave
Wheelersburg OH
45694

Call Sign: KD8EGN
Charles D Bramblett
391 Hansgen Morgan
Rd
Wheelersburg OH
45694

Call Sign: K8CDB
Charles D Bramblett

391 Hansgen Morgan
Rd
Wheelersburg OH
45694

Call Sign: KY4MD
Brian R Barhorst Md
23 Hummingbird Ln
Wheelersburg OH
45694

Call Sign: KC8BBP
Stephen P Donahue
92 Hummingbird Ln
Wheelersburg OH
45694

Call Sign: KC8BBQ
Michael B Donohue
92 Hummingbird Ln
Wheelersburg OH
45694

Call Sign: KA8COD
Carolyn S Williams
975 Kittle Rd
Wheelersburg OH
45694

Call Sign: N8HCG
Cecil C Williams III
975 Kittle Rd
Wheelersburg OH
45694

Call Sign: NW8F
Cecil C Williams Jr
975 Kittle Rd
Wheelersburg OH
45694

Call Sign: KC8BPU
Kevin D Hughes
864 Kittle Rd

Wheelersburg OH
45694

Call Sign: KB8QEH
Dale E Robirds
84 Kristin Dr
Wheelersburg OH
45694

Call Sign: N8JBD
James W Jenkins
1396 Lang Slocum Rd
Wheelersburg OH
45694

Call Sign: KA8PQF
Thomas J Mc Namara
1580 Lawson St
Wheelersburg OH
456949480

Call Sign: KB8WHC
Shelley A Caldwell
65 Lois Ave
Wheelersburg OH
45694

Call Sign: N8WBW
Gary M Caldwell
65 Lois Ave
Wheelersburg OH
45694

Call Sign: WX8G
Gary M Caldwell
65 Lois Ave
Wheelersburg OH
45694

Call Sign: KB8QEE
Danny D Srofe Jr
1214 Pinehurst
Wheelersburg OH
45694

Call Sign: KD8PNT
Jonathan C Baldridge
15 Piquet Rd
Wheelersburg OH
45694

Call Sign: KD8KUL
Paul E Brown
923 Rolf Rd
Wheelersburg OH
45694

Call Sign: K8RAJ
George R Dials
4667 St Rt 140
Wheelersburg OH
45694

Call Sign: WD8PMM
David E Kemper
5003 St Rt 140
Wheelersburg OH
45694

Call Sign: KD8IGD
Mark S Welch
3467 St Rt 522
Wheelersburg OH
45694

Call Sign: W8WXW
Mark S Welch
3467 St Rt 522
Wheelersburg OH
45694

Call Sign: KW8O
Mark S Welch
3467 St Rt 522
Wheelersburg OH
45694

Call Sign: KF8YL
Jesse W Bramblett Jr
163 Sun Vly Ct Unit 1

Wheelersburg OH
45694

Call Sign: KB4XT
Dannie L Tackett
248 Tanglewood Dr
Wheelersburg OH
45694

Call Sign: KD8ONZ
Joseph B Halcomb
Wheelersburg OH
45694

FCC Amateur Radio Licenses in Whipple

Call Sign: WA8WJN
Elmer W Beck
Box 55
Whipple OH 45788

Call Sign: WD8MIQ
Michael D Leonhart
2125 Collins Rd
Whipple OH 45788

Call Sign: KD8PCH
Darlene S Leonhart
2125 Collins Rd
Whipple OH 45788

Call Sign: W8PAN
Darlene S Leonhart
2125 Collins Rd
Whipple OH 45788

Call Sign: WD8PVK
Lloyd E Schneeberger
7040 Dalzell Rd
Whipple OH 457885225

Call Sign: N8CER
Darrel B Grubb
4290 Dalzell Rd

Whipple OH 45788

Call Sign: N8GXM
Mary F Hendershot
7480 Dalzell Rd
Whipple OH 45788

Call Sign: WK8R
Gregory R Robinson
145 Rake Rd
Whipple OH 45788

Call Sign: KA8YZT
Stephen W Beck
2755 Whipple Run Rd
Whipple OH 45788

Call Sign: KC8ZZW
David C Owens Jr
Whipple OH 45788

Call Sign: KC8ZZV
Kelly L Owens
Whipple OH 45788

FCC Amateur Radio Licenses in White Cottage

Call Sign: KD8MPM
Treasa L Himmelspach
White Cottage OH
43791

FCC Amateur Radio Licenses in Willow Wood

Call Sign: KC8AON
Richard S Mc Kee
4183 St Rt 217
Willow Wood OH
45696

Call Sign: KC8NXX

Peggy S Mckee
4183 St Rt 217
Willow Wood OH
45696

Call Sign: KB8YLW
Ronald F Estep
1728 Twp Rd 97
Willow Wood OH
45696

FCC Amateur Radio Licenses in Woodsfield

Call Sign: WA8EGG
James W Ady
46091 78 E
Woodsfield OH 43793

Call Sign: KC8LXL
Robert B Bolen
134 Andover Rd
Woodsfield OH 43793

Call Sign: KB8HYS
George H Nenstiel
178 Andover Rd
Woodsfield OH 43793

Call Sign: WD8RED
Tommy J Robinson
145 Andover Rd
Woodsfield OH 43793

Call Sign: KC8AZP
Patricia A Copeland
182 Andover Rd
Woodsfield OH 43793

Call Sign: N8SC
Steven L Copeland
182 Andover Rd
Woodsfield OH 43793

Call Sign: W8MCC

Monroe County
Communicators
506 Botts Trler Ct
Woodsfield OH 43793

Call Sign: AB8AT
John A Coffey
101 E Church St
Woodsfield OH 43793

Call Sign: KB7QVZ
Richard H Burleigh
438 Easterh Ave
Woodsfield OH 43793

Call Sign: WD8PVJ
Richard W Libby
332 Guilford Ave
Woodsfield OH 43793

Call Sign: NZ8E
James W Heimann
40975 Lick Skillet Rd
Woodsfield OH 43793

Call Sign: K8DIG
Harry F Truax
516 Locust Ln
Woodsfield OH 43793

Call Sign: N8PYR
Kenneth L Burkhart
135 Maple Ave
Woodsfield OH 43793

Call Sign: N8TFK
Janet I Holland
402 Mill St
Woodsfield OH 43793

Call Sign: N8TFL
Gary L Holland
402 Mill St
Woodsfield OH 43793

Call Sign: WA8HTO
Gerald D Fankhauser
219 Oaklawn
Woodsfield OH 43793

Call Sign: KB8UXQ
Ruth D Simpson
44480 Pfalzgraf Rd
Woodsfield OH 43793

Call Sign: KB8UTE
Robert F Simpson
44480 Pfalzgraf Ridge
Rd
Woodsfield OH 43793

Call Sign: KD8MTE
Zachary B Bolin
309 Railroad St
Woodsfield OH 43793

Call Sign: N8MTU
John R Weber
409 S Main St
Woodsfield OH 43793

Call Sign: N8UPV
Dan A Weber
409 S Main St
Woodsfield OH 43793

Call Sign: KC8PXQ
Monroe Ares Group
409 S Main St
Woodsfield OH
437931028

Call Sign: K8DIG
Monroe Ares Group
409 S Main St
Woodsfield OH
437931028

Call Sign: N8MTO
Daniel W Jacobs

40281 SR 26
Woodsfield OH 43793

Call Sign: N8QHA
Marjorie L Jacobs
40281 SR 26
Woodsfield OH 43793

Call Sign: WB8ZUL
James W Hill
39709 St Rt 255
Woodsfield OH 43793

**FCC Amateur Radio
Licenses in Zaleski**

Call Sign: KC8DFQ
Janice R Cottrill
30109 Jamison Rd
Zaleski OH 45698

Call Sign: KC8EFU
Ronald P Molihan
21 N Broadway St
Zaleski OH 456980281

Call Sign: AB8MV
Ronald P Molihan
116 N Broadway St
Zaleski OH 456980281

Call Sign: KB8UIR
Ramon D Cottrill
Zaleski OH 45698

Call Sign: KC8UMD
Charles F Erickson
Zaleski OH 45698

**FCC Amateur Radio
Licenses in Zanesville**

Call Sign: KD8CNB
Michael A Desarro
1032 Adams Cir

Zanesville OH 43701

Call Sign: KD8MQO
John L Montgomery
1830 Adams Ln 15
Zanesville OH 43701

Call Sign: KD8JVQ
Josh B Bennett
3965 Adamsville Rd
Zanesville OH 43701

Call Sign: KD8RII
Jared R Asire
210 Anthony Ln
Zanesville OH 43701

Call Sign: WN8C
Charles L Farmer
3900 Arc Dr
Zanesville OH
437016795

Call Sign: KC8VZI
Pamela L Tracey
2375 Arch Hill Rd
Zanesville OH 43701

Call Sign: KC8AHK
Milton D Tom
1365 Athena C11
Zanesville OH 43701

Call Sign: W8SSC
Milton D Tom
1365 Athena C11
Zanesville OH 43701

Call Sign: KE4DOW
Jerry S Gahagan
3991 Avalon Dr
Zanesville OH 43701

Call Sign: KF4EBI
Valerie L Gahagan

3991 Avalon Dr
Zanesville OH 43701

2985 Broadvue Cir
Zanesville OH 43701

2385 Carmen Dr
Zanesville OH 43701

Call Sign: WD8KFN
Richard G Fuller
84 Beech Rock Dr
Zanesville OH 43701

Call Sign: KD8ETE
Robert T Hardman
3125 Brookside Dr
Zanesville OH 43701

Call Sign: KB8CCH
Douglas C Davy
2735 Center Dr
Zanesville OH 43701

Call Sign: KD8CNG
Ryan M Duty
1080 Beverly Ave
Zanesville OH 43701

Call Sign: KA8UXT
Joseph W Paul
255 Bryan Dr
Zanesville OH 43701

Call Sign: W0RN
Douglas C Davy
2735 Center Dr
Zanesville OH 43701

Call Sign: N8HXR
Ronald E Stevens
1124 Blandy Ave
Zanesville OH 43701

Call Sign: KC8GJC
Dean M Carter
265 Bryan Dr
Zanesville OH 43701

Call Sign: KD8JVR
Bay A Alan
1659 Century Ln
Zanesville OH 43701

Call Sign: KC8SIQ
Elizabeth M Nichols
4165 Boggs Rd
Zanesville OH 43701

Call Sign: KB8HBD
Robert A Hall Jr
290 Bryan Dr
Zanesville OH 43701

Call Sign: KD8ONQ
Jonathan L Lent
2755 Chandlersville Rd
Zanesville OH 43701

Call Sign: WA8YOF
David L Critchfield
4825 Boggs Rd
Zanesville OH 43701

Call Sign: KA8VSS
Gordon B Jividen
980 Bunting Dr
Zanesville OH 43701

Call Sign: WD8NVG
Alvin Leedham Sr
4035 Chandlersville Rd
Zanesville OH 43701

Call Sign: KD8ETC
Joseph A Lusk
440 Bonifield Ct
Zanesville OH 43701

Call Sign: KD8JYS
Sisan E Jividen
980 Bunting Dr
Zanesville OH 43701

Call Sign: W8ZZV
Zanesville ARC
4235 Cherlick Cir
Zanesville OH 43701

Call Sign: KC8ANX
Donald K Clark Jr
3615 Bradly Cir
Zanesville OH 43701

Call Sign: KB8TRF
Kevin R Bailey
557 Cambridge Ave
Zanesville OH 43701

Call Sign: W8TJT
Dwight S Bonifield
4235 Cherlick Cir
Zanesville OH 43701

Call Sign: KB8OGZ
Howard D Frye II
581 Brighton Blvd
Zanesville OH 43701

Call Sign: WY8V
Earl J Hubbard
1790 Candlestick Dr
Zanesville OH 43701

Call Sign: KD8RJQ
Barbara A Bonifield
4235 Cherlick Cir
Zanesville OH 43701

Call Sign: KD8CNA
Cory A Spring

Call Sign: KD8RIR
Max V Kocher

Call Sign: KC8BAB
Barbara A Bonifield

4235 Cherlick Cir
Zanesville OH 43701

Call Sign: KB8KIQ
Carolyn S Sherry
1405 Chevington Cir
Zanesville OH 43701

Call Sign: N8KCN
George M Sherry
1405 Chevington Cir
Zanesville OH 43701

Call Sign: KC8KKR
Roy E Montgomery Jr
1021 Clay
Zanesville OH
437015728

Call Sign: WA8BNR
Oliver W Barnett
3465 Clay Pike
Zanesville OH 43701

Call Sign: KD8ARF
Donald A Newsom
5160 Cliff Rock Dr
Zanesville OH 43701

Call Sign: KB8OGW
Janet S Kiikka
913 Convers Ave
Zanesville OH 43701

Call Sign: KB8OGX
Niel V Kiikka
913 Convers Ave
Zanesville OH 43701

Call Sign: KB8OHA
Deborah M Robinson
921 Convers Ave
Zanesville OH 43701

Call Sign: WA8HFO

Harry D Lewis
1348 Coopermill Rd
Zanesville OH 43701

Call Sign: KD8HKO
Edward E Hedge
2290 Creedmoor Dr
Zanesville OH 43701

Call Sign: KD8OB
John R Bolen
3675 Culbertson Rd
Zanesville OH 43701

Call Sign: N8GDS
Rise N Bolen
3675 Culbertson Rd
Zanesville OH 43701

Call Sign: KC8DOU
Janet S Colvin
725 Deerfield Rd
Zanesville OH 43701

Call Sign: K8SKP
Gale E Colvin
725 Deerfield Rd
Zanesville OH 43701

Call Sign: KD8JUX
Robert G Williams Jr
1420 Dietz Ln
Zanesville OH 43701

Call Sign: KD8OOJ
Adam L Smith
3535 Dona Dr
Zanesville OH 43701

Call Sign: KC8GCO
Michael K Castor
2465 Douglas Dr
Zanesville OH 43701

Call Sign: KC8LVO

Michael D Coulson
107 Downing Dr
Zanesville OH 43701

Call Sign: KC8MKI
Muskingum Valley
Radio Amateur Group
5070 Dresden Ct
Zanesville OH 43701

Call Sign: N8HR
Muskingum Valley
Radio Amateur Group
5070 Dresden Ct
Zanesville OH 43701

Call Sign: WZ8P
Everett H Jackson Jr
5070 Dresden Ct
Zanesville OH
437018841

Call Sign: KB8WBH
Brian F Rich
2219 Dresden Rd
Zanesville OH 43701

Call Sign: N8QFV
David M Weber
2405 Dresden Rd
Zanesville OH 43701

Call Sign: K8UEI
Timothy R Longstreth
3051 Dresden Rd
Zanesville OH 43701

Call Sign: KC8HAP
Lisa M Talley
3325 Dresden Rd
Zanesville OH 43701

Call Sign: KB8ZMG
Ronald G Milner
4125 Dresden Rd

Zanesville OH 43701

Call Sign: KD8JVK
Shawn E Claypool
5962 Dresden Rd Apt 5
Zanesville OH 43701

Call Sign: KA8GHT
Gerald L Barnhart
171 E King St
Zanesville OH 43701

Call Sign: N8ROH
Patrick D Wagner
475 E Lawndale Pl
Zanesville OH 43701

Call Sign: KD8HVZ
Julie A Wagner
475 E Lawndale Pl
Zanesville OH 43701

Call Sign: AC8AD
Patrick D Wagner
475 E Lawndale Pl
Zanesville OH
437013912

Call Sign: KF4UJS
David M Jones
123 E Main St
Zanesville OH 43701

Call Sign: KC8UKK
David M Jones
123 E Main St
Zanesville OH 43701

Call Sign: KB8VQO
David C Redman
2735 E Military Rd
Zanesville OH 43701

Call Sign: WB8JLF
John D Redman

2735 E Military Rd
Zanesville OH 43701

Call Sign: KB8MGP
James F Allen
2655 E Pike
Zanesville OH 43701

Call Sign: KD8RIJ
Zechariah M Bauer
2770 E Pike
Zanesville OH 43701

Call Sign: KA8WZP
John M Jones Sr
3610 E Pike
Zanesville OH
437019625

Call Sign: K8JPN
Robert E King
348 E Taylor St
Zanesville OH 43701

Call Sign: W9MMZ
Fred A Hatfield
2955 Eagle Crest Dr
Zanesville OH
437011693

Call Sign: KC8EIQ
Sean M Jenkins
1002 Eastward Cir
Zanesville OH 43701

Call Sign: WD8BXV
Robert L Ungemach
1920 Ellerman Rd
Zanesville OH 43701

Call Sign: KB8YUK
Lester E Sherwood
827 Eppley Ave
Zanesville OH 43701

Call Sign: KD8RJR
Sirius E Underwood
1846 Euclid Ave
Zanesville OH 43701

Call Sign: KC8HAR
Michael F Morgan
2670 Eva Cir
Zanesville OH 43701

Call Sign: N8TRF
John T Garber
375 Fairview Rd
Zanesville OH 43701

Call Sign: KA8WAJ
Robert A Norman
1200 Fairview Rd
Zanesville OH 43701

Call Sign: KD8JVN
Jared W Parsons
1030 Forest Ave
Zanesville OH 43701

Call Sign: KD8ESK
Anthony R Kinner
4555 Foxfire Dr
Zanesville OH 43701

Call Sign: W8WVO
Robert C Edwards
3730 Frazeysburg Rd
Zanesville OH 43701

Call Sign: KB8ZMH
Cary M Grandstaff
2019 Galena Ave
Zanesville OH 43701

Call Sign: NI8J
Herbert R Hicks
810 Garden Rd
Zanesville OH 43701

Call Sign: N8PFF
Paul A Haskins
896 Garden Rd
Zanesville OH 43701

Call Sign: KK8T
Joe E Grimm
400 Grandview Dr
Zanesville OH 43701

Call Sign: KC8IXU
Scott R Crawford
1107 Greenwood Ave
Zanesville OH 43701

Call Sign: N8TRC
Richard D Crawford
1107 Greenwood Ave
Zanesville OH
437014033

Call Sign: W8LSL
Lawrence E Dearstine
1258 Greenwood Ave
Zanesville OH 43701

Call Sign: WA8AMK
Louis F Dusenberry
717 Grieves Ln
Zanesville OH 43701

Call Sign: W8AMK
Louis F Dusenberry
717 Grieves Ln
Zanesville OH 43701

Call Sign: N8YVH
Walter F Mautz
1390 Hanna Dr
Zanesville OH 43701

Call Sign: KC8CFH
Rhonda E Imlay
575 Harding Rd Apt C
Zanesville OH 43701

Call Sign: KD8RIW
William D Rexroad
33 Hazel Ave
Zanesville OH 43701

Call Sign: W8RSE
Douglass B Taylor
1924 Hazel Ave
Zanesville OH 43701

Call Sign: KC8HAS
Richard E Martin
447 Hedgewood Ave
Zanesville OH 43701

Call Sign: KD8MQN
Allex J Hatfield
448 Hedgewood Ave
Zanesville OH 43701

Call Sign: KB8SHR
Ronald D Learn
3190 Hiawatha Dr
Zanesville OH 43701

Call Sign: KD8ETL
Robert E Matthews
2377 High Point Dr
Zanesville OH 43701

Call Sign: KD8MQU
Dakota L Tom
305 Hillview Dr
Zanesville OH 43701

Call Sign: N8ZJI
Kenneth R Barnhart
866 Homewood Ave
Zanesville OH 43701

Call Sign: KD8HKS
Kevin R Kynnersley
4657 Huggins Rd
Zanesville OH 43701

Call Sign: KC8FSM
Larry D Brink
1434 Indiana St
Zanesville OH 43701

Call Sign: KC8JBI
Mary J Brink
1434 Indiana St
Zanesville OH 43701

Call Sign: KC8PVV
James A Kean
Indiana St
Zanesville OH 43701

Call Sign: KC8VKR
Bobbie L Kean
Indiana St
Zanesville OH 43701

Call Sign: KC8LJH
William D Martin
407 Indiana St Appt I
Zanesville OH 43701

Call Sign: KD8CNO
Ross A Lee
1040 Jersey Ridge Rd
Zanesville OH 43701

Call Sign: N8WCU
Scott E Williams
369 Johnathan Ln
Zanesville OH 43701

Call Sign: K8QDY
Zane G Moore
3165 Kearns Dr
Zanesville OH 43701

Call Sign: KD8HKU
Marcus W West
5100 Knipe Rd
Zanesville OH 43701

Call Sign: KA8ZMQ
Steven W Jones
465 Knox Rd
Zanesville OH 43701

Call Sign: KC8QJ
David L Steahly
3264 Lakewood Dr
Zanesville OH 43701

Call Sign: KD8JVU
Christopher A Reilly
1200 Langan Ln
Zanesville OH 43701

Call Sign: KE8IQ
Paul W Davis Jr
835 Larzelere Ave
Zanesville OH 43701

Call Sign: K8PAM
Virginia M Cable
1045 Lectric Ln
Zanesville OH 43701

Call Sign: K8LAV
Jess T Cable Jr
1045 Lectric Ln
Zanesville OH
437018790

Call Sign: KD8MSP
Jon C Hartmeyer
1110 Lectric Ln
Zanesville OH 43701

Call Sign: KC8TDS
Timothy E Murphy
1235 Lectric Ln
Zanesville OH 43701

Call Sign: KB8JVP
Philip A Hammer
3000 Licking Rd

Zanesville OH 43701

Call Sign: KD8RAT
Lin R Avendano
3410 Licking Rd
Zanesville OH 43701

Call Sign: KG8TC
Larry B Hartsook
3043 Lookout Dr
Zanesville OH
437011642

Call Sign: WD8DQA
Matc ARC
2775 Maple Ave
Zanesville OH 43701

Call Sign: KD8BUE
D Charles Galbraith
28003 Maple Ave Ste
165
Zanesville OH 43701

Call Sign: KC8TVM
Shawn P Mcconnell
2220 Maple Hill St
Zanesville OH 43701

Call Sign: KD8ESL
Shane M Bell
2118 Maplehill St
Zanesville OH 43701

Call Sign: KB8RIM
Danny G Grandstaff
2422 Marion Ave
Zanesville OH 43701

Call Sign: KB8ZXH
Mary J Grandstaff
2422 Marion Ave
Zanesville OH 43701

Call Sign: KC8ORD

Zanesville ARC
2422 Marion Ave
Zanesville OH 43701

Call Sign: K8SXP
Ben M Graham
534 Market St
Zanesville OH 43701

Call Sign: KF2EH
Mark D Haven
842 McIntire Ave
Zanesville OH 43701

Call Sign: KE8YP
Verle G Ridgley
340 Mead St
Zanesville OH
437014750

Call Sign: NY8P
Verle G Ridgley
340 Mead St
Zanesville OH
437014750

Call Sign: KC8GCL
George L Katsampes
3840 Mill Dr
Zanesville OH 43701

Call Sign: W8FRM
Clarence R Acker
3654 Mill Dr
Zanesville OH 43701

Call Sign: WD8AHV
Joseph J Wagner
4668 Millennium Dr
Zanesville OH 43701

Call Sign: W8EBY
Larry M Eby
1378 Mitchell Ave
Zanesville OH 43701

Zanesville OH 43701

Zanesville OH 43701

Call Sign: KD8ESP
John J Fuller
840 Mobile Dr
Zanesville OH 43701

Call Sign: KF8NZ
Steven E Haught
3710 Mona Dr
Zanesville OH
437019444

Call Sign: KD8CNI
Dustin A Hayes
721 Moorehead Ave
Zanesville OH 43701

Call Sign: KD8MQS
Angela D Seward
1445 My Dr
Zanesville OH 43701

Call Sign: KD8JVV
Alic R Kozusko
247 N Blackwood Dr
Zanesville OH 43701

Call Sign: N8OFK
Scott F Ridgley
2780 N Lawndale Pl
Zanesville OH 43701

Call Sign: KA8GPL
Leanna R Imlay
941 N Moorewood Dr
Zanesville OH 43701

Call Sign: KA8GPM
Richard E Imlay
941 N Moorewood Dr
Zanesville OH 43701

Call Sign: KA8GPN
Jeffrey R Imlay
941 N Moorewood Dr

Call Sign: KD8HR
Arthur W Boehme
535 N Ray Dr
Zanesville OH 43701

Call Sign: KD8MQQ
Dillon C Paxson
3255 National Rd
Zanesville OH 43701

Call Sign: KD8JVA
Chris A Shafer
3976 Newark Rd
Zanesville OH 43701

Call Sign: W8EVV
John P Armstrong
1349 Newman Dr
Zanesville OH 43701

Call Sign: KB8MGR
Eric E Thompson
4755 Norfield Rd
Zanesville OH 43701

Call Sign: KD8JVD
Justin G Reilly
7995 Norfield Rd
Zanesville OH 43701

Call Sign: KD8JUY
Chase A Tom
1958 Norwood Blvd
Zanesville OH 43701

Call Sign: KD8MQB
Evan M Moss
5139 Oinecrest Dr Apt 1
Zanesville OH 43701

Call Sign: N8VWS
John W Frank
3652 Old Coopermill Rd

Call Sign: KD8JVJ
Michael L Cole
4505 Old Country Ln
Zanesville OH 43701

Call Sign: WA8HFS
Carl E Carder
4330 Paxton Ln
Zanesville OH 43701

Call Sign: KD8RIN
David K Grubb
5665 Pin Oak Ln
Zanesville OH 43701

Call Sign: NF8Z
Michael D Keeton
5340 Pine Vly Dr
Zanesville OH 43701

Call Sign: KC8CD
Ronald E Allen
5130 Pinecrest Dr
Zanesville OH 43701

Call Sign: KB8VBV
Corrie D Marple
2950 Pinkerton
Zanesville OH 43701

Call Sign: KB8UVS
Terresa S Marple
2950 Pinkerton Rd
Zanesville OH 43701

Call Sign: WA8BNS
Harry E Bell Jr
1660 Potts Ln
Zanesville OH
437016034

Call Sign: KD8HKK
Darrell L Hunt Jr

3085 Primrose Dr
Zanesville OH 43701

Call Sign: KB8WFU
David F Mohler
1328 Race St
Zanesville OH 43701

Call Sign: KC8OIJ
Shane M Tilton
1125 Richey Rd
Zanesville OH 43701

Call Sign: N8BFF
William A Agin
7260 Ridge Rd
Zanesville OH 43701

Call Sign: KB8HBB
Robert L Mast
3490 Riverside Airport
Zanesville OH 43701

Call Sign: NP2DW
Patricia L Walsh
3110 Riverside Airport
Rd
Zanesville OH 43701

Call Sign: KB8JVO
Ray F Collins
3202 Riverside Airport
Rd
Zanesville OH
437011244

Call Sign: W8LCT
Charles J Bruckelmeyer
3350 Riverside Airport
Rd
Zanesville OH 43701

Call Sign: KE8YO
Frederic J Grant III

3450 Riverside Airport
Rd
Zanesville OH
437011246

Call Sign: W8FJG
Frederic J Grant III
3450 Riverside Airport
Rd
Zanesville OH
437011246

Call Sign: KD8ETI
Todd M Ingram
1163 Robin Ct
Zanesville OH 43701

Call Sign: KD8QVW
Brad A Newell
1128 Roosevelt Ave
Zanesville OH 43701

Call Sign: KD8REF
Jennifer A Dilbeck
2586 Rowan St
Zanesville OH 43701

Call Sign: W8ACE
David C Dilbeck
2586 Rowan St
Zanesville OH 43701

Call Sign: KC8IHU
Ricky L Moore
1695 Rubicon Dr
Zanesville OH 43701

Call Sign: KD8ESM
Matthew S Sharp
3240 S River Rd
Zanesville OH 43701

Call Sign: K8LD
Leroy J Dillon
510 S Samuel Dr

Zanesville OH 43701

Call Sign: KD8ESW
Nathaniel A Wharton
3201 Sandhurst Dr
Zanesville OH 43701

Call Sign: KD8MPU
Clarence E Davis
603 Schaum Ave
Zanesville OH 43701

Call Sign: KC8ZT
Richard S Johnston Sr
3130 Sebaugh Dr
Zanesville OH
437011682

Call Sign: KC8YLI
Thomas R Mautz
523 Seborn Ave
Zanesville OH 43701

Call Sign: WA8MYW
Everett R Miskimen
1016 Seborn Ave
Zanesville OH 43701

Call Sign: W8EGG
Harry W Murphy Jr
1116 Seborn Ave
Zanesville OH 43701

Call Sign: KC8DFB
James D Gladman
1041 Sevall St
Zanesville OH 43701

Call Sign: KB8NKI
John A Myer
1068 Sevall St
Zanesville OH 43701

Call Sign: WB8VYG
Edmund J Romito III

170 Shagbark Ln
Zanesville OH 43701

Call Sign: KC8VNI
Brett L Fuller
109 Sherwood Dr
Zanesville OH 43701

Call Sign: KJ8N
Philip C Janke
290 Skyline Dr
Zanesville OH 43701

Call Sign: N8CKK
Beverly J Janke
290 Skyline Dr
Zanesville OH 43701

Call Sign: W8BLW
Bob L Williamson
399 Skyline Dr
Zanesville OH 43701

Call Sign: KB8XZ
Bob L Williamson
399 Skyline Dr
Zanesville OH 43701

Call Sign: WX8J
James W Mayercak
971 Somers St
Zanesville OH 43701

Call Sign: KD8RJD
Craig Wolfinger
513 Spangler Dr
Zanesville OH 43701

Call Sign: W8DVU
Charles W Alexander
547 Spangler Dr
Zanesville OH 43701

Call Sign: K8CFK
John R Wilson

65 Spry Rd
Zanesville OH 43701

Call Sign: KB8HHO
Thomas L Elson
4308 Strattford Cir E
Zanesville OH
437019857

Call Sign: W8ENJ
Russell E Mendenhall
4354 Strattford Cir W
Zanesville OH 43701

Call Sign: KA8JKD
Ernest C Sutton Jr
3445 Sunset Dr
Zanesville OH 43701

Call Sign: K8WVN
William R Rush
1217 Swingle St
Zanesville OH 43701

Call Sign: N8ARC
John C Barclay
1115 Talley Ave
Zanesville OH 43701

Call Sign: KB8OHI
John A Parmi
Tannehill St
Zanesville OH 43701

Call Sign: KC8OZO
George M Brooks
273 Taylor St
Zanesville OH 43701

Call Sign: KD8HKN
Shawn Hoagland
945 Taylor St
Zanesville OH 43701

Call Sign: KD8RIM

Chad A Gill
1100 Taylor St
Zanesville OH 43701

Call Sign: W8FXX
Eugene A Shaw
1185 Taylor St
Zanesville OH 43701

Call Sign: W8LFG
Lillian H Shaw
1185 Taylor St
Zanesville OH 43701

Call Sign: KD8MQV
Daryl W Vines
4490 Tipton Rd
Zanesville OH 43701

Call Sign: KD8MQD
Matt A Vallee
121 Valley Gem Dr
Zanesville OH 43701

Call Sign: KD8RIV
Raju Rana
491 Van Horn Ave
Zanesville OH 43701

Call Sign: KD8ETO
Walter J Myus
539 W Highland Dr
Zanesville OH 43701

Call Sign: KD8EST
Ryan C Steele
5160 W Shore Dr
Zanesville OH 43701

Call Sign: WA8CXS
Delbert B Kirkbride
3375 Wesley Chapel Rd
Zanesville OH 43701

Call Sign: KD8JVP

Jared K Green
814 Westbourne Ave
Zanesville OH 43701

Call Sign: KB8NKH
Janet L Roberts
1407 Westwood Dr
Zanesville OH 43701

Call Sign: KB8JVN
Dale A Roberts
1407 Westwood Dr
Zanesville OH
437017701

Call Sign: KD8ESZ
Orlando T Harrier
2250 Whitman Ave
Zanesville OH 43701

Call Sign: K8ARR
J W Karr
3029 Woodland Dr
Zanesville OH
437018402

Call Sign: KD5KPI
Elizabeth K Conrad
537 Woodlawn Ave
Zanesville OH 43701

Call Sign: KA8UWO
Mary A Wahl
Zanesville OH 43702

Call Sign: WA8BOV
Donald M Wahl
Zanesville OH 43702

Call Sign: KB8ADF
Charles E Hamilton Sr
Zanesville OH 43702

Call Sign: KD8HKF
Emeran G Boehn

Zanesville OH 43702

Call Sign: KB8ZMI
Robert C Burton
Zanesville OH
437022128